# Historic Homes of Bastrop, Texas

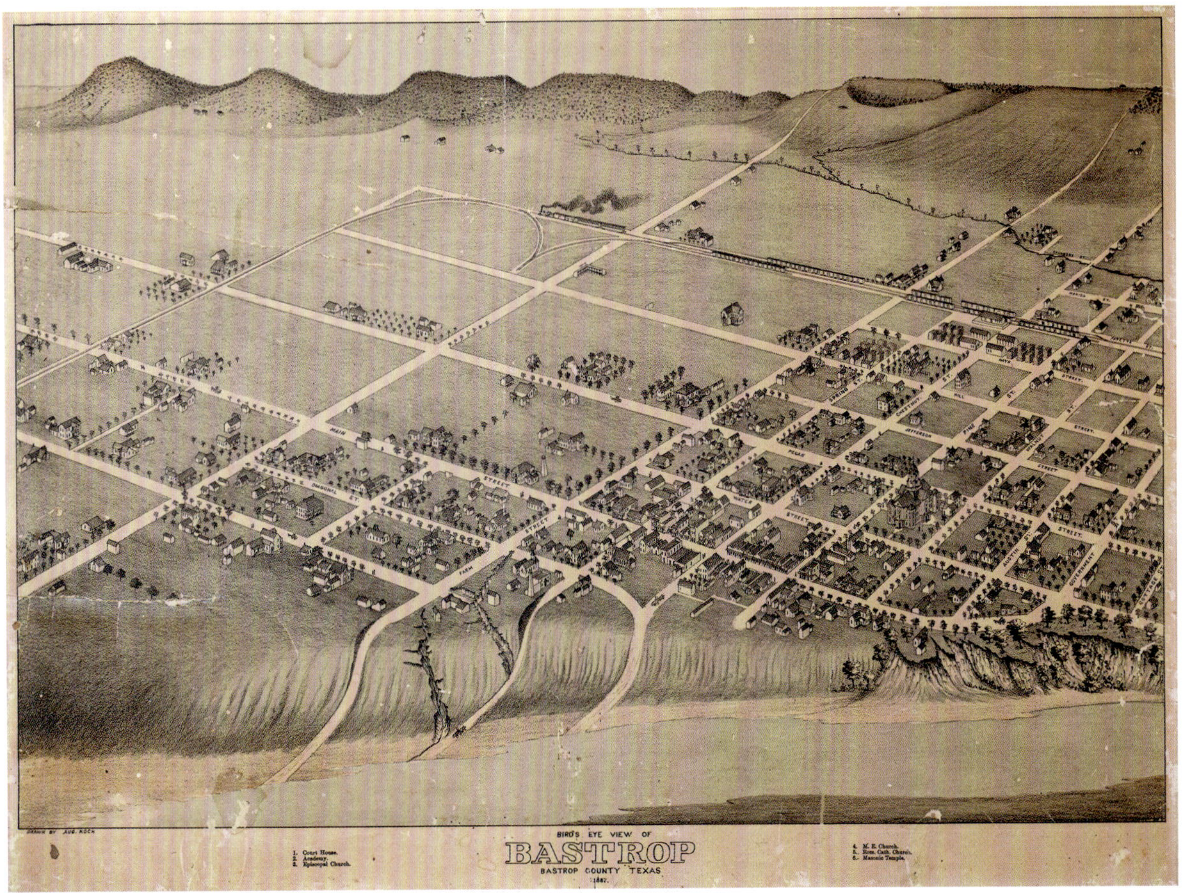


Number Twenty-three
Sara and John Lindsey Series in the Arts and Humanities

# *Historic Homes of Bastrop, Texas*

Robbie Moore Sanders
*with Sandra Chipley*

Photographs by Mark Winslett
Foreword by Marvin E. Beck

TEXAS A&M UNIVERSITY PRESS
COLLEGE STATION

First edition

♾ This paper meets the requirements of ANSI/NISO Z39.48–1992 (Permanence of Paper).
Binding materials have been chosen for durability.
Manufactured in China through Martin Book Management.

Library of Congress Cataloging-in-Publication Data

Names: Sanders, Robbie Moore, 1941– author. | Chipley, Sandra, 1954– author. | Winslett, Mark, photographer (expression) | Beck, Marvin E., 1932–2020, writer of foreword.
Title: Historic homes of Bastrop, Texas / Robbie Moore Sanders with Sandra Chipley; photographs by Mark Winslett; foreword by Marvin E. Beck.
Description: College Station: Texas A&M University Press, [2022] | Includes index.
Identifiers: LCCN 2021043943 (print) | LCCN 2021043944 (ebook) | ISBN 9781623499280 (cloth) | ISBN 9781623499297 (ebook)
Subjects: LCSH: Historic buildings—Texas—Bastrop. | Architecture, Domestic—Texas—Bastrop. | Bastrop (Tex.)—Biography. | LCGFT: Biographies.
Classification: LCC F394.B27 S26 2022 (print) | LCC F394.B27 (ebook) | DDC 976.4/32—dc23
LC record available at https://lccn.loc.gov/2021043943
LC ebook record available at https://lccn.loc.gov/2021043944

Frontispiece map: Courtesy of the Bastrop County Historical Society.

# Contents

# Foreword

## *Marvin E. Beck, AIA Emeritus*

The National Trust for Historic Preservation has designated Bastrop "a distinctive destination." Among the goals of the National Trust is the recognition of a community's great moments in history and important events from everyday life. It recognizes communities with a strong commitment to historic preservation and communities with "diverse and attractive architecture."

This book is the epitome of that goal. Robbie Sanders has assembled, digested, and recorded Bastrop's most recognizable houses into one complete work. She fills those houses with statesmen, Indian fighters, ex-slaves, soldiers, and the ordinary and extraordinary men and women who have made Bastrop their home.

Bastrop, known as Stephen F. Austin's "little colony," was platted in 1832 at the crossing of El Camino Real and the Colorado River. The architecture of Bastrop's early homes is predominantly the result of Anglo-American immigration from the United States into the area, as well as immigration from various European countries, many from Germany. Cypress trees found along the banks of the Colorado and cedar and long-leaf pine from the nearby "Lost Pines" were the most favored building materials for their homes from the 1830s through the first part of the twentieth century.

The story of the pioneering Jenkins family from Alabama is a lesson in Texas history, and the evolution of their early home, the Old Jenkins House at 1710 Main Street, from a double-log cabin in 1830–33 into a house with clapboard siding, a full-length porch, and decorative detail is typical of Bastrop's early structures.

Following the earliest homes were the antebellum houses, which are predominantly of the Greek Revival style. There are several examples from the 1850s, including the two-story Crocheron-McDowall House at 1506 Wilson Street and the Margaret Chambers House at 502 Elm Street, each with a simple portico that frames the first- and second-floor doors. One-story Folk houses from the era include the Dimon-Erhard House at 1402 Main Street and the A. A. Erhard House at 1106 Pecan Street.

In the 1870s and 1880s the railroad was established throughout Bastrop County. It was important because it provided transportation to distant markets for Bastrop's cotton, timber, cattle, and coal. Trail drivers no longer had to drive their herds up the Chisholm Trail, and coal-mining companies were able to supply fuel to universities and factories across the state. With the increase in personal wealth, Bastrop experienced a significant residential boom through the early 1900s. Some homes were modest; some, elaborate.

In general, the more elaborate homes were built in what historians classify as "Victorian style," coinciding with the reign of Queen Victoria of England. Architectural and financial exuberance is expressed in gabled and turreted residences, such as the H. P. Luckett House at 1402 Church Street and the B. D. Orgain House at 1508 Church Street. A number of modest, one-story Victorian cottages were built in the southern part of town.

By the first decades of the twentieth century a few of the more modern styles were being built. The midwestern Prairie style was a drastic departure from the Victorian. It featured wide eaves, horizontal emphasis, a low-hipped roof, and heavy square columns, as seen in the P. C. Maynard House at 1408 Pecan Street and the J. T. Crysup House at 1607 Main Street. The Classical Revival style, also popular in the early twentieth century, is found in the Elbert S. Orgain House at 1704 Main Street, which exhibits two-story fluted Doric columns, a Palladian window, and a classical frieze.

In 1978 Bastrop gained national recognition when it became the first Historic and Architectural Multiple Resource Area in the United States to be nominated for listing in the National Register of Historic Places. In this book, Sanders features families that lived in approximately ninety of those historic homes. She has melded an exceptional collection of architecturally significant homes, photographs, and family stories.

# Preface

*A house cannot say anything*
*Save the truth of those*
*Who have lived in it.*

—RUDYARD KIPLING

This book is as much about the families that lived in Bastrop's historic houses as it is about the houses themselves. Some of the information from oral interviews is based on memories and family lore or anecdotes that are unverifiable. Even so, they are still genuinely part of the stories people associate with the homes. Traditionally, a historic house is named in honor of its first owner or in honor of an owner who made a significant contribution to local, state, or national history. Bastrop's homes and their families meet that requirement. Written here are their stories.

Included are all Bastrop homes designated by the state as Recorded Texas Historic Landmarks. Also included are most, but not all, Bastrop homes listed in the National Register of Historic Places as well as homes identified as a City of Bastrop Historic Landmark as of August 2019. Five of the homes have been recorded by the Historic American Buildings Survey (HABS), a program established in 1933 by the National Park Service to document a representative sampling of America's architectural heritage. Commercial buildings in Bastrop's downtown area are not included here, as this is a story of Bastrop's residential architecture and families. In that light, however, a sampling of commercial, governmental, and religious buildings has been included to provide the reader with a glimpse of the community where Bastrop families lived.

If a building has been recognized by the National Register of Historic Places, the State of Texas Historic Landmark Commission, or the City of Bastrop Landmark Commission, the official name given to that building is used in this book. Otherwise, if a building is not recognized by any of those agencies, an unofficial name is assigned and it is called a "home," not a "house," which is customary for recognized historic structures. Thus, we have names such as the Alf Jung House and the Jewell Hodges Home.

If a building is omitted, it may not have been recognized by one of the agencies mentioned, it may have been significantly altered, or information from written sources or descendants of the early home owners has not been available to me. In some cases, a home was moved into Bastrop from another community. Regardless, there still remain many older homes that should be recognized and are worthy of inclusion in a future book, including homes located in the "New Addition," established in 1942.

Many Bastrop homes were built and designed by carpenters, builders, lumbermen, and the home owners themselves. In only a few instances has the name of a practicing architect been discovered. Known architects include Louis G. Mauer, who designed the H. P. Luckett House, and Arthur Fehr, who designed the Fehr-Haynie-Allbright House. In many cases I have relied on the architectural description of a home as written in the application for listing in the National Register of Historic Places or in the application to the Texas Historical Commission. In some cases, the date of a home's construction may differ from the date I show. I have carefully researched and dated homes through tax and deed records and have noted these differences.

Sandra Chipley and I have collaborated on this book. Sandra has been a trustee for the Bastrop County Historical Society for eleven years and has researched and written home histories for the society's annual Holiday Homes Tour for the past twelve years. She has added immensely to the depth and accuracy of this book.

Robbie Moore Sanders
May 2021

# Acknowledgments

I am grateful to Mary Jane Davis (deceased) for encouraging me to write about Bastrop's old homes in the first place. I would drive through the neighborhoods, Mary Jane on the passenger side, while she told me stories about families and events from a time forty to seventy years earlier.

I am equally grateful to Clyde Reynolds (deceased), local historian and longtime tax assessor and collector, who taught me how to understand Building Blocks and Farm Lots, and gave me his volume of *Assessor's Abstract of City Lots, Bastrop County*, 1892 to 1908. It has proven to be a valuable research tool.

I would like to acknowledge the contribution of photographer Mark Winslett and his Sony a7RIII. Mark's beautiful images capture Bastrop's varied architecture as well as provide a complement to my written descriptions. His dedication to this project was tested several times, especially when he had to pick up bicycles and toys from front yards or had to do battle with wasps and mosquitoes.

I can never repay Carolyn Gurklis Huff, who has read every word of this book. I am sure she has given up trying to teach me when to use a hyphen. Her edits, suggestions, and friendship are invaluable.

I thank Rose Pietsch, Bastrop county clerk, and her team for their patience and assistance as I pored over old courthouse deeds and records. I am indebted to the trustees of the Bastrop County Historical Society (BCHS) who provided access to old photographs and to the museum archives and research library. Carol Kyser and the BCHS volunteers were particularly helpful.

There are many home owners and descendants of home owners who graciously provided additional photographs of their homes and related untold stories of their families and friends. I thank each of them:

> Forrest Adams, Sandy and Ron Barclay, Joe Beal, Henry Bell III, David Boatman, Ann Brown, Jo Ann Cantrell, Chris Cartwright, Forrest Chalmers, Tommy Claiborne, Geoffrey Connor, Pat Crawford, Glenda Dayton, Debbie Denny,

Sharon and Chris Duggan, Mariann Dyer, Joseph Emmert, Jacqueline Hastay, Dan Hays-Clark, Judi Hoover, Ricky Hoskins, Michal Hubbard, Frank Huffman and Lucy Todd, Stephanie Jenkins, Roy Johnson, Sharah Johnson, Deborah Jones, Sally Keinarth, Becky Kelly, Kenneth Kesselus, Richard Kesselus, Kathryn Lang, Vicky Lindsey, Laurie Liriano, Bob Long, Ray Long, Susan B. Long, Clara Maynard, Mary McMurrey, Barry Moncure, Howard New, Doris Oldfield, June Pace, Eliza Perkins, Elizabeth Crysup Pierce, Shawn and Bill Pletsch, Thomas R. Phillips, Charles Rabensburg, Mark Rose, Suzanne Sanders, Terry Sanders, Libby Sartain, Laurie Schneider, Nancy and Tom Scott, Cindy and Reid Sharp, Carol Shull, Annie and Jonathan Taylor, Minifred Trigg, Elaine Weiss, Kay Wesson, Nancy Wood, and the boys at Wednesday-morning coffee.

# Historic Homes of Bastrop, Texas

Colorado
River
Dallas
Austin
BASTROP
Houston
San Antonio
James Chavez
Nov. 12, 2019

# BASTROP, TEXAS

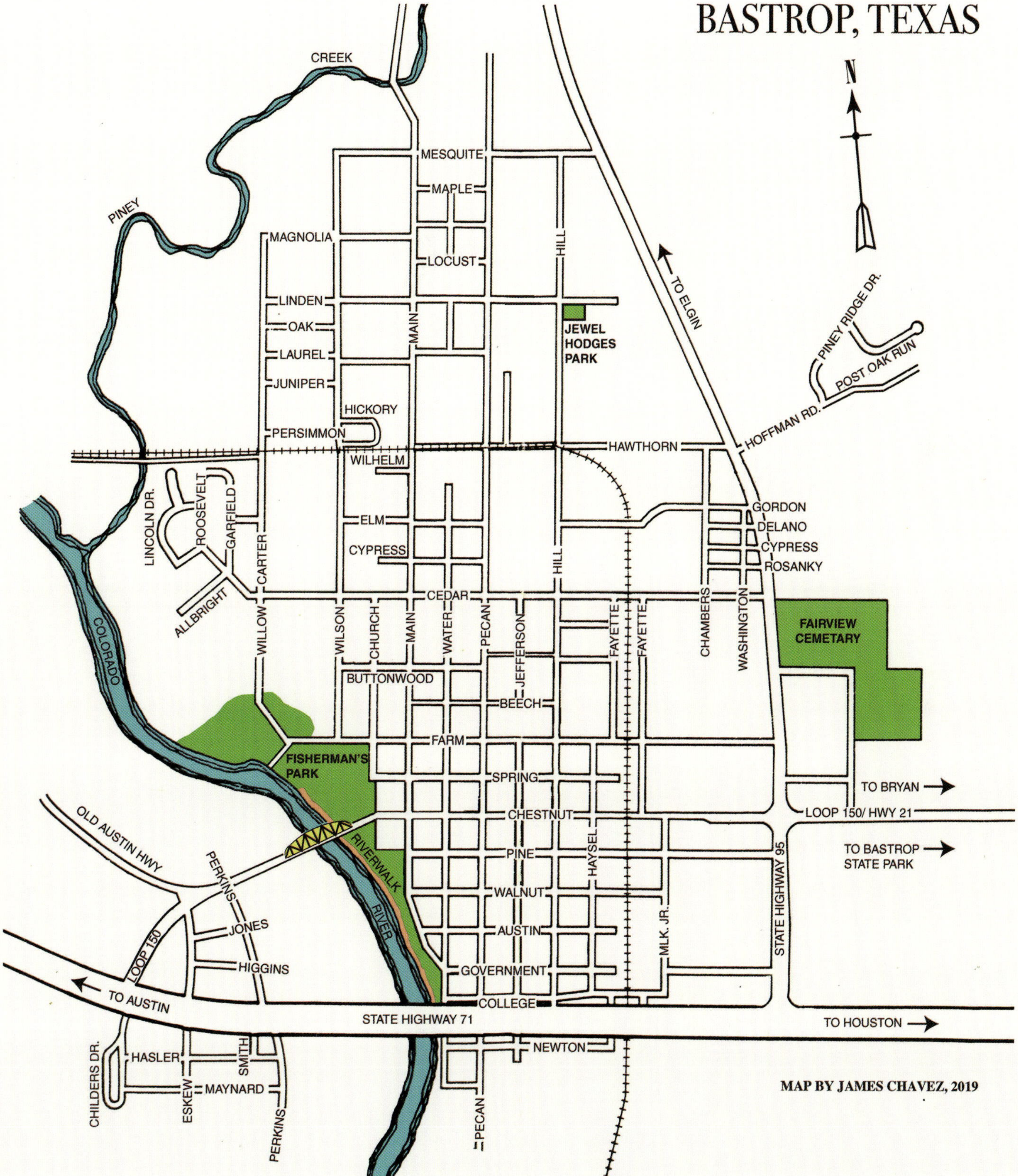


MAP BY JAMES CHAVEZ, 2019

# State Highway 304

## Wylie Hill House

*State Highway 304 / 1856–1857*

In 1835 Abram Wylie Hill, a native of Oglethorpe County, Georgia, purchased land from Sarah Jenkins (in the Jenkins League), which was to become known as "Hills Prairie."[1] Hill fought in the Battle of San Jacinto under General Sam Houston, barely escaping death when a bullet tore through his cap. The *Battle of San Jacinto*, by Henry Arthur McArdle, a painting that hangs in the Senate Chamber in the Texas State Capitol, depicts Wylie wearing this cap.[2]

In 1837 Wylie (age twenty-one) married Evaline Hubbard (age nineteen) and settled on his land, where he built his first home, a log cabin. In 1856–57 the Hills built what the family called "the big house" on the same property. This magnificent example of a Texas Greek Revival plantation home has four tall, brick chimneys, two at each end, with fireplaces upstairs and down. The brick mason was Anton Jung. Years later, his sons, Alf and Gus, rebuilt one of the chimneys, firing the brick on the premises.[3] The upstairs hallway opens onto a small, cantilevered balcony that provides a panoramic view of Hills Prairie. It took three to four carpenters, led by George Orts and Frank Hanke, eighteen months to build the home. The lumber was Bastrop pine, dressed and tongue-and-grooved by hand.[4] The house, when built, was surrounded by three-hundred-year-old live oaks.

Libby Sartain, a descendant of Wylie Hill, and her husband, David, completed a meticulous restoration of the plantation home in 2010. They hired restoration specialists John and Candace Voltz, of Voltz and Associates, Inc., Austin, who used records of the Historic American Buildings Survey (completed in 1933) and the memoirs and

Wylie Hill House, State Highway 304. Courtesy of Libby and David Sartain.

extensive articles written by Eva Hill LeSueur, granddaughter of Wylie and Evaline.[5] Eva detailed almost every aspect of the home's interior—including the hand-painted roller shades, wall coverings, floor stenciling, furnishings, and bric-a-brac.[6] The restoration included a 3,480-square-foot wood-clad addition at the rear of the house, along with the addition of a guesthouse, a pool and pool house, and an open-air kitchen pavilion.

Before the Civil War, thirty-nine slaves worked the Hills' 2,220 acres of cotton. During the restoration process their descendants met with the Sartains, compared notes, shared previously unknown connections, and became friends.[7] The oral history of the enslaved African Americans was passed down and finally published in 2009 by Webster Gregg. Libby Sartain wrote the foreword to Gregg's historical narrative, *From a Prince to a Slave*.[8]

The family cemetery, located on the south side of the home, was also restored and has been designated a Historic Texas Cemetery. Among those buried there are Wylie and Evaline Hill, who died in 1884 and 1893, respectively.

The home is listed in the National Register of Historic Places and is a designated Recorded Texas Historic Landmark.

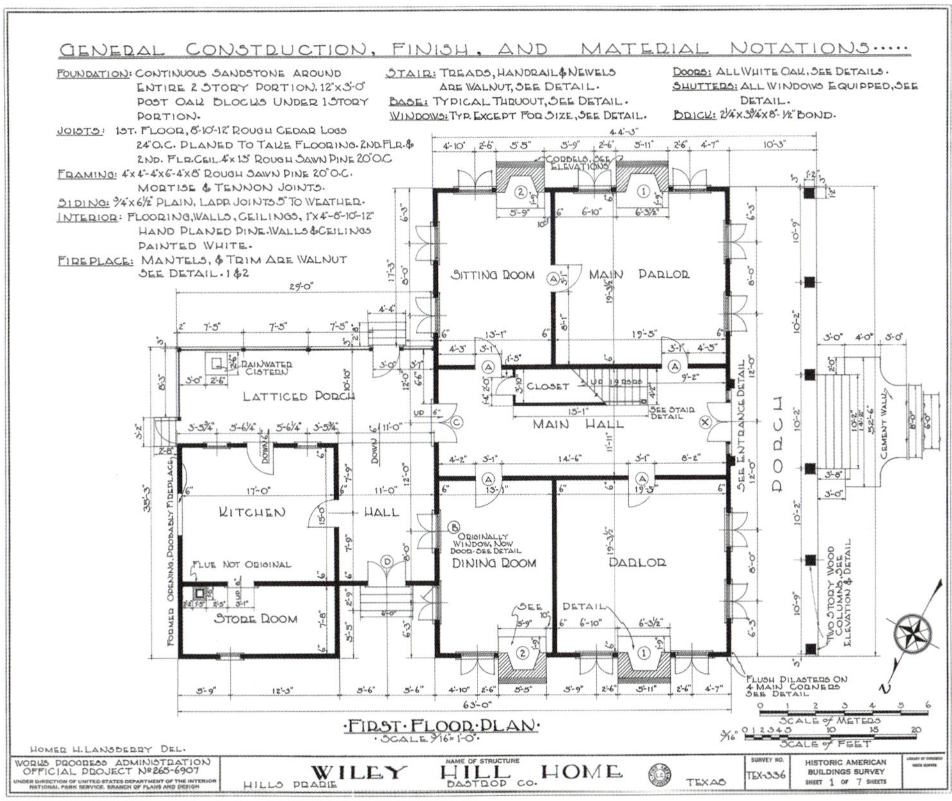


Historic American Buildings Survey, February 9, 1937. Drawing by Homer H. Landsberry.

Replicas of the original hand-painted window shades as described in the memoirs of Eva Hill LeSueur. Photo courtesy of Libby and David Sartain.

## Trigg House

*South of Bastrop, State Highway 304 / 1853*

In 1853 newlyweds Alanson and Ollive "Ollie" Elizabeth Arnett Trigg, came from Tennessee to Hills Prairie and built a two-pen dogtrot cabin of hand-hewn cedar logs on land they leased from Henry McGehee. The Triggs bought 185 acres, which included the cabin, from McGehee in 1857.[9] Children born there were Mary (married William Morris), Della (married Jim Craft), Bettie "Emma" (married Bob Price), Susan (married Charles Jenkins), and William (married Julia Batts). Alanson's brother, Marshall Winchester Trigg, had a farm nearby.

Alanson amassed a valuable estate before he died in 1866. The little dogtrot cabin and land (number of acres undetermined) were valued at $4,000. In addition he owned 240 head of sheep, 7 yokes of oxen, 100 head of stock cattle, 53 pork hogs plus 40 stock hogs, 1 mule, 70 head of horses, 1,600 bushels of corn, 16,618 pounds of cotton, 2 wagons, and 200 bushels of potatoes. One of the accounts due to his estate was $10,208 in Confederate funds.[10]

Ollie's neighbor and distant relative, William "Bill" A. Young, was appointed executor of the estate. Bill, born in Tennessee, had served in the Civil War in Hood's Brigade. He ended the war minus one arm and with the rank of captain.[11] He married Ollie Trigg in Bastrop County on December 20, 1868.[12] They had five children; however, only one survived, John Terry Young, a twin, born July 25, 1868.[13] Ollie and Bill added two rooms to the back of the house and a detached kitchen.

Bill Young died in 1902 and was buried beside Alanson Trigg in the Trigg cemetery. "Ollie would wear widow's garb—usually black. Her dress came all the way to the floor and underneath it were layer after layer of petticoats. As she grew older, her eyesight began to fail, and she spent much of her time in her rocking chair in the open hallway of the home, rocking back and forth and singing gospel hymns or listening to someone read to her. She had a wire line stretched from the back steps to the privy, which was some little distance from the house and this line provided her with both access on her own and a safe place where she could walk for exercise."[14] Ollie died in 1919 and is buried in the cemetery beside Alanson Trigg and Bill Young.

Ollie Trigg Young left her property to her son, John Terry Young.[15] According to John's son, John "had a hard life, for he lived in some very trying times when the community around him was on the decline and cotton farming was on its way out. However, he got the most out of every minute of his life. He loved to play baseball, never missed a square dance and the usual midnight box supper that went with it, getting home about daylight next morning. . . . In his early years he wore a handlebar mus-

Trigg House, South of Bastrop, State Highway 304.

tache, which he later shaved off because it got in his buttermilk, which he dearly loved. He walked with a quick, energetic step . . . striding along, always neat in his dress, with the white tag on his sack of Duke's Mixture smoking tobacco sticking out of his shirt pocket."[16] John married Annie Pierce in 1887 and died in 1945.

John and Annie Young's son, Eugene "Gene," inherited the home. Gene added bathrooms, bedrooms, and closets, eventually selling the house on October 29, 1959, to Ernest Lee.[17] Three months later, Ernest sold the home and the original land (first owned by Alanson and Ollie Trigg) to Kleber Miller Trigg III and his fiancée, Minifred Boyles.[18] Kleber and Minifred had reclaimed the Trigg land. They were married two months later on April 30, 1960.

Kleber was raised "next door," just a couple of miles "down the road," on the land once owned by his grandfather, Marshall Winchester Trigg (Alanson's brother).[19] Kleber was an honor graduate of Texas A&M and a lieutenant with General George Patton's Third Army during World War II. He was a rancher all his life and for thirty-five years the Agricultural Stabilization Conservation Service office manager in Bastrop.[20] Kleber Miller Trigg died in August 1990.

Minifred was a "sophisticated city girl," born in Houston and the perfect example of a "Southern Lady," gracious and elegant. She "took to" life on the ranch and small-town Bastrop. She loved to entertain, hosting many intimate and fund-raising dinners and a Halloween costume party for more than fifty revelers year after year. She enlarged the house, adding a large dining/family room, a patio, and gardens for additional room to entertain. The patio was fenced so the cows could not trample her flowers.[21]

Kleber and Minifred had three children. Their son, Lance, a cattle buyer, died in February 1990; and their daughter, Margaret, an actress in New York, in 2003. Their third child, Kleber "Cheebe," a rancher and cattle buyer, and his mother, Minifred, continue to hold down the home place.

The house is designated a Recorded Texas Historic Landmark, where it is listed as the Trigg Home (Henry E. McGehee House).

## Aldridge-Fitzwilliam House

*South of Bastrop, State Highway 304 / Built 1852, enlarged 1872*

The first portion of this plantation house was erected in 1852 by John Aldridge, a farmer from Tennessee, with servants' cabins located nearby. He and his wife, Eliza Hickerson Thompson Aldridge, had traveled by wagon train, bringing with them their five children, one hundred slaves, a valuable book collection, and several hundred head of cattle. The site was chosen for its proximity to the Colorado River and rich farmland.[22] The original dogtrot floor plan had a back porch leading to a detached kitchen and had a sewing room at the back. "The lumber to build the home was floated across the river from Bastrop and the house was put together with pegs instead of nails."[23]

After John died of typhoid fever in 1861, Eliza and her children moved into Bastrop. Eliza married P. H. Jones but retained ownership of the house, riding out to it from town most mornings. After Eliza's death, her heirs sold the property to Confederate army veteran Captain James W. and Nancy Cartwright Fitzwilliam. The Fitzwilliams added a two-story structure to the original home in 1872 and named the house "Wexford" after the county in Ireland where James was born.[24] James and Nancy's five children were James Henry (married Susie Powell), Alice (married Turner Fowler), Nancy (never married), Frances (married John McPhaul), and John Dennis Fitzwilliam. John married Fannie Goodman in December 1892, and the couple lived at Wexford the rest of their lives. John and Fannie's daughter, Grace, was the first woman faculty member at Texas A&M University.[25] The property remained in the Fitzwilliam family until 1990, a total of 114 years of ownership.

Reid and Cindy Sharp purchased the property in 1990,[26] and the entire Sharp family, including Reid's parents,

Aldridge-Fitzwilliam House, date unknown. Courtesy of the Bastrop County Historical Society.

Claude and Effie Sharp, pitched in on the major renovations that were needed. Using a fingernail-polish brush, Effie, at age seventy, stood on top of tall scaffolding and painted and refreshed the patterned stenciling on the ceiling.[27] Bruce Kana did the renovation's carpentry.

Aldridge-Fitzwilliam House, South of Bastrop, State Highway 304. Courtesy of the Bastrop County Historical Society.

In 1986, with the closest Santa for youngsters being miles away in Austin, First National Bank employees started a party for their children in the bank lobby with Santa being the special guest. In 1991 the Sharps moved the party to Wexford. Today, the affair is not a bank event but is hosted by Cindy and Reid Sharp with help from many "elves," including friends, some bank staff, and even bankers from competitive institutions. Over the years attendance became too large for inside the home, so a separate barn, the Santa House, was built in 2002–3. In 2019 approximately 850 people attended the party, which included holiday music, hayrides, homemade cookies, tamales, taco soup, and crafts. Of course, Santa Claus was the featured guest.[28]

The home is designated a Recorded Texas Historic Landmark.

# Cedar Street

## W. F. Tribble House

*402 Cedar Street / Before 1866*

Sandra Chipley, the current owner (2019), named this home. She wrote, "Usually, an old home is named for its first owner, or for a prominent person, or for the person who owned the home the longest. No name has previously been assigned to this home, and I have taken the liberty of calling it the W. F. Tribble House in honor of William Franklin and Bettie Sue Tribble, who lived here thirty-five years."

The home was built prior to 1866, more than forty years before the Tribbles bought it. The first owner, Phil Claiborne,[1] was a Bastrop attorney and ferry operator. His home was a one-story structure with three rooms. Over time several add-on structures were completed in the rear, forming a U-shaped floor plan.[2] Phil sold the property to P. H. Jones, and it had several subsequent owners until purchased by William and Bettie Tribble in 1906.[3]

The Tribbles married in Tennessee in 1893, came to Texas in 1898, and moved to Bastrop in 1899.[4] After purchasing this home, they immediately began buying nearby parcels of land and soon owned an adjoining forty-seven acres, where they raised mules. Mules were important to the local economy and were sold or leased for use by the railroads, local coal-mining companies, road contractors, and local farmers. According to Sandra Chipley, as of 2019, discarded mule shoes were still being uncovered in the yard of the old Tribble house. In 1911 the Tribbles added the second story, with its dominant Palladian window and five fish-scale-shingled gables, along with other extensive improvements, including an indoor bathroom built on top of the old back porch.[5]

W. F. Tribble House, 402 Cedar Street. Courtesy of Sandra Chipley.

After William died in 1941, Bettie Sue sold the adjoining forty-seven acres to partners J. V. Ash, Joe Crow, and Bruce Allbright, who formed the A.C.A. Housing Company and developed the first subdivision in Bastrop, Riverview Heights. Even though the subdivision has been established for more than seventy-five years, Bastrop's old-time families still refer to it as the "New Addition."

In 1951 the Tribble home was sold to Ferrell and Susie Smith, who owned the Red & White grocery store on Main Street from the early 1950s to the early 1970s.[6] The Smiths built an enclosed porch-like room on the east side of the house and renovated the upstairs into a rental apartment for teachers and police officers. Their home was reported to have had the first color television in town.[7]

Steve and Mary Sonier bought the house in 1989; and in 1993 they, in turn, sold it to L. Charles "Chuck" Kellogg and Sandra Chipley, who had recently returned to Texas from Carson City, Nevada, with their infant son, Jacob. Except for minor modifications and restoration work to the back and side porches, the exterior remains much as it did in 1911. Sandra, a landscape architect, has served as chairman of the Bastrop Parks Board and president of the Bastrop County Historical Society and received the coveted Boy Scouts of America's William T. Hornaday Adult Gold Award for her environmental work at Lost Pines Boy Scout Camp. Chuck, a water-conservation manager for Aqua Water WSC, has served as vice president and president of the Bastrop County Long Term Recovery Team, which was formed after the 2011 Bastrop County Complex fire to rebuild the Bastrop County community for fire survivors who were uninsured and underinsured.

The home is a City of Bastrop Significant Landmark.

## Sarah Jane Orgain House

*602 Cedar Street / Before 1858*

The earliest reference to this home is in a deed dated December 1858, which mentions the "street [Cedar] in front of L. W. Moore's residence."[8] Moore owned the home at 602 Cedar Street. It is believed his home was originally a one-story cottage consisting of the rooms in the back portion of the present house.

Lyttleton "Lyt" Wilde Moore graduated in 1855 from the University of Mississippi as valedictorian with the "highest honors of his class." He was admitted to the bar in 1857 and in the same year married Anna Dunn Wright and settled in Bastrop.[9] Mollie McDowall, born in Bastrop in 1843, wrote in her memoirs that Judge Lyt Moore taught her Sunday school class for a time.[10]

At the outbreak of the Civil War in 1861, Lyt Moore became captain of Company I of George M. Flournoy's Sixteenth Texas Infantry, Walker's Texas Division. Living in the home during the war years were his wife, Anna, and their children, Charles, Ellen, Mary, and Ann. At war's end, he sold the home and moved to La Grange, where four more children were born. There, he was elected to the 1875 Constitutional Convention, which drafted our present state constitution, was elected for three terms to the US House of Representatives, and in 1901 was appointed judge of the 22nd Judicial District.[11] Lyt Moore sold the home to J. H. and Martha Fouchee, who then sold it in January 1867 to Edmund Jones Orgain for twenty-five hundred dollars.[12]

Edmund and Sarah Jane Kimball Orgain came to Bastrop via Tennessee and Williamson County, Texas, with their two sons, Frank and Horace, in 1853.[13] Edmund was

Sarah Jane Orgain House, 602 Cedar Street.

a merchant, and Sarah Jane became one of Bastrop's preeminent educators. For thirty-five years she was principal of a private school, the Colorado Institute, which was attended by students from all over the country. During the Civil War, a bleak period for most other schools, her school flourished, sometimes with more than one hundred pupils in attendance. Later, Edmund assisted in the classroom. "Boys and girls were seated on separate sides of the school room and had separate recesses. When dismissed in the afternoon they marched out in time to *Smith's March* which Mrs. Orgain played on the organ, each pupil turning and bowing to her when he reached the door. It has been said that no child left Mrs. Orgain's school without having learned to read and write well."[14]

Sarah Jane was a charter member of the First Baptist Church founded in 1888. She was the first president of the Ladies Aid Society and a founder of the Ladies Reading Circle in 1897. She was the historian for the United Daughters of the Confederacy and believed in history as a means of broadening the mind. Around 1900 Sarah Jane and Edmund added the two-story front section to the home with two fireplaces.[15] This late-Victorian-styled section has a projecting bay and double gallery in the ell. It has a front pedimented dormer and an ornamented gable with shingling and bargeboards.

Edmund Orgain died in 1905, and Frank died in 1920. Frank had been city secretary in 1901, a banker, and Sarah Jane's partner in many business transactions. She made an outstanding gift to Bastrop of ten thousand dollars to establish the F. A. Orgain Memorial Hospital in Frank's honor. Later, she gave an additional three thousand dollars for two wards within the hospital to serve the Mexican American and African American populations.[16]

Sarah Jane Orgain died suddenly in July 1924 at the age of ninety-three while on a pleasure trip to California. She bequeathed seventy thousand dollars in bonds to Baylor University to establish the Frank A. Orgain Student Loan Fund. The "home place . . . and all the furnishings" were bequeathed to her son, Horace.

The home is listed in the National Register of Historic Places (listed as constructed in 1905) and is a City of Bastrop Historic Landmark.

## Honeymoon Hut

*907 Cedar Street / Circa 1890*

Chester and Mary Erhard built this modest, three-room, board-and-batten cottage for their family cook, Julia Howe, behind their large family home, which faced Pecan Street.[17] After Chester's death in 1929, their son, Earl, inherited the family property, which included the cook's quarters.[18] Earl and Annie Pearl Windrow Erhard had one child, Mary Pearl. From 1938 to 1940, Mary Pearl attended the Mount Vernon Seminary, a finishing school in Washington, D.C. After graduation, she started school at the University of Texas. At a luncheon in Bastrop for officers and wives from nearby Camp Swift, Mary Pearl met her future husband, Captain Kenneth R. Duff, a young orthopedic surgeon who had been assigned to the hospital unit there. They married in December 1942.

Because of the influx of military families into Bastrop during World War II, local residents, including the Erhards, shared their homes or upgraded outbuildings to accommodate the incoming families. Housing was at a premium. While the newlyweds were on their honeymoon, the officer who was renting the Erhard cottage received orders that his unit was leaving. Family friends hurriedly readied the cottage for Mary Pearl and Kenneth and helped with painting, furnishings, and decorations. They found it great fun to be "in on the preparations."[19]

Honeymoon Hut, 907 Cedar Street.

Erhard family cook, Julia Howe, with corncob pipe. Courtesy of Shawn and Bill Pletsch.

When the couple returned, they were greeted with a grand surprise. The cook's cottage had been transformed. Camp Swift's post engineer had made a sign that read "Honeymoon Hut" and nailed it beside the front door. The honeymoon was short. In early 1943 Captain Duff was sent to Europe and Mary Pearl moved back into her parents' Pecan Street residence. After the war, Kenneth and Mary Pearl eventually moved to Houston, where Kenneth began his career as a doctor.

Although Mary Pearl Duff sold the large home on Pecan in 1970, she retained ownership of the Honeymoon Hut. She died in 1989, and Kenneth Duff sold the little cottage to Bryan and Janean Whitten in 1999. The Whittens' home is nearby, and as of 2019, they have never spent a night in the cottage. It is often featured on the Historical Society's Holiday Homes Tour. The Whittens decorate the outside every holiday—Christmas, Valentine's Day, St. Patrick's Day, Easter, Fourth of July, and Thanksgiving—and sometimes during football season with flags and banners supporting Texas A&M University.[20]

Kenneth and Mary Pearl Duff are the grandparents of actresses Haylie and Hilary Duff. Haylie is best known for her roles as Sandy Jameson in the television series *7th Heaven*, Summer Wheatley in *Napoleon Dynamite*, and Amber Von Tussle in Broadway's *Hairspray*. She is host and star of Cooking Channel. Her sister, Hilary, had the title role in the television series *Lizzie McGuire* and expanded her role to become a movie actress, singer, songwriter, fashion designer, and film producer.

The home is listed in the National Register of Historic Places and is a City of Bastrop Historic Landmark.

# Chestnut Street

## Dawson House

*1002 Chestnut Street / Circa 1887–1892*

In 1886 the vacant, corner lot at 1002 Chestnut and the two-story home on the adjoining lot at 1006 Chestnut were owned by Ed Bastian Sr.[1] Between 1887 and 1892, Bastian built a new home on the corner lot,[2] and in 1903 he deeded it to his son, Ed Bastian Jr., and Ed's wife, Julia Hoppe Bastian. The classic one-story Folk Victorian has bracketed eaves, a half-hipped roof, an oriel bay window, and ornamented gables.

In 1904 Ed Bastian Jr. sold the home to Mary Elzner Dawson. Mary and her husband, Wiley Jones Dawson, opened the Dawson Boarding House. Mary did all the cooking for lumbermen, cotton buyers, district judges, lawyers, jurists, and ranchers who boarded at the Dawson House for weeks and months at a time.[3] Mary died in 1933; Wiley, in 1935. Wiley willed his home to his son by a previous marriage, William Benony "Babe" Dawson.

Babe and Alma Julia Kohler Dawson, with their daughters, Mabel and Leah, moved into the home. The girls were in their early twenties at that time. Both daughters married within a few years of moving into the house; however, by 1940 both Leah and Mabel had returned—each with an infant daughter of her own. Leah's husband, Glenn Spooner, died in an automobile accident in 1940, and in the same year Mabel separated from her husband, Wylie Hill LeSueur. Leah and her daughter, Marilee, moved into the Dawson House with Babe and Alma. Mabel and her daughter, Mary Clay, moved into a small home that Babe bought for them directly behind the Dawson House. At the same time, Babe's younger brother, Jessie, moved into a small garage apartment next to Mabel. The Dawson family now numbered seven—all living on the Dawson lot. Babe became "Big Daddy" to them all.

Dawson House, 1002 Chestnut Street.

Marilee wrote about her life as a young girl in the Dawson household:

> Big Daddy [Babe] and Big Mama [Alma] kept us both during the day. I remember sitting on the front porch and watching horse drawn wagons of cotton going down the street to the cotton gin, which was by the depot on Chestnut Street. The cotton gin whistle blew every day at noon. When Mary Clay and I were growing up, we knew everyone in the neighborhood. We would run through yards on errands for Big Daddy or Big Mama collecting eggs, milk, butter and so forth. I remember running barefoot across the hot pavement to Sugar and Curtis Sanders' filling station on Chestnut with tourist courts behind. We loved to get soda water, which was in a big iced container with a lid on each side. If we were extra lucky, they gave us a free candy bar. Mostly, we were sent to get cigarettes for Uncle Jessie.[4]

Mabel and Leah had full-time jobs. Mabel taught school, and Leah worked at Camp Swift during World War II, at the City of Bastrop Utilities Department, and then for the tax assessor's office. After Alma died in 1946, it became Babe's job to raise his two granddaughters while their mothers worked. He solicited the help of Jessie, called "Unc." Jessie was moved from his apartment into the Dawson House to take over the cooking duties. He cooked Babe's favorite foods and had supper ready when the family returned home each evening.[5] Babe enjoyed parenting. He took his granddaughters on walks, pushed them on their tricycles and bicycles, read to them, and taught them to play dominoes and cards. He made the girls very precise, brilliantly colored, miniature bow-and-arrow sets and taught them how to shoot. He also whittled miniature tables, chairs, and toys for them.[6]

Leah Dawson (Spooner/Sanders), circa 1925. Courtesy of Judy Sanders.

Leah and her daughter, Marilee, eventually moved into yet another home owned by Babe. It was a little house directly across the side street (1004 Jefferson Street) from the Dawson House. Leah married Samuel Monroe Sanders in 1949 and had a daughter, Judy, a year later. The Sanders family lived in the little house until 1951, when they traded houses with Babe and Jessie. Mabel and Mary Clay remained in the small home behind the Dawson House. This arrangement lasted for several more years. After Babe died in 1954, and Jessie, in 1961, Leah and Monroe Sanders inherited the home and sold it in 1971.

The home is listed in the National Register of Historic Places (construction date listed as 1905; however, a completion date by 1892 is shown in the *Assessor's Abstract of City Lots, Bastrop County*).

## R. J. Griesenbeck (Sr.) House

*1005 Chestnut Street / Before 1887*

Rudolph "Rufus" Julius Griesenbeck was born in 1854 in New Braunfels, Texas. By 1870 his parents, Julius and Emilie Griesenbeck, had moved their family to Waco, where Julius was a beer brewer, and fifteen-year-old Rufus was an apprentice in his father's business.[7] By 1880 Rufus was a bartender in Bastrop, living with his mother, now a widow, and his brothers Herman, Theodore (called "Pete"), Alfred, Oscar, and Charlie and his sisters Clara and Emilie.[8] Their married siblings, living elsewhere in Bastrop, were Otto and Lina.

On December 15, 1880, Rufus married Amalie Orts, the daughter of George and Elizabeth Fehr Orts. At that time, George was a prominent Bastrop "lumberman," who would later own a lumberyard in downtown Bastrop from 1894 into the early 1900s.[9]

R. J. Griesenbeck (Sr.) House, 1005 Chestnut Street.

In 1887 Rufus bought this property from his father-in-law for nine hundred dollars, the dollar amount indicating there was a home on the property at the time of purchase.[10] The home was an unadorned early Victorian one-story clapboard, with a bay on a projected ell consisting of a simple entablature over triple, angled windows. It has pedimented windows, gingerbread cornice brackets, and a front door with geometric-patterned stained glass in the upper half.

Rufus served as mayor of the Corporation of Bastrop in 1885, was Bastrop County district clerk from 1888 to 1900,[11] and by 1910 was an insurance agent in partnership with W. B. Ransome.[12] Children raised in the home were Emilie, Bruno, Haynie, and Rudolph J. Griesenbeck Jr. (called "R. J." by family and "Rufus" by friends), who followed in his father's footsteps in the insurance business.[13]

Rufus Griesenbeck Sr. died in 1924; Amalie, in 1934. The property was inherited, divided, and sold to descendants for several succeeding generations. A large family room was added on the south (back) in the early 1970s by descendant Bernice Griesenbeck Garrett and her husband, Ashley Jackson Garrett (called both "A. J." and "Jack").[14]

Jack Garrett served in the US Air Force before his retirement in 1968. He was among the top golf competitors while in the air force and was hired as golf pro and operator of the Lost Pines Golf Course in Bastrop State Park. Jack and Bernice ran the park's concession, and Jack gave lessons, rented and maintained carts, collected fees, and did all things associated with the golf course. Jack played with the "Town Bunch," a clique of local men who played golf together four days a week for approximately twenty years. The Town Bunch included Tracy Chalmers, Eugene Wilkins, Robert E. Jenkins Sr., Charlie Rabensburg, Mark "Bubba" Oldfield, Dusty Rhodes, Jug Jenkins, Daniel Boone, Tommy Hendrix, Robert Miller, Joe Quintanilla, and Granville Bunte, who was once bitten on the foot by a copperhead on the ninth hole.[15] After several months of recovery time, Granville returned to the golf course but played shoeless until the swelling went down.[16]

The home was inherited by the Garrett's daughters, Jacqueline Hastay, Barbara Garrett, and Janet Russo, who were the last Griesenbeck descendants to own the home. It had been in the Griesenbeck family 106 years when sold in 1993 to the Best Lil' Hair House, Inc. Owners of the corporation were Laurie and James Schneider and their friend Charles "Charlie" E. Amos III. Charlie eventually sold his shares to the Schneiders.

Laurie and James Schneider retained the historical exterior of the home, but Laurie changed the inside to accommodate her beauty shop. The hairstyling stations were installed in the section with the bay, and the large family room, which had been added in the 1970s, was changed into a nursery, playroom, and kitchen so that Laurie and her employees could bring their children to work. Throughout the years, babysitters were hired to take care of the babies and preschool children. Beauty-shop babies include Shane Pugh, Haley Pugh, Taylor Schneider, James Luke Schneider, Travis Gryder, Dalton Herman Goertz, Rylie Amos, and Sonora Amos.[17]

The house is listed in the National Register of Historic Places (construction date listed as 1910).

## Bastian-Haralson House

*1006 Chestnut Street / 1886*

This home is an excellent example of typical Victorian informal design: it has a centrally located entrance flanked by a bay-windowed projecting parlor on one side and a porch along the remainder of the front. The house exemplifies the architecture of the period with its jigsaw-cut gingerbread detail; wrought-iron balusters; tall, slender windows; various-sized rooms; and second-story porch.[18]

Bastian-Haralson House, 1006 Chestnut Street.

The home's first owner, Ed Bastian, was a local hardware merchant and tinner. When he built the home in 1886, he depended on local workmanship and materials for its construction but brought a carpenter from Chicago to build the free-standing, circular, walnut staircase in the entrance hall.[19] Original outbuildings once included a barn and a combination servants' quarters/smokehouse. Bastian and his family moved to Houston to open a tin shop in 1906 and sold their home to Alex Kleinert, who in turn sold it to James A. and Lula Bass Haralson in 1910. James Haralson was station agent and telegraph operator for the Missouri-Kansas-Texas Railroad Company. His newly acquired residence was within walking distance of his office, and "he maintained a flower garden at the railway station for the pleasure of train passengers traveling through Bastrop."[20]

The Haralsons had five children: Annie Lee, Marguerite, Frances, James, and Paul. Annie Lee and Marguerite lived together in the home at various times throughout their adult years. Each of the two sisters reared their children in the home as well.[21]

"Annie Lee's Room" at the First United Methodist Church on Main Street is named in honor of Annie Lee for her many years of teaching children's Sunday school classes. It is said that on Sunday morning, Annie Lee was "the first in and the last out." Her husband, Henry Alexander, served as Bastrop County clerk for four terms. He died of influenza in 1918, and Annie Lee served out his term until 1920. She continued to work in the county clerk's office until 1968. She died in 1978.

Marguerite was also active in the First Methodist Church (now the First United Methodist Church). She and Annie Lee donated one of the stained-glass windows in the chapel in memory of their parents, James and Lula Haralson. Marguerite's husband, Fred G. Haynie, was Bastrop County school superintendent from 1920 to 1962. After he retired, he opened an insurance business and remodeled the servants' quarters/smokehouse for his office. The building was razed in the early 2000s. Marguerite loved to entertain and was known as an excellent cook. At age ninety-four she hosted her last dinner party in Bastrop, the occasion being her departure for El Paso to live with her daughter, Marguerite Haynie Sanderson. Marguerite Haynie died in El Paso at age one hundred in 1991.

Haralson stained-glass window, First United Methodist Church.

### Marguerite Haynie's Pecan Pie

1 cup broken pecans
2 eggs, well beaten
1 cup white Karo
2 tbs. melted butter
1/4 cup sugar
2 tsp. vanilla

Mix above ingredients together and pour into a slightly baked pie shell. Place a few whole pecans on top to decorate. Bake at 400 degrees for 10 minutes. Reduce heat to 250–300 degrees until set, 20 minutes or longer. (Courtesy of Evelyn Holm, January 15, 1993)

The home is listed in the National Register of Historic Places and has been designated a Recorded Texas Historic Landmark (listed as the Haralson House). It is a City of Bastrop Historic Landmark.

## George W. Davis House

*1010 Chestnut Street / 1907*

After George W. Davis married Edna Gill in 1897, the couple lived with Edna's parents (707 Pecan) for ten years until George hired Joseph Pfeiffer to design and build this home. Its one and one-half story frame features a central truncated roof with four main projecting gables with Carpenter Victorian trim. Situated on a corner lot, the Chestnut Street facade is a mirror image of the Hill Street facade. The windows are of special interest because of the inclusion of diamond shapes with four-inch-square stained-glass borders.[22] As of 2019 the pine Eastlake woodwork is in excellent original condition and includes forty-two-inch wainscoting in the hall and dining room. There are oak mantels, working ebonized transoms, and original electrical fixtures throughout the house.

"Five Freaks." Mary Jane Davis, center, and high school girlfriends, 1925. Courtesy of William Terry Sanders.

George Davis was a farmer, rancher, sheriff, and Bastrop County tax collector. He was the grandson of early settler S. V. R. Eggleston, who was killed by Indians in 1839 in the front yard of his home on Water Street.[23] Edna was the granddaughter of early settler Robert Gill, who arrived in Bastrop in 1840 and for whom Gill's Branch is named. After the death of George Davis in 1926, Edna was appointed tax collector to fill his unexpired term. She was elected to serve one term and then retired.

George and Edna had two children: Robert Jonathan Davis, who was born in 1897 and died in 1933 while living in Richmond, Texas; and Mary Jane Davis, born at high noon on August 30, 1909. Mary Jane was a busy teenager, performing in high school one-act plays and vaudeville skits. She was a piano student of Ivor Young and played in public recitals in 1924, 1925, and 1926. She sang a solo as part of her high school graduation in May 1927.[24] In 1931 at age twenty-two, she won first place in the "Bridge Game Contest" in the *Houston Chronicle*,[25] and she was named centennial queen when Bastrop County celebrated its centennial in 1932. After attending the University of Texas and working as a counselor at the Scottish Rite Dormitory on the UT campus for a number of years,[26] she returned to Bastrop after her mother died in 1951.

Although Mary Jane had not studied library science in college, she was the librarian at Bastrop Junior High School. During the mid-1960s, she checked out books from the

George W. Davis House, 1010 Chestnut Street.

University of Texas library to self-educate and drove to Austin every Saturday for three years to attend a library science workshop, resulting in accreditation of the school from the State Department of Education.[27] She was the junior high librarian for approximately ten years until the early 1970s. She told the students, "If you can't abide by my rules, don't come into my library."[28]

Mary Jane never married and insisted that she be called "Miss Mary Jane Davis." Although in her late eighties when she died, she was listed in the telephone book as "Miss Mary Jane Davis." She lived in her childhood home until her death in 1998.

Although the house is no longer a private residence, subsequent owners and tenants in the historic home have retained the original architectural and decorative elements. Local attorney Kathryn Rogers purchased the home in 1998 and moved her law practice to the house in 1999. She made minor repairs and added central air and heat. The home continues to be professional office space.[29]

The home is listed in the National Register of Historic Places and is a City of Bastrop Historic Landmark.

# Church Street

## Albert Erhard Home

*1207 Church Street / 1851*

The first owner of this early home was James R. Nichols, a blacksmith, who built a three-room structure on the lot he purchased from John D. Hogan in 1851.[1] During the Civil War James joined with local gunsmith N. B. Tanner, who had a contract with the Texas Military Board "to produce five-hundred Mississippi-type rifles . . . Nichols reputed to be the best barrel man in the State."[2] In December 1863, after completing 294 rifles and bayonets, James complained to the board that he was not being paid sufficiently: "To make gun barrels & bayonets [any] longer at [dollar amount unclear], I beg to decline. . . . I have a family to support, which is my only care." After this letter, there is no evidence that Tanner and Company sold any more rifles to the Confederate States of America.[3]

Albert Erhard was in business with his father, Cayton Erhard, in the C. Erhard and Son drugstore and inherited the store when his father died in 1884. The same year, Albert and Josephine Garth Erhard purchased the house for $1,225. They enlarged the home in 1898 and in 1902 hired contractor Joseph Pfeiffer to add a second floor.[4] With the second story added, the structure became a simplified Queen Anne Victorian with a cross-gabled hipped roof. The bottom corners of the second-story projection are highlighted with a decorative fan-shingle pattern, while the first floor below is a cutaway bay. Patterned fish-scale shingles accentuate the gable surfaces, and half-size square columns support arched spandrels across the front porch.

Albert died in 1931, and his son, Harry, inherited the store and home. For more than seventy years, local townspeople laughingly remembered Harry Erhard. He had a

Albert Erhard Home, 1207 Church Street.

Fan-patterned shingles.

"large" personality. Neil Gurwitz, at age ninety, still remembered the first time he met Harry: "He had a pipe between his teeth, turned upside down."[5] Many remembered that Harry bought rattlesnakes from the local kids for twenty-five cents each, which he caged in the back of his store and used the venom in various pharmaceuticals. Occasionally, Harry would fry a snake on a burner in the back of the store and serve it to his customers and friends. When Harry died in 1963, three generations had owned the drugstore—from 1865 to 1963. The store burned in 1980.

Harry and Maude Erhard inside his drugstore, 1942. Courtesy of the Bastrop County Historical Society.

Harry Erhard died in 1964. His wife, Maude, who died in 1975, willed the home to their children, Albert Erhard and Bonnie Erhard Zunker.[6] The Erhard children sold their home to Effie and Claude Sharp in 1976. Claude Harris "Red" Sharp was among the first group of Bastrop County men drafted in World War II and was among the first American troops to land at Salerno Beach, Italy. He earned two Bronze Battle Stars and returned home to train troops at Camp Wolters, Texas. After the war, he served in the National Guard, retiring with the rank of lieutenant colonel.[7]

With war's end, Bastrop residents turned out to watch veterans play at the new baseball field—Fireman's Park—where Red played shortstop and was nicknamed "Lightning." Claude and Effie married in 1947. During their retirement years, they restored the Albert Erhard Home.[8]

Effie worked as secretary for the Bastrop County Agent's (Agricultural Extension) Office. For thirty-six years she was a source of information and direction for visitors to the courthouse: "Because of her quick wit and sharp tongue, she was a source of news and merriment for visitors and county employees alike."[9] Effie died in 2010; Claude, in 2011.

## H. B. Combs House

*1208 Church Street / 1911*

Henry Burris Combs, a prominent local physician, and his wife, Maude, commissioned their home to be built by the Wilbarger Lumber Company in 1911.[10] They had eclectic tastes, and their home has been described as an "eclectic architectural mix"—a fusion of Neoclassical elements with an essentially Victorian house plan with an interior that is both Neoclassical and Arts and Crafts.[11] The mix may be ascribed to not only the original owners' tastes but also the increasing availability of manufactured building components in standardized patterns and styles that could be ordered from cata-

H. B. Combs House, 1208 Church Street.

logues. Local designers, builders, and contractors increasingly had access to building plans and components that might be customized for individual clients.

In 1892 Henry Combs graduated from Vanderbilt Medical College. He strayed from the family tradition: his father and four of his brothers were dentists, while Henry chose to be a surgeon. He became well established in the Bastrop community and was co-owner of the post office building at Main and Pine Streets and a director of the Citizens State Bank. He served as the bank's vice president from 1909 until 1945.[12]

In 1897 he married Dorothy "Maude" Olive, the granddaughter of pioneer Texans Thomas W. and Margaret Wilbarger Chambers. Maude's mother, Belina Chambers Olive, died tragically in May 1905. She was fatally burned at her home in the northern part of Bastrop when her clothing caught fire while she was lighting a match, her husband having gone to the barn only a few minutes before to do the morning milking. Belina Olive ran into the yard, attracting the attention of her husband and neighbors, but their efforts to save her from the engulfing flames were in vain. Her son-in-law, Henry Combs, was summoned immediately, but unfortunately the burns were beyond his medical skill. She died a few hours later.[13]

Henry and Maude had no children of their own but in 1906 took under their protective wing a thirteen-year-old orphan, Marcario (Mike) Juarez, who worked on the Combs's farm located behind their house. When Mike married Encarnation (Connie) Morales in 1913, the Combses hired her to cook, clean, and help Mike maintain the property. Mike and Connie Juarez had twelve children, each of whom Henry Combs delivered and took the honor of naming—many after members of the Combs and Olive families. The children's names include Dorothy Maude Juarez and Henry Juarez, named for Maude and Henry Combs. Evidently Henry ran out of family names because there was even a child named after the governor of Texas, Dan Moody.[14]

Maude died in 1938; Henry, in December 1956. His sister, Laura Combs, lived in the house until 1961. Subsequent owners include S. M. and Rosemary Hardt, O. W, "Happy" and Marie Glenn, and Mark and Celeste Rose, who undertook major renovations in 1993.

Carlos and Laurie Liriano moved to Bastrop with their sons, Scott and Michael, from Metairie, Louisiana, while their daughters, Christy and Carmen, remained in graduate school at Louisiana State University. The Lirianos purchased the house on October 26, 2012, and moved in just in time to celebrate Christmas there.[15] Carlos and Laurie established the Lost Pines Toyota Dealership.

The house is listed in the National Register of Historic Places and is a City of Bastrop Historic Landmark.

## Hall-Sayers-Perkins House

*1307 Church Street / 1852*

The historical marker for this home describes it as an American primitive colonial home. It was built by Constant K. and Margaret Hall after they purchased the lot for three hundred dollars in 1852. The home began as a one-story settler's home built of heart pine that was completely hand-pegged and notched. It was a two-room cottage with a dogtrot hall and two fireplaces. Constant Hall was part owner of the Risher, Sawyer, Hall stage line, which controlled sixteen passenger and mail lines in the state.[16]

Dr. David and Inda Sayers purchased the homestead from the Halls in 1870 for twenty-five hundred gold dollars.[17] David had previously moved to Bastrop in 1851 from Mississippi after the death of his first wife, Mary Peete Sayers. He then married Inda (Indiana) Scott in Bastrop in 1854. Children raised in the home were Jessie, Elizabeth, Tom Green, and Samuel S.[18] David Sayers died in 1886. His descendants have spoken of his benevolence,[19] which is reflected in the inscription etched on his headstone in Fairview Cemetery: "The Afflicted Poor Never Appealed to Him in Vain."

Hall-Sayers-Perkins House, 1307 Church Street.

Longtime home owner Catine Perkins believed that the house was "not fine in the aspect of ever having riches or carvings."[20] In 1905 the descendants of David Sayers sold the home to a dentist, Nathan (Than) G. Fowler, and his wife, Beulah, who had five children: Turner, Leola, William, Ethel, and Daisy. In 1910 the couple contracted with Joseph Pfeiffer to add the second story. A charming story about Than Fowler appeared in the April 14, 1921, issue of the *Bastrop Advertiser*:

> Dr. N. G. Fowler, Bastrop's Rhode Island Red king, has recently had shipped to him a rooster that seems to take the prize from all the roosters in town. When the fowl was shipped into town and brought upon Main Street last week he had quite a number of gentlemen admirers. The rooster was in a large box and when he stood up to crow his head was well above the box and the rest of the crowd. Dr. Fowler took the bird home, put it in one of his ordinary chicken

> yards, and it was not very long until the Dr. found that he had to take down one of the cross fences in order that his new fowl might have room to turn around. In other words, all of the chicken apartments in the doctor's yard have had to be enlarged. Even the doctor's visions have been enlarged to the extent that he now fancies himself as being the champion chicken raiser of the county.[21]

Major Robert L. Perkins Jr. and Catine E. Perkins purchased the home with a handshake on April 14, 1959, the day of their eighth wedding anniversary, and the couple with their newborn daughter, Eliza, and two young sons, Lucian and David, moved to Bastrop soon afterward.[22]

Robert Perkins was called "Scoop" from his days on Guam during World War II because of his ability to get the "scoop" on whatever was happening on base. He served in the air force for twenty years, many of them as a navigator on B-52 bombers, and was stationed at Bergstrom Air Force Base in Austin when the home was purchased.[23] In 1962 Texas was still segregated, and many Bastrop kids still speak of the time when Robert brought two green military buses to Bastrop, making sure the Cub Scouts, both white and African American, got to visit Bergstrom Air Force Base and tour the B-52s, KC-135s, and other military planes.[24] Patient and dedicated, he worked an additional twenty years as a high school physics teacher in San Antonio, commuting back and forth to Bastrop. He loved being in his workshop and built many of the pine shelves that hang in the house today.

Catine was known for her prolific garden. She spoke of herself as an "illusionary farmer" and dug the soil relentlessly, endlessly bringing in cow and chicken manure, cottonseed hulls, pine needles, and sandy loam.[25] People drove for miles to see her beds filled with irises, daylilies, poppies, antique roses, and culinary herbs. An advocate of organic gardening, she worked in the garden until her late eighties, still making her own daily rosemary, thyme, and other teas that she drank for health. She held herb classes for the young staff at Whole Foods when it first opened in Austin and supplied herbs to some of the top Austin restaurants at the time. A self-taught scholar, she was quite outspoken—delving into cultures, world and American history, and politics.[26] Robert died in 2009; Catine, in 2016. Their descendants continue to own the home today (2019).

The house is listed in the National Register of Historic Places and is a designated Recorded Texas Historic Landmark (listed as the Joseph L. [*sic*] Sayers House).

## Harriet Erhard House

*1401 Church Street / 1889*

Harriet Erhard built this Victorian house, which faces Church Street, in the backyard of her first home, which faces Main Street. Her new home, built around 1889,[27] reflects her generous inheritance from her husband, early settler and veteran Cayton Erhard, who died in 1884. The one-story, frame home has five chimneys, a bracketed bay window, small brackets under the eaves, two attached porches with Juliet metal awnings, a stained-glass front door, and curved bargeboards on the gable end.

Harriet moved into the home with her youngest children: Eugene, age nineteen, and Cora, age twelve. Neither child married, and all three lived in the home throughout the remainder of their lives. Harriet died in 1903; Eugene, in 1956; and Cora, in 1969.

Harriet Erhard House, 1401 Church Street.

(Eugene and Cora were buried side by side in Fairview Cemetery, but only one headstone spans their two graves. Both names are etched on the stone, which leads people to believe incorrectly that they were married.)[28]

Cora preserved her father's scrapbook and papers, which included his reminiscences of the Texan Santa Fe Expedition of 1841. The scrapbook and papers were placed in the archives of the University of Texas Library, now the Dolph Briscoe Center for American History, and were published in the *Southwestern Historical Quarterly* from July 1962 to April 1963.

The home lay vacant for thirty years prior to its purchase by Clint Hille in 1996. Deed restrictions stipulated that Cora's framed high school diploma must remain hanging in the foyer throughout the life of the house. Hille added a guesthouse, pool, and gardens.[29] As of 2019, subsequent owners have continued to hang Cora's diploma in the foyer.

The house is listed in the National Register of Historic Places (as the Cayton Erhard House although Cayton never lived here) and is a City of Bastrop Historic Landmark.

## H. P. Luckett House

*1402 Church Street / 1892*

This home is a classic Queen Anne design and one of Bastrop's most photographed historic structures. It occupies part of what was once the campus of the Bastrop Academy—later the Bastrop Military Institute—in operation from 1851 until midway through the Civil War. The house, built in 1892 by Humphrey P. and Fannie Haynie Luckett, replaced the old academy building. Many of the structural support boards in the attic are recycled lumber from the Military Institute. Numerous initials and dates are carved and written on the boards.[30]

Evidence suggests the house was designed by architect Louis G. Mauer, the brother of well-known Texas architect Henry C. Mauer. The contractor was W. T. Parks.[31] Featured are a steamboat-style wraparound veranda fronting the first and second floors, oriel bay windows, gingerbread fretwork, and an overall lightness characteristic of the American interpretation of Queen Anne architecture. The roof is multigabled, and each gable is faced with a different pattern of fish-scale shingles and carved verge boards. The foyer is dominated by a grand, split stairway and the original, elaborate iridescent wallpaper. The original French carpet remained in the living room as of 2019.

Humphrey Luckett was twenty years old when he came to Texas in 1867 after graduating from the Louisville College of Medicine in Kentucky. Two years later he married Frances (Fannie) Haynie, and the couple moved to Bastrop. Fannie was the daughter of

H. P. Luckett House, 1402 Church Street.
Courtesy of Elliott Gurwitz.

H. P. Luckett House, circa 1900.
Courtesy of the Bastrop County Historical Society.

Elegant double entry to the stairs.

One of three fireplaces in the H. P. Luckett House.

Austin physician and politician S. G. Haynie and the granddaughter of the renowned Reverend John Haynie. Humphrey became well established in the Bastrop medical community and was a founder and member of several medical associations. He served as the city health officer and became known throughout the state as an authority on yellow fever. In 1905 he went before the city council and declared a "systematic war on mosquitoes" by pressing for enforcement of all sanitary ordinances, especially the Mosquito Ordinance, and the closing of public watering troughs to protect Bastrop from the threat of yellow fever.[32]

Humphrey was a director of the First National Bank from 1890 to 1923 and vice president from 1917 to 1923. Besides his professional accomplishments, he had the distinction of owning the first automobile in Bastrop County. A stroke ended his career in 1918. He died in 1925; Fannie, in 1930. In 1936 their heirs sold the house to Alex Waugh for two thousand dollars.[33]

Alexander C. "Alex" Waugh was a mining engineer who graduated from the Colorado School of Mines. He was in partnership with his father, Robert "Bob" Waugh, in the Waugh Coal Company, located about ten miles north of Bastrop.[34] In 1923 Alex married Lucile Booth. In the late 1930s Lucile donated the decorative iron cresting on the roof of their home to Fairview Cemetery for use in its entrance gates. Ownership of the house passed to the Waugh's only son, Alex Waugh Jr.

In 1983 the home was sold to Christine "Chris" and Donald Cartwright, who dedicated more than twenty years to carefully restoring the home, and as of 2019 it appears much as it did during the Lucketts' lifetime. The ornate ironwork was returned to the Cartwrights in 2000 when the old cemetery gates were removed and replaced with new ones. Don Cartwright died in 2004, and Chris continues to maintain the home and make it available for private tours and the Historical Society's Holiday Homes Tour.

The house is designated a Recorded Texas Historic Landmark and a City of Bastrop Historic Landmark.

## Allen-Bell House

*1408 Church Street / 1854*

When Major Robert D. Allen was summoned to Bastrop by his father (Colonel Robert Thomas Prichard Allen) to be commandant of the prestigious Bastrop Military Institute, a portion of his trip required travel from New Orleans to Galveston on the ill-fated steamship *Opelousas*, which collided with the *General Chambers*. Many lives were lost, but Robert Allen, his mother (Julia), and twelve-year-old brother (John Howard) were saved. They were adrift three hours; Julia Allen clung to the side of a lifeboat with her

Allen-Bell House, 1408 Church Street.

son supporting her until they were all rescued. Thus, Robert Allen began his new position in Bastrop as a hero.[35]

In addition to being a commandant and hero, Robert was a respected mathematics professor and was quickly hired to tutor young women in Bastrop, among them Laura Sims. Laura's parents, Samuel W. and Julia Harman Sims, built this home in 1854. After math lessons turned into marriage, Laura and Robert lived with her parents from 1859 to 1866. As the number of cadets at the Bastrop Military Institute declined during the Civil War, the institute closed, and the Allens moved to Kentucky and reopened the Kentucky Military Institute.[36]

In addition to being named for Robert Allen, the house is named for Mary Ann Mathews Bell. Mary Ann married Durant Hatch Bell Sr. in Memphis, Tennessee, before moving to Gregory, Arkansas. In 1859 the Bells and their children, Sarah (Sallie), J. Hunter, Samuel Wesley, William Jerome, Henry Newton, and Durant Hatch Jr., arrived in Bastrop County in an area that later became known as Sayers, just north of Bastrop.[37] Durant Sr. died of a fever on August 1, 1860, and Mary Ann bought acreage in the Sayers area and began farming and ranching.[38]

Located behind the Allen-Bell House is the law office of Robert Lynn Batts, future law professor, federal judge, and University of Texas regent.

Arched board-and-batten fascia.

Mary Ann's oldest son, Hunter, was killed in January 1874 while playing cards in the nearby community of McDade. He was in a card game with Wild John Lawrence, who had previously killed thirteen men. When Hunter accused Wild John of cheating, they both jumped up from the table, and Hunter, who was wearing a cumbersome buffalo-skin coat, reached for his pistol. It got tangled in the coat as he fired, missing its mark.[39] Wild John shot Hunter three times in the right shoulder. The shots were fatal. Wild John "was arrested and turned over to the Town Marshal, but in the night Lawrence escaped."[40]

In 1886 three brothers, Sammy, Henry "Man," and Durant Bell, bought this home for their mother.[41] Of special interest is the home's elegant exterior treatment. The walls are vertical board-and-batten with the battens joined at both top and bottom by arch-like cuts in the fasciae.[42] When the Military Institute was dismantled in the 1890s, two cadet barracks were moved to the west side of the house to create two bedrooms. Although covered from view, the names and dates of several cadets are written above the bedroom ceilings.[43] Located on the southwest side of the home is a small building that was used as the private law office of Robert Lynn Batts from 1886 to 1891.[44] Robert Batts later was named chairman of the Board of Regents of the University of Texas and, still later, chief counsel for Gulf Oil.

Three of Mary Ann's sons became law officers: William Jerome was a Bastrop County deputy sheriff, sheriff, and a deputy US marshal; Durant Hatch was Bastrop mayor, postmaster, and Bastrop County deputy sheriff; and Henry Newton "Man" was Bastrop County deputy sheriff or sheriff (1886–90) for twenty-one years.[45] Their brother Sammy was a deputy sheriff on several occasions but was better known for being proprietor of Bastrop's Iron Front Saloon. His partner in the saloon was Otto Amthor, who for a number of years lived with the Bell family in this home.[46] It is presumed Otto named his son, Willie Bell Amthor, in honor of this family.

Sheriff Man Bell inherited the home from his mother. In 1895 Man married Ella Hicks Baxter Batts, the sister of Robert Lynn Batts. The home was next owned by Henry Newton Bell Jr., who married Mildred Smith from Caldwell, Texas. Henry Jr. was a veterans affairs officer in Bastrop County.[47]

The current owner of the home (2019) is Henry Newton Bell III, the fifth generation of Bells to own the home. Henry III married Pamela Roberts from San Antonio, the daughter of architect Reginald and Billie Wurzbach Minckner Roberts. Henry and Pamela Bell's children are Regina Eleanor McFarland and Henry Newton Bell IV, "Cuatro." Grandchildren are Kathryn Tennie McFarland, John S. McFarland III, and Henry Newton Bell V.[48]

Henry III is an attorney admitted to practice before both state and federal courts, including the US Supreme Court. He is a life fellow of the Texas Bar Foundation and a member of the International Bar Association of London. He is a member of the

Sons of the Republic of Texas and Sons of the American Revolution. He retired as a colonel from the JAGC, US Army Reserve. He is past lord chancellor of the Knights of the Symphony (Austin) and is former co-president, with his wife, Pamela, of the English-Speaking Union, Austin Branch.[49]

The house is listed in the National Register of Historic Places, is a designated Recorded Texas Historic Landmark (named the H. N. Bell Home), and is a City of Bastrop Historic Landmark. It has been featured in various publications, including the 1967 *Texas Parade Magazine* and Amon Carter Museum's "Texas Houses of the Nineteenth Century."

## Rufus A. Green House

*1501 Church Street / Before 1888*

Rufus Alexander Green was a familiar figure in Bastrop for forty years prior to his death in 1893. He partnered with Alf Jung in a local brick company, operated a drugstore with W. J. Miley, and was a builder and banker.[50] He drove members of the popular Bastrop City Band in parades and community events in his large wagon drawn by four white horses.[51]

The Rufus A. Green House was a one-story cottage with high ceilings and wide cedar flooring when purchased by Rufus and Sue Trigg Green in 1888. Rufus, a builder by trade, upgraded the home and converted the outbuildings into a kitchen and bathroom. Rufus also built the historic 1890 First National Bank building located at 1016 Main Street. He was one of the bank's original directors and stockholders and held a considerable number of bank shares. After his death in 1893, the bank shares were inherited by Sue and his unmarried daughter, Minnie.

In November 1894 Minnie married William Bland Ransome. Four years earlier, "Ransome arrived in Bastrop with $10.00 and one change of clothes. He had attended business school in Illinois and landed a job as a clerk for the Bastrop firm of Bell and Erhard."[52] William, Minnie, and Sue lived together in the home. Sue eventually sold her share of the home to her daughter and son-in-law. Sue and Minnie's bank shares were transferred to William, and he was appointed to First National's board of directors in 1903. Sue remained in the home until her death in 1911.

Automobiles were beginning to appear in Bastrop about 1910, and Ransome wanted one. Minnie told him, "You can't have a car until you build me a house." Ransome's solution was to remodel their home as it is today (2019).[53] He added the upper story and dramatic two-story classical columns but left the lower floor basically as it had been.[54] It is not known whether or not he got his automobile.

Rufus A. Green House, 1501 Church Street.

Rufus Green, driver for the Bastrop City Band. Courtesy of the Bastrop County Historical Society.

William B. Ransome's name appears on the cornerstone of Bastrop's Methodist Episcopal Church South, now the First United Methodist Church. He was church treasurer for fifteen years and a trustee when the church was built in 1925. Stained-glass windows in the church were donated in honor of William and his in-laws, Rufus and Sue Green. In addition to ranching, William had financial interest in the Coca-Cola Bottling Company and owned Ransome and Company Insurance. He served as president of the bank from 1930 until his death in 1951.[55]

The home is listed in the National Register of Historic Places and is a City of Bastrop Historic Landmark.

## J. M. Holt House

*1507 Church Street / After 1852*

The first owners of the home at 1507 Church Street were Henry and Catherine Thompson Perkins, who bought the lot in 1852 from John D. Hogan and built a one-story home on the property.[56] Henry was a carpenter by trade and served as a trustee for School District 1, one of Bastrop County's twenty-three school districts.[57] Henry and Catherine Perkins lived in the home until their deaths in 1897 and 1901, respectively. Their children inherited the home, and their daughter, Dora Perkins Partain, sold it in October 1906 to John and Mattie Holt.[58]

John Milton Holt had married Mattie Ellen Litton Turner four years earlier on November 19, 1902, and a month later purchased the stock and inventory of Meyers Brothers' Green Flag Grocery located on the northeast corner of the intersection of Main and Chestnut Streets.[59] Together, John and Mattie operated their new business, J. M. Holt & Co., a dry goods store. They employed Mattie's brothers, John Oliver Turner and Dale (Tisdale) Turner.[60] (Two other brothers, Nash and LeGrand Turner were famous horse jockeys in Paris, France.)

After buying the Perkins house, John and Mattie added a second story before moving into the home two months later in mid- to late December 1906.[61] They replaced the square columns with round Doric ones and enlarged the front porch. A smaller, second-story porch sits above a decorative pediment over the front entry. At the second-story roofline, asymmetrically located left of center, is a dormer with shingled sides and triple decorative windows. The overall effect on the facade is the stepping down of the rooflines—from the dormer line at the left, to second-story porch roof, then to the first-floor roof on the right. Less than two weeks later, on December 26, John died of appendicitis. John and Mattie had been married only four years and had two young girls, Bernice Nash Holt and Julia Kathryn Holt.

J. M. Holt House, 1507 Church Street.

The home was originally one story as shown in a photo of Catherine Perkins (left) and her daughter, Dora Perkins Partain, circa 1900. Courtesy of Robbie Sanders.

After John's death, Mattie continued to own and work in the dry goods store, and John Oliver Turner became its manager. Mattie Holt died on July 3, 1916, and her sister, Callie Turner Sessums, was appointed the guardian of her two minor daughters. John Oliver Turner took over the business and operated it for many years for the two Holt children.

Mattie's probate in the Bastrop County clerk's office listed the home's value at four thousand dollars. In April 1930 the Holt house was "conveyed to the Citizens State Bank for indebtedness of the J. M. Holt Company to said bank."[62] The bank sold the house to John R. and Neppie Allen in 1936.[63]

The home is listed in the National Register of Historic Places (dated as built in 1910) and is a City of Bastrop Historic Landmark.

## B. D. Orgain House

*1508 Church Street / 1888*

Twenty-five-year-old Dru (Drusilla) Johnson left her home state, Tennessee, "to see something of other lands and peoples,"[64] and in January 1869 she accepted a teaching position at the Colorado Institute in Bastrop. She soon met a promising young lawyer, Captain Benjamin Darby Orgain, and they married on December 27, 1870. In her memoirs, *From Dawn to Eventide,* Dru wrote, "One thing we planned for and worked for from the first, was the possession of a commodious and comfortable home."[65]

The Orgain house has more than forty-seven hundred square feet on the first two floors alone and was "the place" for many social and cultural gatherings. Each of six fireplaces and mantels is different, incorporating carved wood, tile, spindle work, marble, and mirrors. There are stained-glass windows throughout, and walk-through windows lead to several small smoking porches. The music room, library, and parlor can be closed off by massive pocket doors. The architectural elements include wraparound galleries on two levels and an intricate, filigreed arch in the entry foyer.[66]

Benjamin Orgain, as a young boy, lost an arm after he was accidentally shot while out hunting with several other young boys. This loss may have influenced his decision to become a lawyer since many other professions were not practical for him. In addition to practicing law, Benjamin was county attorney from 1878 to 1880 and was a founder of the First National Bank of Bastrop. He served as its president from 1890 to 1916.[67]

Dru Orgain was an active member of the Methodist Episcopal Church South and interested in the affairs of Bastrop. In 1897 she became founder and first president of the Ladies Reading Circle, the founders of the Bastrop County Historical Society and museum.

B. D. Orgain House, 1508 Church Street.

One of her other interests was the city burying ground.[68] Unhappy with the city aldermen for the lack of care given to the cemetery, Dru boldly appeared with a contingent of women at council meetings and demanded action. During one particularly difficult meeting, the exasperated aldermen threw up their hands and cried, "You do it!"[69] Thus, Dru became the first president of the Bastrop Cemetery Association, an organization that operated the cemetery for 124 years until it was turned back to the city in 2005.

After the death of Benjamin in 1917, Dru wore a tall black turban with a widow's veil for the rest of her life—winter and summer for fourteen years. When she died in 1931, all the stores in Bastrop were closed for her funeral.[70] Family members sold the home in 1947.

The home is listed in the National Register of Historic Places, is designated a Recorded Texas Historic Landmark, and is a City of Bastrop Historic Landmark.

# Elm Street

## Margaret Chambers House

*502 Elm Street / Before 1857*

This home, named for Margaret Chambers, is the first residential structure in Bastrop County to acquire a historical marker from the Texas Historical Commission (August 10, 1962). Constructed with native cypress, pine, and cedar, this Texas Greek Revival home has three wood-burning fireplaces, heavy square columns with simple capitals, and handmade pegged doors and woodwork. On the north side are original "nine-over-six" windows. Shutters are hung on the interior side of all windows throughout the house.[1]

Margaret Barker Wilbarger Chambers was first married to early colonist Josiah Wilbarger. They settled west of Bastrop on the north side of the Colorado River in what is now called Wilbarger Bend. In 1830, while Margaret waited in Matagorda, Josiah built a log cabin surrounded by a stockade for protection against hostile Indians. When the cabin was built, Josiah sent an Indian fighter to guide her to their new home. Margaret made the journey on horseback with a baby, John, on her lap, a feather bed tied on the back of the saddle, and a carpet bag on the saddle horn. The guide seldom spoke and rode well ahead, often out of sight. There were times she was instructed to dismount, hide in the thickets, and keep the baby silent. They often changed directions when signs of Indians were detected on the trails. After their safe arrival at the cabin, her husband and his hunting companions gave a hasty greeting and begged her to cook something to eat. This hardy pioneer woman soon had a huge fire in the fireplace and an iron pot on a hook over hot coals where she prepared venison and bear meat.[2]

Margaret Chambers House, 502 Elm Street.

Margaret Chambers House, 1942. Courtesy of the Bastrop County Historical Society.

Josiah was scalped by Indians in 1833,[3] which he survived, and he died in 1844. Margaret married Colonel Thomas W. Chambers in 1846.[4] He had come to Texas with the Kentucky Volunteers who had ridden from Princeton, Kentucky, to join General Sam Houston at the Battle of San Jacinto. However, the battle was over by the time they arrived. Thomas was a lawyer and legal adviser to the Wilbargers.[5]

Margaret donated two thousand dollars to the construction of the Methodist Church and Bastrop Academy buildings in 1851.[6] Thomas died in 1855, and Margaret purchased this home on three acres from David Coulson for two thousand dollars in 1857.[7] She lived here with her children from both marriages. Her oldest child, John Wilbarger, the baby who traveled to Wilbarger Bend on her lap, became a Texas Ranger and was killed by Indians in 1850, dying on the Texas plains.[8]

Margaret's youngest daughter, Fenora Chambers, sold the home to Walter M. and Anna Norment in 1910. Their daughter, Rubelle, and Rubelle's husband, James L. McMillan, purchased the property in 1945. One of the early settlers who once owned the land was Bartholomew Manlove, the first mayor of Bastrop.[9]

The building is listed in the National Register of Historic Places (named the Bartholomew Manlove House), is a designated Recorded Texas Historic Landmark, and is a City of Bastrop Historic Landmark.

# Farm Street

## Burger House

*703 Farm Street / 1868–1869*

Richard "Dick" Burger emigrated from Germany to the United States in 1850 and by 1860 was living in Bastrop.[1] In 1861 at age eighteen he enlisted as a private in the Confederate Army and served in Terry's Texas Rangers. He was twice wounded, served for the entire war, and arrived home exactly four years after he left.[2] In 1868 he married Clara Linke and purchased this newly built home from W. C. and Sallie Powell.[3] Dick worked as a clerk at P. O. Elzner's Mercantile in Bastrop. He was an original stockholder in the Casino Association, which hosted concerts, plays, banquets, and other social functions at its regional cultural center, the Casino. He was a member of the city council, the Democratic Party, and Terry's Texas Rangers Veterans Association and later a store owner in partnership with C. B. Garwood.[4]

The wood-frame home features a Greek Revival floor plan. When constructed, the first floor consisted of a dog-run hallway with a parlor to the west and the Burgers' bedroom to the east. The kitchen, outhouse, and carriage storage building were all detached from the main structure.[5] A second story was added in 1885,[6] most likely to accommodate the Burger children, August and Mina. Porticos are centered on the front at both levels and are supported by square columns extending from the base of the lower porch to the entablature.[7] The home has eclectic architectural features on the first- and second-story facade. It has a low-pitched, hipped roof and brackets under the eaves.

Burger House, 703 Farm Street.

Burger House, photo circa 1895. Courtesy of Kenneth Kesselus.

The single-family residence was converted into a duplex in 1942 to accommodate the influx of people into Bastrop due to Camp Swift, a newly constructed military training facility north of town. In 1976 the property was sold by Burger descendants to Richard Alan Hawkins, who began rehabilitating the house, including replacing the original knob-and-tube wiring and removing the wall that had been added to convert the home to a duplex.[8] The house was sold in 1979 to Judith and Thomas Hoover, who continued the rehabilitation. Jonathan and Annie Taylor purchased the home in 2009 and remain committed to its preservation and upkeep.[9]

The home is listed in the National Register of Historic Places and is designated a Recorded Texas Historic Landmark.

## Ernest and Julia Hasler Home

*909 Farm Street / Circa 1909*

This home was built on a large corner lot for Ernest F. and Julia Rabensburg Hasler.[10] The original house plan was L-shaped with a bay window at the front northwest corner, a porch along the front facade, and back porches along the back of the ell.[11] By the late 1930s the floor plan consisted of a large foyer with a central hallway leading to the back of the house, and the backyard boasted pecan trees, sweet peas, and a flower garden.

Ernest and Julia Hasler had two girls, Bernice and Marie. The family would sit at night in their beautiful backyard and sometimes walk back and forth to the nearby houses of aunts, uncles, and cousins.[12] Bernice married Robert E. Jenkins, and Marie married Harvard McLeod. Ernest inherited an interest in the Hasler Funeral Home, later called Hasler Brothers Funeral Home. Ernest died in 1938, and Julia took over her husband's business with the help of her son-in-law, Robert E. Jenkins.

The funeral home was located upstairs in a two-story building on Main Street (Hasler's Corner) that housed all of the Hasler family businesses. World War II changed that. With the lack of workers, and a demand for cots where soldiers from nearby Camp Swift could "sleep it off" before returning to their barracks, Julia moved the funeral business from Hasler's Corner into her home to free up the upstairs for the

Ernest and Julia Hasler Home, 909 Farm Street.

new enterprise. (Soldiers paid fifty cents per cot for a few hours' sleep.)[13] Being widowed and living alone, she remodeled her home to accommodate the funeral business. Her private apartment was on the east side of the house, and the funeral home was on the west. No additional parking was allotted because most people were within walking distance of the services.[14]

Robert, who had been helping her in the funeral home, joined the army, so Bernice quit her teaching job to help her mother. One of Bastrop's finer moments is credited to these two women. There is a historic marker in Fairview Cemetery that reads:

War Babies Guardian Angel, Memorial Day, Fairview Cemetery.

> WAR BABIES
>
> During WWII, over 300,000 troops were trained seven miles north of Bastrop at Camp Swift. Many women moved to Bastrop for a few months to be near their soldier one last time before his deployment overseas. Some of these women, upon the death of a child, had no money for burial. Assistance was provided by the owners of the Hasler Brothers Funeral Home who bought fabric from the local "Five & Dime" store to line small wooden coffins and purchased doll clothes for the deceased infants. The children were buried free of charge in this area of Fairview. When the mothers returned to their homes in distant towns or states, the graves were forgotten. It is believed there are at least 16 War Babies in unmarked graves. Their names are unknown.

In 2005 the Bastrop County Historical Society placed small crosses where the children are thought to be buried. The society also installed a large statue of an angel and named it the War Babies Guardian Angel. Often, flowers can be found at the base of the statue or in the arms of the angel. No one knows who places them there.

When Marie's husband died in 1945, she and her daughter, Judy McLeod, moved in with Julia for a year; her son, Harvard McLeod Jr., stayed nearby with an aunt and uncle.[15] Marie and Bernice inherited the property from their mother when she died in 1959 and sold the house and business in 1964 to Carl and Margaret Cooper from Bell County for thirty thousand dollars.[16] This historic home, with its poignant story, had been owned by Ernest and Julia Hasler and their descendants for fifty-five years.

The structure remained in place through subsequent owners; however, it fell into decline until 2014, when it was moved several feet west to create an additional residential lot on the corner of the property. Robert and Vicky Lindsey purchased the old home in 2016 and began a major restoration project.[17] They placed the home on the Historical Society's 2018 Holiday Homes Tour and welcomed approximately four hundred guests who toured the home.

## Dr. C. A. Grimes House

*1201 Farm Street / 1904*

Charles Anderson Grimes, a graduate of Meharry Medical College in Nashville, Tennessee, was twenty-three years old when he came to Bastrop County in 1895.[18] He was the first African American physician in the area. In 1904 he married Laura Madison and built this modest clapboard home on vacant property he purchased for two hundred dollars from R. Burger.[19] He began a private practice for the west end of the county and in the Piney Creek community and "as far as a horse and buggy could carry him."[20] He was, however, one of the first African Americans in Bastrop to buy a Model-T Ford.[21] Charles practiced medicine in Bastrop County for thirty-five years. He died in 1935; Laura, in 1959.

The home is listed in the National Register of Historic Places (dated 1885).

Dr. C. A. Grimes House, 1201 Farm Street.

# Hoskins House

*1310 Farm Street / 1898*

Moritz Gloeckner immigrated to the United States from Germany in 1859 and acquired his citizenship in Bastrop County in 1865.[22] Moritz, a merchant on Bastrop's Main Street, married Bertha (Bettie) Michel in 1879, and they had four children: Frank, Anton, Mary, and Helen. Moritz purchased the property for his home in 1895,[23] and by 1898 he and Bertha had built a new house. In the years 1895, 1896, and 1897 the property was appraised at $350. In 1898 the appraised value jumped to $1,000, indicating a house was built on the property during that year.[24] Built in a typical Folk Victorian ell plan, the gables have fish-scale shingles with pediments supported by decorative brackets atop the first-floor double windows.

Helen Gloeckner, a schoolteacher, inherited the home from her father in 1917 and married Emil Prokop later the same year.[25] She sold the home to Herman Brown in 1920. After a series of owners, including Arthur and Willie Mae McPhaul, Paul G. Lehnick, Selma Lehnick Veselka, and V. B. Ferguson, the house was sold to Bevy and Lottie Wainscott Hoskins in 1950, who deeded the house to their son, Ira Raymond Hoskins, in 1960.[26]

The following history of Ira Hoskins is taken from one written in 2002 by an unknown author. The history is located in the City of Bastrop's Planning and Zoning Department in the files of the Landmark Commission.

### HOSKINS HOUSE

> Ira R. Hoskins was born in Red Rock, to B. V. and Lottie Hoskins on April 17, 1908. It was 1927 when Ira got his first taste of law enforcement. He went to Richmond, Texas and hired on with the penitentiary there guarding prisoners.
>
> Ira married Orlean Rucker in 1931 and returned to farming. In 1933 with his wife and first son, they returned to penitentiary work at the Harlem #1 State Farm near Richmond. Over the next 10 years, Hoskins established himself as one of the finest dog men in East Texas. Still working for the pen, he was deputized by the Texas Rangers, and Fort Bend County law officers all over the territory enlisted him to track escaped "trusties" with his pack of blue ticks and black-and-tans.
>
> Ira and his family returned to central Texas in 1942 when Ira's mother developed cancer. He drove a shuttle bus for the Camp Swift soldiers for a year and then in 1942 took work as a switchman for the M. K. T. Railroad in Smithville.

Hoskins House, 1310 Farm Street.

Ira first ran for sheriff against incumbent E. D. Cartwright in 1948. He lost, lost again in 1950 but in 1952 was elected to the first of his five terms in office. The next four years Ira and Orlean lived downstairs in the jailhouse (which is still standing next to the Bastrop County Courthouse). The sheriff made $350.00 a month and his one deputy earned $275.00. Ira hired Jimmy Nutt as his first deputy. The two "had a run in" shortly thereafter and Nutt turned out [meaning Nutt ran for Sheriff]. Hoskins was reelected in 1954 (then the sheriff's term was only two years) and again for four years in 1956. It was the same Jimmy Nutt who in 1960 returned to take the office away from Ira and to hold it for 16 years.

Hoskins mounted campaigns to regain his job in 1964, and in 1968 went back to switching trains, to get his 16 with the railroad. He and Orlean also opened the Ranch House Café in the 1960s. In 1976 Ira won in a field of 9 candidates, reclaiming the job after a 16-year retirement.

Ira and Tommy Moseley of Elgin vied in the 1980 race, and Moseley won. Ira, not to be undone, came back strong in 1984 in a race that included not only incumbent Moseley, but Judy Edwards (past investigator in Hoskins' office) and

> Smithville police [chief] Frank Calabrese, Ira took his old friend Moseley to the run-off and won by 500 votes.
>
> Ira was diagnosed with leukemia and expired in December 1987. He is buried at Fairview Cemetery along with his spouse Orlean for nearly 54 years.

In 1990 the home was deeded to Ricky Dean Hoskins and Sherri Hoskins (divorced in 2004).[27] The home, now owned by Ricky, has been in the Hoskins family almost seventy years.

The home is a City of Bastrop Historic Landmark.

## Willis Miley House

*1320 Farm Street / Circa 1890*

Built about 1890 by Alfred and Julia Griesenbeck (and Alfred's mother, Emilie), the homestead was conveyed to contractor Joseph R. Pfeiffer in 1911 for material and work due on the home. The Griesenbeck home was sold to Willis Oliver Miley in 1918.[28] The one-story Folk Victorian has a combination board-and-batten and clapboard exterior. It has an L-shaped front porch, two-over-two windows with pediments, cornice returns at the gabled ends, and sidelights with a transom over the front door.

Willis O. Miley and Dora Elizabeth Davis were both born at Reid's Bend, a rural community near Bastrop. They married in 1907 and had one child, Cora (married V. B. Ferguson). Willis Miley was a drayman for the Railway Express Company and was a civilian guard at Camp Swift, a World War II army training camp located north of Bastrop, until his retirement two years prior to his death in August 1947.[29]

Dora continued to live in the home until her death in 1973. She rented out spare rooms, once to the parents of Melinda Larson. In 2017 Melinda wrote in her application to the City of Bastrop for a historical marker: "My mother and father rented a room from Mrs. Miley in the 1940s. . . . The house was gifted to me by my husband around 1996. . . . This house means the world to me."[30]

The home is listed in the National Register of Historic Places and is a City of Bastrop Historic Landmark.

Willis Miley House, 1320 Farm Street.

# Hill Street

## Mina-Bastrop Pioneers' House

*1005 Hill Street / 1836–1837*

The Mina-Bastrop Pioneers' House, built beside the Old San Antonio Road, was first owned by Greenlief (Greenleaf) Fisk and Mary Ann Manlove Fisk, the daughter of Bartholomew Manlove, Bastrop's first mayor. Mary Ann gave birth to her first child while escaping from Mexican general Santa Anna's advancing forces during the historic 1836 Runaway Scrape, when frightened settlers across Texas fled eastward after the fall of the Alamo. General Santa Anna divided his army and sent six hundred troops led by General Antonio Gaona up the Old San Antonio Road to Bastrop; he turned the rest of his army toward Harrisburg. Helpless women and children fled for their lives toward Louisiana. After receiving word of Santa Anna's defeat at the Battle of San Jacinto on April 21, 1836, families returning to Mina-Bastrop found the Mexican Army had taken everything that had been left behind, and Indians plundered or destroyed anything left by Gaona's army.[1]

The home is locally known as the "San Jacinto House" because it was owned by two veterans of the Battle of San Jacinto, Jesse Halderman and Campbell Taylor. Harriet Craft Halderman moved into the house in the 1840s with her first husband, Jesse Halderman. After his death in 1850, Harriet married Campbell Taylor, and they too lived in the home. Harriet was the sister of two other San Jacinto veterans, James A. Craft and Russell B. Craft. The structure is typical early-Texas architecture and was built as a traditional dogtrot with dormer windows; a long, sloping roof covering a gallery on the south; and narrow stairways rising to a half story floored with wide planking. The foundation of the house is constructed of giant cedar logs, and the chimneys are of locally made brick.

Mina-Bastrop Pioneers' House, 1005 Hill Street.

A legend told by Fisk descendants is that in January 1836 David Crockett spent a night in this home while on his way to the Alamo. His gun was broken and required the expertise of a gunsmith, so he remained in the home overnight for the repairs to be completed.[2] The *Bastrop Advertiser* printed a slightly different story. It stated that Crockett's gun was broken, and the repairs required that he stay overnight. The article explained, "Crockett and his 'b'ar huntin' friends' spent the night in the jail-house at Mina (present Bastrop) charged with 'disturbing the peace and disorderly conduct.'. . . It is not known whether Davy's fiddle tunes and uproarious stories disturbed the tranquility of Mina, or if a friendly sheriff trumped up the charges so the 12 Tennessee volunteers could sleep indoors."[3]

The home later served as a stagecoach inn. An avenue of flowering shrubs and roses, reaching from Chestnut Street to the inn, greeted travelers as they approached their stop. Guests included General Sam Houston and other notable Texans. At the time of her death in 1911, Harriet had lived in the house for seventy years. She is buried in Fairview Cemetery between her two husbands: Halderman on her right and Taylor on her left.

In 1984 the house became the property of Royce and Mildred Namken. The house was rental property until 2010 when Mildred Namken, along with family members Wally and Janet Namken and Patsy Trigg, mounted an extensive restoration and renovation of the property.

The home is listed in the National Register of Historic Places (listed as the Campbell Taylor-Greenlief Fisk House) and is designated a Recorded Texas Historic Landmark (listed as the Mina-Bastrop Pioneers' House).[4] It is a City of Bastrop Historic Landmark.

## T. C. Osborn House

*1102 Hill Street / 1881*

Thomas Claiborne (sometimes Claiborn) "T. C." Osborn married Suzanna Isabell "Belle" Smithwick in 1878, and together they built this single-story Greek Revival home in 1881. Lumber for the house was hauled by wagon from the train depot at McDade, Texas. They also built several large barns, a smokehouse, and a washhouse with a furnace and large cauldron for scalding clothes.[5]

The Osborn family provides a short course in Texas and Bastrop history. T. C.'s grandfather Benjamin came to Texas in 1825 from Tennessee as a colonist with Stephen F. Austin. T. C.'s father, Thomas, married Mary Augustine McCullough, a cousin of the famous Texas Ranger Ben McCullough. T. C.'s wife, Belle, was born in Bastrop County at Gravelly, on Alum Creek, in 1857. Her father, A. A. Smithwick, was an early circuit rider Methodist preacher and cousin of Noah Smithwick, author of *The Evolution of a State*.[6]

T. C. was born in Hog Eye (now named Elgin) on August 12, 1850. Between 1871 and 1883 he rode the Chisholm Trail seven times. T. C. pursued several business ventures in Bastrop, including a partnership in the late 1880s in the Iron Front Saloon at 1009 Main Street. He eventually dissolved the partnership because of the strenuous objections of Belle.[7] In 1906 T. C. bought the farm of Colonel G. W. "Wash" Jones and spent the rest of his life raising cotton and cattle. He rode his horse from his Hill Street home to the farm and back each day until 1939, two months before his death at age eighty-eight. Belle lived in the house until her death on February 1, 1955. At that time, she was the oldest native-born citizen in the state of Texas.[8]

T. C. Osborn House, 1102 Hill Street.

The home changed many times: outbuildings were removed, bedrooms and bathrooms were added, and it was remodeled and "modernized" by a succession of owners. In the 1970s and 1980s owners began the process of restoring several of the original features of the house. Craig and Cynthia Pence purchased the home in 1990, continued the restoration process, and put it on the 2006 Bastrop County Historical Society Holiday Homes Tour.[9]

The home is a City of Bastrop Historic Landmark.

## Reynolds House

*1108 Hill Street / 1851*

Originally built by Thomas Blackstone Rector in 1851, this early-Texas home was a wedding present from Rufus Sidney Green to his daughter, Frances Marietta, upon her marriage to A. B. Reynolds in 1874. Green gave each of his children on their wedding day a home, a farm, a thousand dollars, a horse and a buggy, and a gold watch and chain. To Marietta he gave an extra thousand dollars because he did not want her to work. To his fourth child, Dave, a bachelor, instead of a home, he gave a tailor-made suit, which was rare in those days.[10]

In 1912 Marietta deeded the house and the half block it still sits on to her son, Sidney David ("Siddie"), in exchange for his taking care of her for the rest of her life. Siddie and his wife, Daisy, had four children: Dan ("Rusty"), Clyde, Sid, and James Arthur ("Hop"). The elder Sidney farmed the land and by 1941 had turned his small dairy farm into the largest retail dairy in Bastrop County.[11] Clyde Reynolds inherited

Reynolds House, 1108 Hill Street.

Cousins Sid Reynolds and Margaret Jones in front of the Reynolds House, circa 1908. Photo courtesy of Minifred Trigg.

the home. He served as the Bastrop County tax assessor-collector and was Bastrop's fire chief for many years. Clyde's wife, Dula Bell Webb, died in 1980. Clyde, a local historian and Bastrop County Historical Society member, bequeathed the house and property to the society in his estate.[12]

When the society sold the property in 2017, it remained much as did when it was originally built. Its central double entry doors, framed by sidelights and pilasters, open into an enclosed porch and a large central dogtrot-like hallway. The only changes include the addition of bathrooms, the upgrading of the kitchen throughout the years, and a two-story cottage-style addition to the rear of the house, constructed by restoration expert and carpenter Clay Terrell in 1987.[13]

The house is listed in the National Register of Historic Places by its address only.

## Alf Griesenbeck House

*1302 Hill Street / 1911*

Alfred "Alf" Griesenbeck was born in Waco, Texas, in 1864 and, when still a child, came to Bastrop with his widowed mother, Emilie, and eleven siblings in a wagon.[14] He married Julia Augusta Miller in 1889; their six children were Hiram, Juanita, Otellia, Alfred, Julia Helen, and Marcia. The *Bastrop Advertiser* wrote of Julia, "Her home and her family were the center of her happiness."[15] Alf was in partnership with W. B. Ransome, and

Alf Griesenbeck House, 1302 Hill Street.

together they bought the Bastrop Water, Light, and Power Company, which was sold to the Texas Public Utilities Company fifteen years later. He devoted much of his attention to farming. When the Texas Farm Bureau Cotton Association was organized, he became one of the Bastrop County charter members and for several years was a director of the Texas Farm Bureau Federation.[16]

This grand Neoclassical Revival frame home was built for the Griesenbecks by contractor Joseph Pfeiffer "with only the barest of instruction."[17] It is two stories, has a square plan with a hipped roof, and has projected gables with two Palladian windows. The second-floor balcony is incorporated in the gables. It has Doric columns and simple balustrades. Alf died in 1926; Julia, in 1950.

J. Gordon and Lily Clara Shuddemagen Bryson bought the house in 1923, after having lived for years on the first floor of their private family hospital, the Bryson Sanitarium, where Gordon was the chief surgeon, house physician, intern, orderly, and laundry man. That same year, he worked with W. B. Ransome to form a nonprofit corporation to finance a new hospital. The hospital became a reality when Sarah Jane Orgain donated ten thousand dollars in memory of her son, F. A. Orgain. Later, she gave an additional three thousand dollars for two wards within the hospital: one for Mexican Americans and the other for African Americans.[18]

Gordon graduated from the University of Texas medical school in Galveston, and during his thirty-seven-year career became one of the best-known general practitioners in Central Texas.[19] He served as mayor of Bastrop from 1946 to 1950 and school board president for several terms. At the age of seventy-two, he returned to the university to study history. Two books resulted: *Reminiscences of a Country Doctor,* first published in 1963 and reissued in 1965 under the title *One Hundred Dollars and a Horse*; and *Shin Oak Ridge,* published in 1965.[20]

Lily Bryson oversaw various changes to the rambling old house, including the addition of many lavatories/bathrooms (the house had one bathroom and an outhouse when they bought it), several closets, and a laundry chute, all needed to accommodate their six children. Her daughter, Shudde Bess, wrote that Lily was "smart as a whip, a scholar" and that she "did dad's lab work until they got a tech, administered anesthetics for him, and trained to be an X-ray technician so she could do that for him, too."[21] Gordon Bryson died in 1968; Lily, in 1983 at age ninety-nine.

The house is listed in the National Register of Historic Places and is a City of Bastrop Historic Landmark.

## W. E. Maynard Sr. House

*1310 Hill Street / 1911*

In August 1910 William McIntosh Andrews and his wife, Mary Ellen, purchased a vacant lot (the future 1310 Hill Street) from W. E. and Mollie Maynard.[22] W. E. had inherited the lot in 1892 from his father, C. B. Maynard.[23] William Andrews was the son of a Bastrop minister, Ridden Andrews, and Mary Ellen was the daughter of J. W. Kennedy, owner of the Kennedy Cotton Gin and Grist Mill in Bastrop. After they married in 1901, William was employed at various gins in Central Texas. By 1910, when the couple purchased the lot, they were living in Brenham, where William was working as a "cotton clerk" in a "cotton office."[24] It appears the couple bought the lot in preparation for their return to Bastrop where William was to become proprietor of a cotton gin.[25]

William hired contractor Joseph Pfeiffer to build their new home at a cost of thirty-five hundred dollars.[26] This Prairie-style home with Craftsman details is a two-and-one-half-story frame home with a hipped roof, projected hip dormers, two chimneys, Doric columns, and a front door with sidelights and transom. In July 1913, after owning the home for just over two years, William and Mary sold the land, now with a new

W. E. Maynard Sr. House, 2019, pending restoration.

W. E. Maynard Sr. House, 1310 Hill Street, circa 1917. Courtesy of Mary Maynard McMurrey.

house, back to the original landowners, W. E. and Mollie Maynard, for forty-five hundred dollars.[27]

William Edward "W. E." Maynard, born in 1858, attended the Bastrop Academy, Dr. Burleson's School in Waco (now Baylor University), and Emory and Henry College in Virginia. He was admitted to the bar in 1878 and elected Bastrop city attorney, serving five consecutive terms. In 1881 he married Mary Ann "Mollie" Clements of Virginia.

W. E. and Mollie had eight children, three of whom died young (Claude Clay, Virgie Deal, and Ben McCord). When W. E. and Mollie moved into this home, four of their surviving children (Maude, Powell, Janette, and Edward) were married and living in homes elsewhere. Their youngest child, C. B. Maynard II (named for his grandfather), was eight years old and lived with them. Mollie lived in her new home less than a year when she died June 13, 1914.

Young C. B. was sent to the San Marcos Baptist Academy boarding school, and his father lived alone in the large home until 1916, when W. E. married Evelyn Barnes from Temple. Evelyn and her twenty-one-year-old daughter, Maud Barnes, joined the household. It is believed that the handsome porte cochere was added to the home's south side under Evelyn's guidance.[28] During her years in the home, Evelyn became president of the Ladies Reading Circle and supported W. E.'s efforts as trustee and steward of the First Methodist Church. W. E. is listed on the cornerstone of the 1925 Methodist church, and together they donated one of the large stained-glass windows in the church sanctuary.

Maud Barnes had been married barely over a year to Harry Johnson when she died in 1923. After W. E. died in 1926, Evelyn had no family left in Bastrop and returned to Temple. The home was inherited by W. E. and Mollie's two daughters, Janette Maynard Reynolds and Maude Maynard Seeligson. Janette and her husband, Jake, bought Maude's share and moved into the home. Janette, too, became president of the Ladies Reading Circle. Jake served as an alderman on the Bastrop City Council and was secretary and treasurer of the First Methodist Church. Janette and Jake Reynolds sold the house ten years later to Janette's brother, C. B. Maynard II.[29]

C. B. Maynard II married Mary Lucy Rivers in 1931. They had two daughters, Lucy Rivers Maynard (called Lucy Rivers) and Mary Clements Maynard (called Mary Clements). Maynard served in the Forty-First Texas Legislature, was Bastrop County attorney, and was the Bastrop County judge when he bought the home in October 1940. The Maynards immediately began making improvements. The wooden porch steps were replaced with concrete; Lucy Rivers and Mary Clements pressed their handprints, dated 1941, into it. Ornamental latticework was added to the porte cochere, and pink Queen Anne's lace was planted.[30]

Tragedy struck in October 1942 when Lucy Rivers Maynard was abducted while on her way home from school. The eight-year-old fourth-grader was found the next morning suffering from exposure and injuries from the attack. She died the following morning. Private George S. Knapp, stationed at Camp Swift, an army training facility near Bastrop, confessed to her murder and was hanged on March 19, 1943.[31]

The war may have served as a needed distraction for the grieving family. In January 1943 Maynard resigned as county judge and joined the army, serving as a lieutenant colonel in the Judge Advocate General's Department.[32] Lucy remained in the home and rented space to wives of soldiers who were training at Camp Swift. (After completion of their training, troops were deployed to Europe, and families came to Bastrop to be with their soldier one last time before his departure.) Lucy rented out the northwest bedroom and redesigned a bath into a combination kitchen-bath. Lucy would later tell an amusing story of one woman who arrived from "back East" with a Great Dane. When questioned why she had brought the large dog, the woman explained that it was for her protection because "she was worried that Texas still had Indians."[33] Lucy did not like dogs but allowed the dog to stay, and little Mary Clements Maynard (about seven years old) acquired a playmate. Mary Clements, in her eighties, still loves Great Danes.

C. B. and Lucy moved to their ranch (Sweet Lucy Ranch) north of town and gave the home to Mary Clements and her husband, Allen McMurrey, in 1964.[34] The pink Queen Anne's lace still bloomed on the trellis each summer.[35] Mary Clements and Allen (divorced in 1984) sold the home in 1974 to Charles and Marilyn Kuhn. More than forty years later (2017), Charles and Marilyn sold the home to Mary Clements's son, William McMurrey.[36] The home was once again owned by members of the Maynard family.

The home is listed in the National Register of Historic Places.

## John D. Claiborne House

*1402 Hill Street / Circa 1889*

In 1887 John and Mattie Black Claiborne paid $450 to J. C. Buchanan for a vacant lot in the residential section of Bastrop because they planned to move their large family from their farm near Alum Creek into town.[37] They built a large, two-story home on the lot. However, by 1900 the family was back on the farm,[38] and in 1902 they sold the home to the First National Bank for twenty-five hundred dollars.[39] Family lore is that the Claibornes abandoned the house and moved back to their farm because they were disenchanted with "city" life and a growing Bastrop.[40]

After a series of owners, Cleo Albert "Dude" and Bess Andrus Long bought the home for forty-five hundred dollars in September 1946. The two-story home is clapboard with an ell on the north side. A bay with four windows projects from the ell. The Longs installed plumbing and electricity and added a covered porch with two-story pillars on the front (east) and a sunroom on the south.[41] At the time they bought the home, Dude owned the Western Auto Associates Store and continued its operation until he retired in 1975. (He had previously owned the Farm & Home store.) He was a member of the Chamber of Commerce and Lions Club, a founder of the Young Democrat Club, an avid fisherman, a community leader, and executive director of the Bastrop Housing Authority at the time of his death in December 1978.[42]

Bess Long worked in the store as a sales clerk and bookkeeper and was the Western Union telegraph operator, sending and receiving messages for the town. She may be remembered more for her years directing the Kid Kollege. Bastrop preschool children would go to the Longs' home, where Bess taught them "fine arts"—music, drama, art, and Spanish.[43] During the summer, young school-age children joined in and would dress up, practice good manners, and at the end of the summer perform a pageant on the front lawn for their parents. There are many now in their seventies who fondly remember their Kid Kollege years and being chosen to be the king or queen of Bastrop, Little Boy Blue, Little Red Riding Hood, or one of many other storybook characters presented at the pageants. Susan Long, a preschooler in the Kid Kollege, inherited the home from her mother, Bess, in 1986.

The home is a City of Bastrop Historic Landmark.

John D. Claiborne House, 1402 Hill Street, late 1940s. Courtesy of Susan B. Long.

Bess Long's Kid Kollege, circa 1949. Forrest Adams (king), Mary Murchison (queen). Left to right: unknown, unknown, Bobby Jenkins, Ray Long, JoAnn Griesenbeck (Cantrell), Bess Long, Ann Loveless (Kurio), John Powell Ash, unknown, unknown, Sandy Wright (Kibby), William "Terry" Sanders, Bob Long. Courtesy of Terry Sanders.

## Richard J. and Annie Brieger House

*1508 Hill Street / 1910*

The Texas Historical Commission building marker reads: "Theodore and Mary Hasler, owners of a general merchandise store, hired architect Gus Brieger to build this house for their daughter Annie and her husband (Gus' brother) Richard J. Brieger. Built about 1910, the late Victorian Queen Anne style house was home to the Briegers and their five children, and often the setting of social gatherings. During World War II, it also provided temporary housing to wives of soldiers from nearby Camp Swift."

An article in the *Bastrop Advertiser* on July 28, 1911, reported that the new home of R. J. Brieger had been "completed within the past year." The building is listed in the National Register of Historic Places and is designated a Recorded Texas Historic Landmark. It is a City of Bastrop Historic Landmark.

Richard J. and Annie Brieger House, 1508 Hill Street.

## Jewell Hodges Home

*2310 Hill Street / Circa 1986*

This modest 1986 ranch-style home is not a National Register home, a City of Bastrop Historic Landmark, or architecturally significant. It is important, however, because it was the home of one of Bastrop's most powerful and influential African American leaders, Jewell Washington Hyder Hodges.[44] Jewell was born in 1917 in Bastrop and attended local segregated schools. When her first husband, Oscar Hyder Sr., died of pneumonia, leaving her with two small children, Oscar and Lullaby, she left Bastrop at age twenty-seven and moved to the East Coast looking for a better life for herself and her children.[45] Jewell "lived in Springfield, Massachusetts with her second husband, Eugene W. Hodges, for the next 41 years, enjoying a career in fashion merchandising. She worked for the same company for 30 years, taking early retirement at age 60 in order to care for her mother."[46]

After her mother's death, Jewell returned to Bastrop in 1986 and began a second life in her hometown as "a strong and independent woman who immediately went to work to improve the lives of everyone around her."[47] She founded the Bastrop County Emergency Food Pantry and its accompanying senior support center, which is named after her. She was active in Church Women United, a group that endeavored to bring all races together. She was also instrumental in starting the Martin Luther King Jr. Celebration, the MLK Jr. Scholarship Fund, and the Housing Authority, which provides affordable housing in Bastrop. Jewell was precinct chair of the Bastrop County Democratic Party for many years.

Jewell Hodges, circa 1990s. Courtesy of the Bastrop County Historical Society.

The National Mothers of America, a group aimed at championing women by honoring, educating, and serving mothers at home, named her 2013 Mother of the Year in Texas.[48] That same year Jewell Hodges died at age ninety-five and was buried in nearby Cedar Creek in the Shiloh Cemetery.

After her death the City of Bastrop honored Jewell's accomplishments and legacy by developing and naming a park near her former home after her.[49] The one-acre pocket park on Linden Street has a play area with picnic tables, small barbecue pits, and basketball courts.

Jewell Hodges Home, 2310 Hill Street.

City of Bastrop
Jewell Hodges Park.

# Jefferson Street

## Kleinert-Hoppe House

*806 Jefferson Street / Circa 1887–1890*

The Texas Historical Commission building marker reads: "Located among a number of homes built in the 19th century by German immigrants to Bastrop, this house was built between 1887 and 1890 for Charles and Maria Kleinert. Fellow German immigrant and local innkeeper A. L. Hoppe bought the property in 1890, and it remained in his family until 1961. A fine example of eclectic Victorian-era design, the house features pedimented architraves, jigsawn porch details, and a distinctive octagonal bay."

Charles Kleinert was a Bastrop merchant and wheelwright. In 1889 he was elected to the newly formed board of directors of the Bastrop Bridge Company, which is credited with establishing Bastrop's first bridge over the Colorado River in 1890. Albert L. Hoppe operated a meat market on Main Street in 1889 and a bakery in 1900. At the time of his death in 1917, he was managing the Bastrop Inn.[1]

The home is listed in the National Register of Historic Places and is designated a Recorded Texas Historic Landmark.

## W. E. Maynard Jr. House

*1313 Jefferson Street / 1928*

In 1926 W. E. "Ed" Maynard Jr. and Elsie Maynard had been married six years when the vacant lot on Jefferson Street was given to them by Ed's father, W. E. Maynard Sr. (who

Kleinert-Hoppe House, 806 Jefferson Street.

W. E. Maynard Jr. House, 1313 Jefferson.

lived on adjoining property on Hill Street).[2] The couple built a new house that was completed in April–May 1928.[3] It was a modest single-story, hipped-roof bungalow with an asymmetrical front entry.

Ed and Elsie raised two children in the home, William "Billy" Edward III and Betty. Ed served on the Bastrop City Council and was a Bastrop Independent School District trustee. He was the Mobil Oil agent from 1923 to 1961 and transported petroleum products to more than fifteen service stations and numerous farms, developing lasting friendships with area farmers. He also owned a Mobil station where the Bastrop post office now stands (1106 Main Street).[4]

After retirement, Ed worked for ten years to compile an accurate listing of all persons buried in each of the county's cemeteries. The names were listed alphabetically, including inscriptions on tombstones, and then bound into volumes to be used for reference.[5] These volumes were incorporated into the cemetery surveys completed in 1987 by Audrey Rother. Ed died at age eighty-nine on January 2, 1980.

Bastrop and Bastrop County history were Elsie's love. She was a charter member of the Bastrop County Historical Society and the first chairman of the Bastrop County Historical Survey Committee (now the Bastrop County Historical Commission.) She concentrated her efforts locating and securing markers for historical sites in the county and medallions for historical buildings and homes. The inclusion of 131 Bastrop sites and structures in the National Register of Historic Places is the result of her efforts. Elsie died in 1978.

The home was inherited by Billy and his sister, Betty.[6] They redesigned the recessed entry so that it was flush with the front facade. Stained glass salvaged from the razed Bastrop Catholic Church was installed on both sides of the front door. A deep porch spanning the entire front of the house was added along with a central arched portico, supported by corbels, over the front steps.

Betty Jeanette Maynard was a professor at Southern Methodist University and a diplomat with the US State Department. She died in 2001. Billy married Clarabelle "Clara" Louise Curtis on January 16, 1982, and Clara joined him in the old family home.[7] It has been in the Maynard family more than ninety years.

When the Bastrop County Historical Society began its capital campaign for the renovation of the old City Hall building at 904 Main as a new museum, Billy and Clara made a major financial contribution in 2012. In recognition of their generosity, the Maynard River Room was named in honor of Elsie, Ed, Betty, Clara, and Billy Maynard.

The house is a City of Bastrop Historic Landmark.

# Main Street

## Old Cornelson-Fehr House

*702 Main Street / 1850*

The Texas historical building marker reads: "Originated 1850 as frame cabin of John Cornelson. Enlarged after 1854 by Joe Fehr, who used brick from Lottmans' kiln, east of town. Texas Legislature in 1954 designated building and area an historic shrine of Texas. Now Bastrop County museum."

John Cornelson purchased the site for this building for $80 in 1850 from the Corporation of Bastrop. He built a frame cabin and sold his property for $480 in 1853 to Christopher C. McGinnis, a lawyer and Bastrop County judge (1866–67), who sold the property in 1854 to Joe B. Fehr, an emigrant from Germany. Its various uses over the years include a tannery for making saddles, harnesses, and leather goods for Confederate soldiers during the Civil War; a furniture factory; residence of a river ferryboat operator; three apartments during World War II; and hay storage.[1]

The Bastrop County Historical Society purchased the building for a museum in 1952. The building had been the home of the society for more than sixty years when it was sold in 2013 to Baham Interests, Ltd. Partnership, which expanded the building and property into apartments and office space.[2]

The building is listed in the National Register of Historic Places (listed as the John Cornelsum [*sic*] House) and is designated a Recorded Texas Historic Landmark (listed as the Old Cornelson-Fehr House).

Old Cornelson-Fehr House, 702 Main Street, photo circa 1970. Courtesy of the Bastrop County Historical Society.

Old Cornelson-Fehr House, 2019.

## Richard Starcke House

*703 Main Street / 1913–1915*

In 1913 Richard Starcke tore down his parents' old family home and built a new home on the same site, which is this grand, modified four-square, with Prairie-style influence as evidenced by the continuous horizontal lines, deep porch and overhang, and bulky railing. This was a very modern home at that time, as Victorian architecture had all but disappeared.[3]

Richard Starcke was born in Guadalupe County, Texas, and was four years old when his family moved to Bastrop in 1863. He married Mary "Angie" Shutter Smith in 1897. By 1890 brothers Richard and George Starcke were partners and respected merchants in a variety of businesses on Main Street. They owned R & G Starcke Hardware Store and were agents for steel-wire picket fencing.[4] With their father, Carl Starcke, they owned Starcke's Pharmacy and were the manufacturers of Starcke's Chill and Fever Tonic. By 1900 Richard and George had opened Starcke Brothers Orange Crush Bottling Works.

Richard Starcke House, 703 Main Street.

Richard died in early November 1931. Angie married twice more: to James H. Pearcy and then to S. B. Goode. She loved the home she had built with Richard and remained there with her subsequent husbands until her death in 1961 at age ninety-two.

There were several owners after Angie. However, the house finally fell on hard times and the Citizens State Bank foreclosed on the property in 1966. That same year, Lieutenant Colonel Johnnie and Ernestine Moncure Zinn were living in New Mexico and planning Johnnie's retirement from the army. Ernestine was dispatched to Bastrop, her childhood home, with instructions to find a house. Ernestine decided to bid on 703 Main, but at the auction she got "excited" and started bidding against herself. She bid two thousand dollars more than necessary. She went to the bank, head down, and explained to bank president Charlie Eskew what she had done. Eskew laughed and allowed her to buy the home for the price established before she began bidding against herself.[5]

Johnnie had a distinguished military career, serving in World War II, Korea, and the early years of Vietnam. After retiring and moving to Bastrop, he taught school for a year and became principal of Bastrop Junior High. Ernestine and Johnnie loved to play bridge. Ernestine hosted her ladies' bridge club, and she and Johnnie hosted couples' bridge, which eventually turned into poker.[6] The couple lived in the home until 1987.

Following the Zinns, several owners operated the house as a bed-and-breakfast, until 2017, when Colonel Michael and Sheri Kinslow purchased the home for a private residence. Michael is a survivor of the 9/11 Pentagon terrorist attacks, served one year in Afghanistan, and served almost thirty-two years in the US Air Force.

The home is listed in the National Register of Historic Places.

## P. O. Elzner House

*802 Main Street / 1885*

Paul Otto Elzner was eleven years old in 1858 when his family came to Bastrop from Germany. An energetic young man, Otto became one of Bastrop's leaders and was reported to have been "actively involved in anything that would benefit the town."[7] He married Mary Rabensburg in 1875. Otto and Mary's home, with its steamboat, gingerbread porch and elongated double-hung windows, is identified as transitional Victorian. It fronts Main Street, but more important to Otto was the excellent view of the Colorado River from the backyard. The sloping site on which the house is built posed a problem for foundation work. It was solved when large cedar tree trunks, cut at differing lengths, were used as piers, "creating a unique basement area under the house."[8]

P. O. Elzner House, 802 Main Street.

Gingerbread on the front porch of the P. O. Elzner House.

Bastrop's Main Street, circa 1898. Photo taken at the intersection of Main and Spring Streets, looking south. Elzner's Corner, established in 1876, is on the left. Bastrop's population was approximately twenty-one hundred residents. As of 2019 the same two blocks are the heart of Bastrop's downtown business district. Elzner's Corner is still a prominent commercial building. Photo courtesy of the Bastrop County Historical Society.

Otto owned two cotton gins in town and established Elzner's Corner, a large mercantile store located only two blocks away from his home. He could watch from the rear of the house as wagons loaded with merchandise for his store crossed the river by ferry or as cotton, which was floated from upriver, was received at the docks located just behind the home.

Otto was among the civic leaders who established the first bridge (1890) across the Colorado River at Bastrop. He was a director of the First National Bank and served as a city councilman, city treasurer, and mayor pro tem. In 1889 he partnered with David Green to build the Bastrop Opera House, which was considered the finest in the state at that time. An amateur musician, Otto was one of twelve members of the Bastrop City Band, which rode down Main Street in a wagon drawn by four white horses. The bandwagon was a familiar sight in Bastrop in the 1870s and 1880s.

Otto's son, Bruno A. Elzner, inherited the home in 1918. At Bruno's death in 1957, the house passed to Bruno A. Elzner Jr. and his wife, Marcia. The old Elzner home was deeded to H. E. and Gladys Dubois in 1968.[9]

The home is listed in the National Register of Historic Places (the address is listed as 800 Main Street and the construction date as 1890). The home is designated a Recorded Texas Historic Landmark and is shown by the City of Bastrop Landmark Commission to be located at 802 Main Street and constructed in 1885.

## S. L. Brannon Sr. House

*1301 Main Street / 1915*

Sidney Lee "S. L." Brannon wrote: "In the year 1894 when I was 19-years-old, many boys my age were going to Texas, some staying and some returning with fantastic reports of the western state. I got the 'bug' for 'going West young man,' and I came to Texas." S. L. left Tennessee and first arrived at Mesquite, Texas, population three hundred, working odd jobs until arriving in Bastrop County in 1895. He began teaching in September 1898 at Gay Hill near Elgin and, in the same month, married "that pretty brunette," Cora Lynn Hemphill. In 1900 Brannon purchased a half interest in a drugstore in McDade, where he learned the pharmacy trade. He bought, and later sold, a drugstore in Elgin and in 1913 opened S. L. Brannon Drug Company in a newly constructed building at 1014 Main Street in Bastrop.[10]

S. L. Brannon Sr. House, 1301 Main Street.

S. L. and Cora Brannon built their frame home in Bastrop in 1915, only two blocks from his drugstore. Here they raised four children: Jack, S. L. Jr., Fay, and Clara. The home is a one-and-one-half-story, simple late Victorian residence with a typical L-shaped gallery on square columns. Amazingly, there are five hipped dormers. Three matching entrance doors with transoms are spaced at different locations around the gallery.

After S. L. retired, he loved to reminisce about his years in the drugstore. He told the story of the day Cora was canning a large batch of peaches. She ran out of sugar and sent their young daughter Fay to the drugstore with instructions to scoop up the necessary sugar from the sugar barrel. Fay returned home and poured her sugar into the peaches. They all had to be thrown away. Fay had scooped from a barrel of Epson salt.[11]

S. L. was a city councilman, mayor, and president of the Chamber of Commerce, and he was a pharmacist for forty-four years—more than thirty of them in Bastrop.[12] He retired in 1944, and his longtime employee L. C. Price became proprietor of the store, which was renamed L. C. Price's Drug Store.[13] S. L. died at age ninety-six in 1971; Cora, in 1972. The Brannon estate sold the home to Bobby and Sharon Boatright in 1973.

The home is listed in the National Register of Historic Places.

## White-Turner House

*1307 Main Street / 1890*

John and Martha L. White signed an agreement with Wilbarger Lumber Company for their new home in Bastrop in March 1890, and four months later John began advertising his business in the *Bastrop Advertiser*. He advertised himself as a contractor providing "Plans, Specifications, and Estimates." The agreement with Wilbarger was to "construct a dwelling, said house to be built according to plans and specifications in possession of said John W. White . . . , said house to be in value not less than Twelve Hundred Dollars."[14]

Constructed of cypress and heart pine, White's asymmetrical Victorian-style cottage features gingerbread and elaborate woodworking typifying Queen Anne Victorian houses from 1875 to 1910. In the attic above the kitchen is a large copper-lined water reservoir capable of holding twelve hundred gallons and pipes of what apparently was a carbide-gas lighting system. Two outbuildings, at one time a carriage house and servants' house, are constructed in a style similar to that of the principal house, suggesting they were built at, or near, the same time as the home.[15] A separate structure was moved from the Jenkins property on Pecan Street in the 1990s to serve as a garage.[16]

White-Turner House, 1307 Main Street.

Juliet awning over stained-glass-bordered windows, 1307 Main Street.

The front facade has one-over-one windows that extend to the floor, with the top half bordered with stained-glass squares. Many windows throughout the home have the same stained-glass pattern. A Juliet metal awning is above the twin windows and small porch in the projected ell.

Thirty-three-year-old Martha White died in January 1892, less than two years after the home was built, and John sold it in February 1894 to N. G. and Beulah Fowler. He no longer advertised his business in the newspaper and apparently moved from Bastrop. In 1900 the Fowlers moved one block west into the David Sayers house on Church Street, later named the historic Hall-Sayers-Perkins House. They sold their home to Otto and Clara Amthor, who had been married one month earlier. Otto and Clara owned the Iron Front Saloon, which was conveniently located only three blocks away at 1009 Main.

The next owner was Kate Hamilton Turner. Kate and Calvin Turner had owned and lived in the Turner Hotel (aka the Exchange Hotel) on Chestnut Street from 1895 until Calvin's death in June 1901. It was improper for a single woman to live among the male boarders, so Kate's son, Allen "Nash" Turner, bought the home for his widowed mother in November 1901. In 1902 a double wedding took place in Kate's Main Street home. It was lavishly decorated with ferns, palms, carnations, and roses for the marriage of her daughter Callie to A. W. Sessums, a businessman from Elgin, and her daughter Mattie to John Milton Holt.[17] John and Mattie soon thereafter operated a business in Bastrop, J. M. Holt & Co.

Kate was described as a very tall, slender woman who sat on the front porch swing reading her Bible. When her sight began to fail, her young granddaughter, Mary Belle Turner (later married Walter Gore), read to her.[18] After Kate died in 1925, the Turner family continued to own the home until 1937.

Nash Turner was born in Utley, near Bastrop. He had a remarkable talent for horsemanship. In 1900 he was ranked among the top-ten leading jockeys in the United States and in 1906 was the eleventh leading rider in France. He won some of the largest purses in Europe. After his riding career ended, Turner became an owner and trainer in France. His stables near Paris became a showplace, but after World War I he suffered financial reverses and returned to the United States. He stayed in Bastrop with his mother in 1920–21 but returned to France in 1922 to spend the rest of his life training horses at his stables at Maisons-Laffitte. He died of a heart attack in 1937. His name is recorded in the Racing Hall of Fame at Saratoga Springs, New York.[19]

William J. and Louise Schewe bought the home in January 1938. William was proprietor of the Bastrop Furniture Company—selling items such as rugs, dressers, buffets, and china closets. As was the custom in most small towns and rural communities, wooden coffins were also purchased from the local furniture store. William was an undertaker, and his undertaking business was also in the store (as was customary). He kept a large ledger from September 1917 to March 1940 that listed a deceased person's name, age, sex, race, name of father, mother's maiden name, cause of death, and place of burial. Titled *Bastrop County Death Records*, the ledger was published by Save Texas Cemeteries, Inc. and Jim Cox in April 2000 and is of historical interest to researchers and genealogists.[20] Sadly, listed in the ledger is eighteen-year-old Wm. Schewe Jr., who died of the 1918 flu while serving in the military in San Antonio. The day after his death, he was brought to Bastrop, where the Bastrop Furniture Company is listed as the undertaker. William J. Schewe died in 1953. Louise continued to live in the home, doing fine sewing and dressmaking.[21] She died in 1968. The Schewe family owned the home more than thirty years.

Later owners include Nell H. Reedy (1969), D. L. and R. M. Baggett (1972), William C. (Chris) and Cheryl O. (Cherry) Dickson (1976), and Charles and Trudy Barden, who began extensive restoration in 1979. Brenda and Gerald R. Wagner purchased the home in 1984, painted it pink, and operated an elegant bed-and-breakfast, the Pink Lady Inn. Owners Jack and Sarah Else purchased the house in 1992 and painted the exterior yellow with green trim and multicolored highlights.

Frank Huffman and Lucy Todd bought the home in 1998 and continue to own it today (2019). Frank has served as a trustee and president of the Bastrop County Historical Society and is a research fellow at University of Texas at Austin. Lucy is an artist and volunteer for the Lost Pines Art Center and serves on the MLK Jr. Scholarship Committee. The home is often featured on the Historical Society's Holiday Homes Tour.

The home is listed in the National Register of Historic Places (listed as the White House), is designated a Recorded Texas Historic Landmark, and is a City of Bastrop Historic Landmark.

## Amthor House

*1308 Main Street / 1911*

Otto Amthor and Clara Perkins were married in Bastrop in 1900 and had three children: Frances, Willie Bell, and Nell. On October 2, 1911, Otto and Clara contracted with the J. L. Wilbarger Company to "erect a dwelling house" for fifteen hundred dollars. The home is clapboard with a front gallery that features heavy, square columns; a front door with sidelights; and a beveled, three-panel transom. An angled bay window is on the north side. Otto and Clara also owned a local business, the Iron Front Saloon, located at 1009 Main Street. Their business partner was Samuel Bell. It is presumed that Otto and Clara named their son, Willie Bell Amthor, in honor of their friend and partner.[22]

Amthor House, 1308 Main Street.

Willie Bell Amthor was seventeen years old in September 1920 when he enlisted in the US Marines. By December 1921 he was in Managua, Nicaragua, and with a large group of marines got into a brawl inside a cantina with a captain of the Nicaraguan presidential guard. Ultimately, three Nicaraguan police were killed, as well as three civilians and three marines. Many of the brawling marines were arrested. A naval tribunal aboard the USS *Galveston* found Corporal Amthor and two others guilty of killing the Nicaraguan police. Amthor and three others jumped ship and killed four more police before their recapture.[23] Amthor's accumulated sentence was twenty years.[24] He was incarcerated in the US penitentiary in Atlanta, Georgia, on March 22, 1922; however, he was released five years later in July 1927. Amthor eventually moved to California, where he was a mechanical engineer. He married Lela May Drake in 1935.

During the years Willie Bell Amthor was in prison, Otto and Clara divorced (1925), and Otto deeded the house to Clara. It is not known when the Iron Front Saloon closed, but Otto became a grocery merchant in Bastrop. Clara married Alfred Heitman, and they lived in the home. There were several subsequent owners, one of whom left it vacant for more than ten years. It was once a home for unwed mothers as well as a Christian home for children.[25] Extensive restoration and remodeling were undertaken in 2003 by owners Michael and Patricia Beeman. They added a large family room, a large deck on the back of the home, and extensive landscaping.[26] Robert Kuhn bought the home in 2014. He was raised in Paige, Texas, and, before retiring to live in Bastrop was a practicing attorney in Austin. He would probably say his claim to fame is that he was the executive producer of the original version of the classic horror movie *The Texas Chainsaw Massacre*.[27]

The home has been designated a City of Bastrop Significant Landmark.

## Dimon-Erhard House

*1402 Main Street / Circa 1851*

Moses O. Dimon purchased three acres from John D. Hogan for three hundred dollars in April 1851.[28] Moses was a dry goods merchant in Bastrop who advertised throughout the 1850s in the local newspaper. His store building was described as "capacious . . . and filled with immense stocks of merchandise."[29] Unfortunately, his business was destroyed in 1862 when a devastating fire burned every building on two blocks of down-

Dimon-Erhard House, 1402 Main Street.

The Dimon-Erhard House, circa 1905. Children left to right: Merton Erhard, Nelda Erhard (Price), Hal Jones, Kathryn Jones, and Florence Erhard (Arbuckle). Photo courtesy of Robbie Sanders.

town Main Street.[30] In 1865 Moses and Eloisa Dimon moved to La Grange and sold their home to Cayton Erhard for two thousand dollars.[31]

Cayton Erhard, his younger brother, Adolph, and their parents settled in Bastrop in 1840. Both parents died the next year, leaving the brothers orphaned. They were taken in and protected by a local hotelier, James Nicholson. In 1841 eighteen-year-old Cayton was among the Bastrop men who joined the ill-fated Texan Santa Fe Expedition and were captured and imprisoned by Mexican forces. In his reminiscences published in 1884, Cayton wrote: "That terrible 90-mile desert without water, food, or firewood; it was indeed a journey of death."[32]

In March 1843, "after suffering cruel hardships, Erhard returned to Texas, where he rejoined the Nicholson family in Bastrop. Four years later, with his own savings and a loan from friends, he moved to San Marcos,"[33] where he was elected the first county clerk, became the first postmaster, and opened the first drugstore in the state of Texas.[34] He married Harriet Smith in 1851. They had three children while living in San Marcos: Albert, Rosalie (Clopton), and Louis. In 1865 Erhard moved his family to Bastrop, bought the home of Moses Dimon, and opened C. Erhard Drug at 921 Main Street. Two more children were born in Bastrop, Eugene and Cora.

Upon his death in 1884, Cayton's wishes were "to be buried after sundown, about dark, by torch light. . . . I would desire that a band of music accompany my body to the grave. . . . I would like to have that little cannon at the court house hauled out and fired, and let it announce . . . in deep tones of thunder, that another of Texas' early settlers, a Veteran is gone."[35]

Cayton Erhard, circa 1875. Photo courtesy of Robbie Sanders.

A photo taken about 1905 shows the Erhard home to be substantially the same as it is today (2019). It is a one-story, pre–Civil War, Folk house in the National style, with a combination board-and-batten and clapboard exterior. It has a shed roof, multiple gables, a deep front porch with two matching front doors, and a long porch along the south side.

After Cayton's death, Harriet built a new home at 1401 Church Street for herself and the two younger children, Cora and Eugene.[36] She allowed her son Louis, a jeweler on Main Street, and his wife, Martha, to remain in the old home place.[37] Their children, Merton, Nelda, and Florence, were born here.

In 1919 the home was sold to Joseph and Ivor Wilbarger Young.[38] Ivor enclosed the porch on the south side for a music room, where she gave piano lessons to young students.[39] Ivor's mother, Emily Wilbarger, died in October 1939, and Ivor and Joe moved across the street into Ivor's childhood home to help her father.[40]

Ivor and Joe rented out the Dimon-Erhard home to military families and contractors throughout the war years. The home and barn (with hayloft) were remodeled and rented to as many as four families at a time.[41] Bastrop County swelled from three thousand to ninety thousand people during the war years because of Camp Swift. Thus, housing was scarce.

The home was sold in 1957 to Delmar Woody and Mildred Clardy for seven thousand dollars.[42] Woody owned and operated the Bastrop Meat Market, and Mildred remodeled the home's interior to accommodate three or four elderly people. The home is considered by Bastrop old-timers to be the first "old-folks home" in Bastrop.[43]

Robbie and William "Terry" Sanders purchased the home in 1993.[44] It remains (2019) unchanged except for the addition of a porch off the kitchen and the conversion of the barn into a garage. In 2005 Robbie teamed with architect Marvin Beck to build a stone gazebo in Fairview Cemetery for the purpose of listing all war veterans buried there and displaying histories of all Republic of Texas persons buried there. She was commissioned a Yellow Rose of Texas under Governor George W. Bush, was awarded Citizen of the Year, has received the Community Builder Award and the Nell Herndon Award (from the Historic Landmark Commission), and was trustee for the Bastrop County Historical Society for approximately fifteen years. Terry was a Bastrop City

Council member during a period of significant reinvestment in city infrastructure and new commercial development on the city's west side. He owned Sanders Exxon and a convenience store, Terry's Corner. Now retired, he continues to run cattle on ancestral land in the Watterson Community.

The home is a City of Bastrop Historic Landmark.

## Brooks-Wilbarger House

*1403 Main Street / 1851*

Built of heart pine in 1851 by Colonel A. M. and Althea Brooks, the home is described as Colonial style in the early Classical Revival period. It features a central hallway, hipped roofs, cornices emphasized by bands of trim, sixteen pairs of cypress shutters, identical windows with six-over-six panes, and a two-story entry portico fronted by eight prominent square cypress columns. The house was sold to William T. Allen in 1861,[45] and James "Harvey" and Dorothy Olive Wilbarger bought it in 1866.[46]

Harvey Wilbarger died in 1869, leaving Dorothy to raise their seven children: Josephine, Mary Frances, Laura, Annie, James Lee, Kate, and Claudia.[47] Dorothy remained in the home and filled the children's lives with cultural pursuits: endless hours of music practice, sculpting, painting, reading, and writing. She set the standard for refinement in Bastrop. The youngest daughter, Claudia Wilbarger Norvell, is recognized as "The Savior of El Camino Real" and honored by having her portrait hung in the Senate Chamber in Austin. The honor is for her research and efforts to save the Texas Camino Real, Old San Antonio Road, from oblivion.[48] The King's Highway Chapter of the Daughters of the American Revolution, organized in Bastrop in 2016, held its first meeting in this house in honor of Claudia's work.

After Dorothy Wilbarger died in 1926, her son, James Lee, inherited the family home. James Lee established several lumberyards in the county, including the successful J. L. Wilbarger Lumber Company in Bastrop. He owned numerous cotton farms, was active in real estate and finance, and helped organize the Bastrop Chamber of Commerce. In 1893 James Lee married Emily Harris, who dazzled Bastrop with elegant parties and teas. She set strict standards for morals and manners. Among her words of wisdom were, "You don't have to pursue happiness. . . . It just sort of creeps upon you while you are helping others."[49] Their two children, daughters Ivor and Lee, inherited the home. It had been in the Wilbarger family for 113 years when sold by Ivor Wilbarger Young in 1976 to Andrew Zilker Thompson.[50]

Andrew was on the boards of both the Witte Museum and the McNay Art Museum in San Antonio. Although he did not live in the home, he furnished it with his personal

Brooks-Wilbarger House, 1403 Main Street.

collection of early-Texas furniture and household items and made it available to the Bastrop Chamber of Commerce for private tours.

Following Thompson were owners Thomas R. and Marilyn "Lyn" Phillips, who owned the home from 2000 to 2012. Lyn Phillips served on the Texas Higher Education Coordinating Board, and Tom Phillips was chief justice of the Texas Supreme Court and a member of the Texas Historical Commission. Tom recognized that the date of construction for the Brooks-Wilbarger House (1842) displayed on the Texas Historical medallion on the home was incorrect. His research proved that the construction date was actually 1851, and the Historical Commission corrected its files and replaced the medallion with one displaying the proper date.[51]

The next owners were Sharah and David Johnson and their children, Claire and Zane, whose home had burned in the 2011 massive Bastrop County Complex fire that destroyed 1,645 homes and 34,356 acres and caused two deaths.[52]

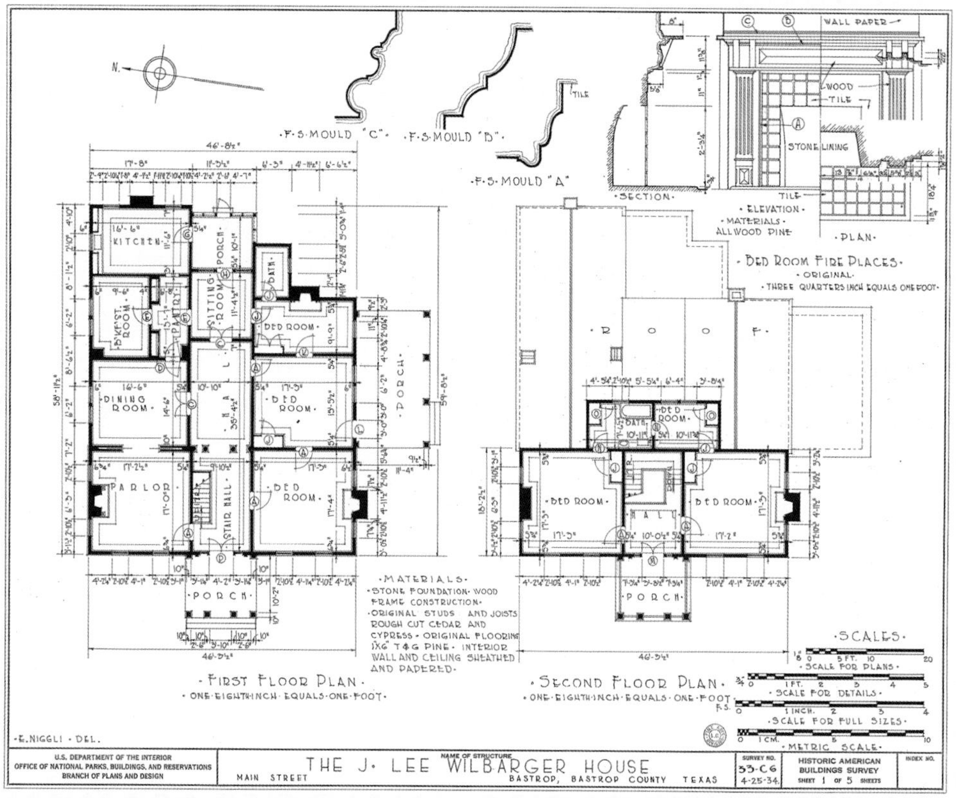


Historic American Buildings Survey, April 25, 1934. Drawing by Emil Niggli.

Brooks-Wilbarger House, south elevation, March 12, 1934, Historic American Buildings Survey. L. C. Page Jr., photographer.

Much of the lore surrounding the home is associated with Harvey Wilbarger's father, Josiah Pugh Wilbarger, whose survival of a scalping is the best-known encounter between Native Americans and Anglo settlers in Central Texas.[53] Josiah died in 1844 before the house was built.

The home is listed in the National Register of Historic Places and is designated a Recorded Texas Historic Landmark. The Brooks-Wilbarger House is included in the Historic American Buildings Survey (HABS).

## Moncure House

*1601 Main Street / 1910–1911*

Cassius Lee "C. L." and Hattie Nuckols Moncure purchased this parcel of land from J. L. Wilbarger in 1910 for the sum of seven hundred dollars and hired a carpenter, P. J. Zurburg, to build their home for three thousand dollars.[54] Hattie was proud to have electric lights all over the house and a closet in every bedroom.[55] The home's simple rectangular plan is enhanced by Prairie-style elements. It has a deep porch with wide eaves, a central gabled dormer, a second-story balcony with balustrade, two projecting chamfered bays with windows, and an offset front door with transom and sidelights.

Leah Moncure, circa 1960. Courtesy of Texas Department of Transportation.

C. L. and Hattie were married in 1888 and had four daughters: Ruby (b. 1889), Julia (b. 1892), and twins, Grace and Leah (b. 1904). Hattie was the proprietor of a millinery store, and C. L. was a civil engineer and the county surveyor. He slept with a pistol under his pillow every night.[56] C. L. died in 1942; Hattie, in 1952; and Ruby (married to Robert Moore), in 1947.

Julia graduated from Bastrop High School at age fifteen and immediately studied for her teaching certificate. She began teaching at various schools within the county and then taught and worked within the Houston Independent School District for thirty years. She moved back to Bastrop and taught second grade from 1944 to 1959.[57] Julia lived with, and took care of, her mother in the old home.

After becoming a teacher, Grace Moncure married Samuel Adam Kunkle in Houston. They later moved to Port Arthur, Texas, where Sam worked as a supervisor at the Texas Company's (Texaco) oil refinery.[58] After Grace's daughter, Martha, was grown and her husband had died, she moved back to Bastrop and into the house with her sister Julia.

Moncure House, 1601 Main Street.

Leah Moncure, who had been born with a heart defect that caused her to be what was termed a "blue baby,"[59] earned a degree in civil engineering from the University of Texas in 1937 and became the first female to be licensed as a professional engineer in the state of Texas. She moved to Austin in 1945 and worked in the Right of Way Division of the Texas Highway Department. She was also the first female Life Member of the National Society of Professional Engineers.[60] After retirement in the 1960s, she moved back to Bastrop to live in her childhood home.[61] Leah's health deteriorated as a result of her congenital heart defect.[62] She died at age sixty-seven in 1972; Julia, in 1980.

Grace was the last surviving sister of the Moncure household. She lived in the house until she moved into a nursing home in 1987. When Grace sold the house in 1989 to Brian J. and Kathy S. Butler, it had been in the Moncure family for seventy-eight years. Grace died in 1991.

The Texas Historical Commission awarded an undertold Texas historical marker for the site honoring Leah Moncure. It is a City of Bastrop Historic Landmark.

## J. T. Crysup House

*1607 Main Street / 1911*

When the Citizens State Bank was founded in Bastrop in 1909, it was in need of a "banking expert." James Travis "J. T." Crysup, former president of the Crockett State Bank in Crockett, Texas, was persuaded to become Citizens State Bank's cashier and daily operations manager. In addition to those duties, he became a stockholder and member of the board of directors.[63]

J. T. and Elizabeth "Lillie" Hart Crysup bought a vacant lot on Main Street from C. L. and Hattie Moncure in June 1911 for $550.[64] They built a two-story frame house with a porte cochere on the south side, a double hipped roof, and projected portico and

J. T. Crysup House, 1607 Main Street.

gallery. The Prairie-style structure was built with one-over-one windows and strong horizontal lines at the base and between the floors. (At some time during the life of the home, the porte cochere was enclosed.) J. T. and Lillie's only child, James Charles (called Charles), was born three years after the house was built.

In addition to his banking business, J. T. was instrumental in organizing the Bastrop Furniture Company and was a stockholder of the Powell Oil Mill (a cottonseed oil mill). In 1923, due to illness, he was forced to retire from active business.[65] He was fifty-two years old when he died two years later. Lillie was publicity chair of the Bastrop County American Red Cross and a member of the Women's Missionary Society. To celebrate the end of World War I in 1918, she gave a large Christmas party in their home, which she announced in the newspaper. In 1926 she purchased and renovated the Bastrop Hotel. Under her management, it was reborn to its former glory. By 1937 "the elite of Bastrop gathered at the hotel for lunch on Sundays after church services. Mrs. Crysup was a wonderful cook who put some very fine meals on the table."[66] Lillie died in 1941.

Subsequent owners include Mary Galloway Tullis and her son, Robert Alanson Tullis Jr., followed by John Clark and his son and daughter-in-law, Frank and Doris. In 1979 Joseph "Joe" H. and Ann B. Emmert moved to Bastrop and purchased the home in 1980.[67] Their daughters, Sarah and Kate, were raised here. Joe entered into partnership with Curtis McDonald and practiced dentistry in Bastrop for more than thirty-five years before retiring on January 1, 2016.

Joe and Ann moved to their ranch south of Bastrop on Highway 304 and turned the old Crysup home over to their daughter, Sarah Emmert; her husband, Pete Redfearn; and their grandson, Brett Joseph Redfearn. Their daughter, Kate Emmert; her husband, Adrain Henke; and their children, Max and twins Ruby and Gus Henke, live in California. Today (2019) the Emmert family has occupied the home for approximately forty years.[68]

The home is listed in the National Register of Historic Places (listed as constructed in 1918) and is a City of Bastrop Historic Landmark.

## Elbert S. Orgain House

*1704 Main Street / 1914–1915*

Elbert and Louise Nichols Orgain, married on November 18, 1914, received this stately home as a wedding gift from Elbert's father, Benjamin Darby Orgain. This Classical Revival–style home is two and one-half stories and has Palladian windows in the front gable, a double gallery, fluted Doric columns, and corner pilasters.[69] When under construction, a worker's ten-year-old son, Joe Angel, fell from the roof and amazingly

Elbert S. Orgain House, 1704 Main Street.

walked away unharmed.[70] The home has three operable coal-burning fireplaces with original brick flues, appropriate because Elbert was a partner in a coal-mining operation, the Belto Coal Company, north of Bastrop. He was also a downtown businessman, selling insurance and owning a cleaning and pressing business.[71] Elbert died in 1944 at age fifty-four.

When Elbert died, he willed his three automobiles to Louise.[72] It is not known whether or not Louise could drive at that time. However, by the 1950s and 1960s she was driving, but very badly. Bastrop's oldest citizens, even today (2019), remember saying, "Hit the ditch; here comes Louise." It seems she never stopped at a stop sign and never slowed down, honking if someone was in her way.[73] Louise also collected bottles and lined the windows of the cleaning-and-pressing business with them. They are said to have been colorful and varied.[74] Louise died in 1969; and her son, Franklin Darby Organ, in 1972. The home sold in 1974.

Drawing discovered during renovations in 2019, signed by one of the original carpenters, Wm. Schilling, in 1915.

Historic Robert Lynn Batts House moved in 1998 from 609 Pecan Street.

Subsequent owners include Wayne and Cathy Smith, Wilfred and Dooley Navarro, Ursula and Ken Frost, Sammy and Lisa Lerma, and Ron and Sandra Barclay. The Barclays undertook major renovations and in 2019 added an elevator on the north side. To make way for the elevator, a section of the north wall was opened, exposing a board that had been signed and dated by twenty-one-year-old William Schilling, one of the original carpenters when the home was built in 1915. A second signature and drawing by Schilling were discovered on an exposed brick chimney wall inside the renovated attic area.

This home served as the setting for a Christmas movie, *Angels Sing*, released in 2013 and starring Harry Connick Jr., Kris Kristofferson, Lyle Lovett, and Willie Nelson. To accommodate the needs of the production, neighbors left their outdoor Christmas decorations up for seven months, through July.

Another home on the property is the historic Robert Lynn Batts House, which was moved in 1998 from 609 Pecan Street to the south side of the home to be used as a guesthouse. The Batts House, which began as a typical Greek Revival–style cottage, was built by Andrew Jackson and Julia Priscilla Rice Batts in 1860. Their son, Robert Lynn Batts (1864–1935), was raised in the home and was a lawyer in Bastrop until 1892. He was assistant Texas attorney general, a special assistant attorney general of the United States, and a law professor at the University of Texas. He was judge of the Fifth Circuit Court of Appeals and a University of Texas regent. Batts Hall at the university is named in his honor.[75]

The Elbert S. Orgain House is listed in the National Register of Historic Places and is a City of Bastrop Historic Landmark. The Batts House was listed in the National Register of Historic Places and named the Judge R. Batts House.

## Old Jenkins House

*1710 Main Street / Circa 1830–1833*

Edward and Sarah Jenkins settled near Bastrop in 1830 on their league of land on the west side of the Colorado River near present Hills Prairie. In 1833 Edward was murdered and scalped (killer unknown) while he was working in the fields.[76] Sarah, pregnant at the time, moved to Bastrop with her three little children into this small log cabin. In 1836, after Santa Anna's defeat at San Jacinto, Sarah and her family converted the cabin into the typical pioneer double-log cabin with a log floor. A kitchen was built separate from the house and later connected to the main structure.[77] Later, the logs were covered with siding, and a small front porch was added. This charming Texas cottage is the oldest home in Bastrop.

Old Jenkins House, 1710 Main Street.

In 1835 Sarah married Reverend James Northcross, who died with William B. Travis and Davy Crockett at the Alamo.[78] A month later, her son, thirteen-year-old John Holland Jenkins, pleaded to join General Sam Houston's army as it marched to face Mexican general Santa Anna at San Jacinto. Sarah reluctantly gave him permission to go. However, before the battle began, young John was persuaded to return to Bastrop to help his mother as she readied her escape from advancing Mexican forces (the Runaway Scrape). Though he did not participate in the Battle of San Jacinto, John Jenkins is credited with being the youngest soldier in the fight for Texas independence.[79] John served in frequent Indian campaigns under General Edward Burleson and Captain John H. Moore and served in the Confederate Army during the Civil War.[80] Between 1884 and 1885 he wrote his personal reminiscences of life in pioneer Texas. Today, *Recollections of Early Texas* is one of the state's most widely read historical resources.

Seven generations of the Jenkins family lived in the home. For sixty years the kitchen was ruled by a Tonkawa woman named Aunt Puss, who had been captured at an early age and lived with the family as cook and maid. Many believed that the Tonkawa practiced cannibalism, so Aunt Puss took advantage of that belief. When the children who were reared under her rule misbehaved, she threatened to turn them into "Jenkins soup."[81]

The home is listed in the National Register of Historic Places and has been designated a Recorded Texas Historic Landmark.

## Waugh House

*1801 Main Street / Before 1859*

Early owners of this property were Eli and Millie McCoy (1857), Malkijah and Frances Highsmith (1859), James and Helen Jones (1860), and Chauncey Johnson (1861). It is unclear who was first to build on the property; however, Malkijah Highsmith's purchase price of $850 for six acres indicates there was a home on the property by 1859.[82]

Later owners W. E. and Mollie Maynard purchased the home in 1885. During the twenty-two years they owned the home, they added a new Victorian gingerbread front with elaborate jigsawn balustrade and square chamfered columns. They "enlarged, improved and beautified in keeping with the period."[83] Improvements included ornate fireplaces, hand-carved archways, and stained-glass windows. The home is a rare example of symmetrical Victorian architecture in Bastrop.

The Waugh House is named for Robert M. "Bob" Waugh, who together with his wife, Winnie Blackmon Waugh, purchased the home in 1917. Bob came to Bastrop in 1912 as the active vice president of the Calvin Coal Company. Their new mine at Calvin was located approximately five miles north of Bastrop. Bob had been a mining engineer in Glasgow, Scotland, before immigrating to the United States.[84] In 1918 Bob and his son, Alexander, also a mining engineer, joined in a partnership and established the Waugh Coal Company. Alex was pit boss.[85]

Winnie Waugh was organizer and, for eight years, president of the Bastrop Public Schools Mothers Club, which in 1931 became the Parent-Teachers Association. She continued as president of that organization for another twelve years. She helped organize the Negro Mothers Club and volunteered for the Red Cross for many years. She was a fifty-year member of the Order of Eastern Star; a member of the United Daughters of the Confederacy, Bastrop Ladies Reading Circle, and Lost Pines Garden Club; and a charter member of the Bastrop County Historical Society.[86]

Waugh House,
1801 Main Street.

Bob died in 1944. Winnie continued to live in the home until 1964, when she moved to Bonham, Texas, to live with her daughter, Helen Waugh Leatherwood. Although Winnie died in Bonham in 1972, her descendants continued to own the Bastrop home, the last one being great-granddaughter Suzanne Sanders Bentz and her husband, Chris, who sold it in 1991. The home had been in the Waugh family seventy-four years.

The house is listed in the National Register of Historic Places and is a City of Bastrop Historic Landmark.

## Pfeiffer House

*1802 Main Street / 1901*

The Texas Historical Commission building medallion attached to the Pfeiffer House reads: "A native of Bastrop, Joseph R. Pfeiffer (1876–1944) erected many homes and buildings in the town. He built this turn-of-the-century residence for his bride Freda (d. 1960) in 1901. Hoping to display his skill as a builder and attract future business, he made the house a showcase of fine materials and craftsmanship. Pfeiffer, who operated a lumber company and mill, later enlarged the dwelling to accommodate his family of six children."

This home is a fine example of late Victorian, or turn-of-the-century, architecture. Its facade features a corner front entry porch that is comfortably balanced between cross gables. The porch has square columns with gingerbread embellishment and an overhead balustrade that spans the distance between the gables. The gables are decorated with fish-scale shingles and a carpenter's sunrise/sunset above their windows. Pfeiffer designed and constructed the 1906 Fowler-Jenkins House (1302 Pecan Street) with many of these same elements.

Joe, as did other local builders, "drew his ideas of stylish design from so-called pattern books." He added many of his own ideas to show his building skills; he served as his own architect, contractor, and foreman.[87] "Uncle Joe" either built or remodeled many homes in Bastrop and was superintendent of construction for Bastrop State Park.

The original structure had five rooms (including a kitchen) and a sleeping porch. With the advent of plumbing, the sleeping porch was converted into a bathroom. The Pfeiffers occupied the home from the date of their marriage, December 1901, until Joe's death on July 31, 1944, and Freda's on March 7, 1960. The home was sold to Ernest and Clara Goertz in 1961, to Joe Echols in 1971, and to John McPhaul in 1973.[88]

Although interior changes and decor are seldom noted in descriptions of National Register homes, stenciling applied by owner Bobbie Felts Terrell is worthy of mention. After Bobbie, an artist and historian, purchased the home in 1975, she stenciled colorful flowers on the walls of the downstairs bath. Stenciling is an old art form often used by the "working farm wife" to achieve a look similar to wallpaper, which only the affluent could afford.[89] Bobbie's stenciling continues to decorate the walls of this and several other homes in Bastrop (2019).

The home was sold to Charles Melvin and Marilyn Whites in 1979.[90] Under the ownership of the Whites, the Pfeiffer House was the first bed-and-breakfast in Bastrop and among the first in Central Texas. Charles Melvin (called by both names)

Pfeiffer House, 1802 Main Street.

Stenciling in the Pfeiffer House by artist and historian Bobbie Terrell. Photo courtesy of Kathryn Lang.

joined the Evening Lions Club in 1984 and today (2019) at age eighty-six is still an active member. He was treasurer for the restoration of the historic 1914 Kerr Hall, originally the social center for Bastrop's African American community. Marilyn, in keeping with her love for history and historic homes, served as a trustee for the Bastrop County Historical Society and was a member of the City's Landmark Commission from 2002 to 2016.[91]

The building is listed in the National Register of Historic Places, is designated a Recorded Texas Historic Landmark, and is a City of Bastrop Historic Landmark.

# Pecan Street

## Alf Jung House

*508 Pecan Street / Circa 1895*

Alf (Adolph) Jung and his twin brother, Gus, were born in Bastrop in 1857. The boys worked with their older brother, Joe, and their father, Anton, in their brickyard outside town. The family made their own bricks and worked together as brick masons and builders. They built both residential and commercial buildings in Bastrop.[1] Alf married Emilie Lister in 1884. His parents, Anton and Anna Jung, deeded the lot for this home to him in March 1891.[2] Alf, probably with the help of his father and brothers, built this brick home a few years later. (They had previously worked together to build a brick home for Joe Jung at 909 Pecan.)

This one-story, red-brick Folk Victorian home features several porches with simple scroll-cut brackets. It has a double gable and a T-shaped floor plan with windows that have segmental brick arches and ornamental lintels. Because the house sits on a corner lot, the Jungs designed it to have a distinctively different "front-entry" porch on each of its street facades. Still standing (2019) a few feet from the house is an outbuilding thought to have been a kitchen or smokehouse. By 1934 it was being used as an "auto house," an early term for a garage. The woven roll-top wire fence and its iron support railing are believed to be original. Adjoining land was deeded to Alf by his mother in 1898. Alf died in 1920; Emilie, in 1936. Their children sold the home to Richard Whitworth (called R. W.) and Bertie Lee Hancock Smith.

During the Depression years of the 1930s, R. W. moved from his McDade family farm into Bastrop to work as a janitor for the Bastrop Independent School District. R. W. and Bertie purchased the home in 1943, and it remained in the Smith family until

Alf Jung House, 508 Pecan Street.

2010, when it was purchased by an attorney, Tina Zapalac, for use as her law office.[3] After Tina married John Alan Nixon in 2011, the home was converted into a headquarters for their company, Nixon Engineering, and their various other businesses.

The home is listed in the National Register of Historic Places and is a City of Bastrop Historic Landmark.

## W. F. Schaeffer House

*608 Pecan Street / Before 1887*

The W. F. Schaeffer House is built on the site of a livery stable that served customers of Rice's Ferry, which crossed the Colorado River approximately where Highway 71 crosses the river today. Travelers would leave their animals overnight if the ferry had closed for the evening.[4] Constructed before 1887, the home was purchased in 1898 by Willie Friedrich Schaeffer, the son of a Bastrop tinsmith.[5] The original four rooms eventually expanded into a traditional "T" floor plan with a gabled roof and siding milled from trees harvested from the shores of the Colorado River. Drinking water was collected in a cistern that is now concealed beneath the living room floor. The centerpiece of the front yard, a beautiful crape myrtle, was planted by Willie's wife, Willie Ann Middleton,

W. F. Schaeffer House, 608 Pecan Street.

in 1899 and is still surviving in 2019. While Willie F. Schaeffer died in 1915, "Miss Willie" continued to live in the home until her death in 1968 at age ninety.[6]

In September 2011 the home became a refuge for three families who suddenly became homeless when their houses burned in the Bastrop County Complex fire. The fire burned more than 34,365 acres and 1,645 area homes and resulted in two deaths. The fire spared Bastrop's west side and downtown residential area, and, according to Sally Keinarth, one of those seeking refuge, "Folks began snatching up houses for lease and even to purchase. Rental houses were all taken within 48 hours."[7]

At the time of the fire, the W. F. Schaeffer House was a rent house owned by T. Jay and Maxann Collins. Fire victims Sally and Art Keinarth and their sons, Payne and Jake; Ella and Mark Bedford and their sons, Sebastian and Guy; Sharah and David Johnson and their daughter, Claire, all moved into the Schaeffer home together. Family and friends donated air mattresses, cots, blankets, dishes, clothing, folding tables, and chairs—all manner of household items.[8] The families lived together many months until each family either purchased or built a new home. The children, ages thirteen to sixteen, thought it great fun and named the group the Keinfordsons.[9]

The home is listed in the National Register of Historic Places (dated 1913) and is a City of Bastrop Historic Landmark.

## Prokop Home

*703 Pecan Street / 1918*

Newlyweds Emil and Helen Prokop inherited the property for their future home from Emil's father, Michel A. Prokop. In 1918 they built this comfortable single-story bungalow featuring square porch columns, wide overhangs, and a wraparound veranda.[10] After moving into their new home, Emile and Helen rented out their older house next door (701 Pecan Street) for additional income.[11]

In direct contrast to the ornate Victorian styles that had been prevalent in Bastrop, the home features simplicity. The bungalow has five large, square rooms. The front door opens directly into the living room, unlike the dogtrot or long entry hall of many early-Texas homes. The structure rests on pier-and-beam construction with large square piers of old Austin common bricks. Early (for Bastrop) indoor plumbing boasted a footed cast-iron bathtub.[12]

Emil Prokop and his brother, Frank, worked as cobblers in their father's shoe store making boots and shoes. The Prokops rented a building on Main Street until 1887, when they built the Prokop Building at 913 Main Street. The brothers continued to own and operate the business after their father's death in 1916. The Prokop Bootery was

Prokop Home, 703 Pecan Street.

later converted to a general merchandise store.[13] The building is still (2019) prominent on Main Street and owned by the Prokop family.

Emil died in 1934. Helen, a schoolteacher, remained in the house. During World War II she added a temporary kitchen onto the back and rented a much-needed apartment to families of soldiers stationed at Camp Swift, a military training camp six miles north of Bastrop. Helen remained active in her church and social events of the town.[14] She died in 1971.

After Merle Arnold Prokop, a nephew, inherited the home, it became rental property. Fortunately, the house remained intact, and very little "remuddling" occurred.[15] The house was purchased in 1985 by H. G. Terrell and his son, Clay, who was a local restoration expert. He restored much of the home to its original condition. The home was sold to Clay's sister and brother-in-law, Terry and Jim Hamm, in 1995. The home's current owners, Shawn and Lindsay Kana, purchased it in 2016.[16]

## Rabensburg House

*707 Pecan Street / Before 1869*

Robert Gill and Mary Jane Thompson were married in Travis County in December 1867,[17] and in 1869 they bought this home on Pecan Street from Pryor N. and Anna Harris.[18] The home was originally one story with a Greek Revival floor plan.[19] Robert Gill, a Confederate soldier for four years, was a butcher and merchant on Main Street. Gill's Branch, which flows under Chestnut Street in the 1500 block, is named for Robert's family. Robert's parents settled on the east side of the branch in the 1840s.

Mary Jane Thompson was born in Knottingley, Yorkshire, England, in 1848 and came to Austin in 1852 with her parents and brothers, Ben and Bill, and a little sister, Fanny.[20] Ben Thompson became an infamous gunslinger, gambler, and city marshal of Austin. Mary Jane attended the Amelia Barr School for Young Ladies and the B. J. Smith School.[21] As a bride she moved to Bastrop and became interested in civic and social affairs.[22]

Robert and Mary Jane Gill had three children: Edna Earl, Robert Jr., and Walter. Their daughter married George Davis in 1897, and the couple lived here with Edna's parents for approximately ten years before building their own home at 1010 Chestnut Street. George Davis was Bastrop County sheriff from 1890 to 1904. During his years as sheriff, there were two famous murder trials: Tobe Cook, who murdered Ida Bell Moore,[23] and Aleck Brown, who murdered Jane Wilkins.[24] It became the duty of Sheriff Davis to hang both men. His friends encouraged him to leave town and appoint someone else to carry out the hangings, but years later George explained to his daughter, Mary Jane: "No, I took the oath of office to fulfill my obligation, and I had to stay here whether I believed in it or not."[25]

Robert Gill died in 1918; Mary Jane, in 1940 at age ninety-two.[26] They sold the home to Ed Roe in 1910.[27] Roe sold it to Jesse Dawson, who sold it to Edward Jacob "Ed" and Katherine "Kate" Watson Rabensburg in March 1920.[28] The Rabensburgs added a half story, the projecting bays, an L-shaped porch, Doric columns, and the central front gable with its Palladian window.[29] Ed owned the IGA grocery business and store building on Main Street.[30] He refused to drive, and for approximately twenty years Kate was his chauffeur.[31] Ed died in 1967; Kate, in 1980. When their descendants sold the home to Edward L. "Dusty" and Sonya McBride Rhodes in 1983,[32] the home had been in the Rabensburg family for sixty-three years.

The home is listed in the National Register of Historic Places (dated 1915) and is a City of Bastrop Historic Landmark.

Rabensburg House, 707 Pecan Street.

## Scottie Chambliss Jenkins House

*801 Pecan Street / 1890*

This clapboard Victorian home, with its central porch, was given as a wedding gift to Robert Lane and Scottie Chambliss Jenkins in 1890. The builder was John White. Robert died in 1891, and Scottie married James H. Davis in 1897. She lived in the home until her death in 1970 at age ninety-nine years.

The only child of Scottie and Robert Jenkins, a daughter, "Miss Bob" (1891–1980), was born in the home and lived there her entire life. For twenty-three years, Miss Bob was choir director at the First Methodist Church. She was employed at the Bastrop County Tax Assessor's Office and later in the office of the county clerk. On the north side of the home was her large azalea garden, and every spring when the garden was in full bloom, it became a "drive-by destination" for Bastrop residents.[33] She married Will Rogers (1885–1970) in 1913.

Will Rogers was Bastrop's colorful mayor for twenty-two years, retiring in 1964. He was mayor during the chaotic days of Camp Swift, when Bastrop became a boomtown overnight. Throughout the years he became a sort of trademark for Bastrop by char-

Mayor Will Rogers riding in a Main Street parade, circa 1950s. Courtesy of the Bastrop County Historical Society.

Mayor Will Rogers and his gentleman's Stetson, 1942. Photo courtesy of the Bastrop County Historical Society.

Scottie Chambliss Jenkins House, 801 Pecan Street.

acteristically wearing cowboy boots, a Stetson perched on the side of his head, and a broad grin. Among his major accomplishments were the development of Bastrop State Park, securing the location for the Lower Colorado River Authority's Sim Gideon Power Plant at Bastrop, and the development of the city sewer system.[34]

Mayor Rogers often consulted with his friend Lyndon B. Johnson about city matters, and because of their friendship, in 1959 Will organized a fish fry at the Bastrop American Legion Hall so that Lyndon Johnson could announce his candidacy for US president. For the fish fry local fishermen were allowed to dynamite and/or telephone fish in the Colorado River while Game Warden Harold Farley turned a blind eye. When telephoning, a fisherman would string electric wires in the water, connect them to an old-style crank telephone, and turn the crank. Fish were shocked by the electrical current, momentarily stunned, and floated to the top. Over a two- to three-week period, approximately two thousand fish were caught and taken to the large concrete reservoir that collected evaporated water from the cooling towers for the local ice house. The reservoir, about forty feet square, was big enough to keep the fish alive until the afternoon of the fish fry. Among the ten or twelve designated fishermen were Ira Frieda, Jack Claiborne Jr., Jerry Woehl, Pat Hoffman, James "Tooter" Myers, Ray Davis, Alvin McAfee, and Slim Henderson. Thousands were fed, but to no avail. Johnson lost the Democratic Party nomination to future president John F. Kennedy.[35]

The home is listed in the National Register of Historic Places, is designated a Recorded Texas Historic Landmark, and is a City of Bastrop Historic Landmark.

## Griesenbeck House

*805 Pecan Street / Circa 1901*

Theodore Peter "Pete" Griesenbeck married Minnie Thedin on January 10, 1893, when he was twenty-one and she was nineteen.[36] Together they had five children that were raised in this home: Willfred Griesenbeck Robinson Baugh, Ethel Griesenbeck Tarver, Lula Nell Griesenbeck Bays, Jack John Griesenbeck, and Theodore Leland ("young Pete") Griesenbeck. Pete enjoyed ballroom dancing, roller skating, and acting in productions at the Old Bastrop Opera House. He was among the many Bastropians who went ice skating on the Colorado River when it froze in 1899.[37]

In 1901 Pete bought the vacant lot at 805 Pecan from his sister-in-law, Sarah Thedin Lockett.[38] He then bought a one-room church,[39] which he moved onto the property and, within a few years, added a living room, dining room, large L-shaped hall, kitchen, three bedrooms, and a bath. The house now (2019) has another bathroom and bedroom and a screened porch on the back. It is not known when these last additions were made.

Sarah Lockett lived in the home with her sister and brother-in-law, Minnie and Pete,[40] and owned a "confectionary and a fancy grocery establishment" on Bastrop's Main Street.[41] After Sarah's death in 1904, the confections building changed ownership and was sold in 1910 by J. L. Wilbarger to make way for a new building, the Citizens State Bank of Bastrop.[42] Pete and Minnie owned and operated the grocery business at 926 Main Street; at the same time Pete operated his three farms, which were located outside Bastrop. In 1911 they rented out their grocery store building and started a new business.[43]

According to a family member, Pete made and sold the first hamburgers in Central Texas. Pete's Hamburger Shack was located at 1019 Main Street in what is now a wide-paved driveway between two buildings into the alley. The Hamburger Shack shared the small driveway with Max Leath's summer outdoor movie theater.[44] Pete's hamburgers

were famous. He had a set sequence for assembling them that he insisted be followed: first the mustard, then the mayonnaise, lettuce, pickles, tomato, and finally a fried egg or cheese next to the meat on buns that were always warmed. Courting young couples drove into Bastrop from the surrounding area to enjoy Pete's hamburgers at one or two o'clock in the morning.[45]

Griesenbeck House, 805 Pecan Street.

In 1917 or 1918 Minnie went to Galveston to visit her married daughter, Willfred. Minnie fell in love with the Galveston homes on stilts and, after her return to Bastrop, put her own home up on ten-foot-high stilts. (The terrible Colorado River flood of 1915 may still have been fresh on Minnie's mind.) The family wash was done with wash pots and scrub boards in the shady area under the raised house. This area also served as a garage for the family cars and as hay storage for Pete's cattle. During the Depression years in the 1930s there were many homeless people in Bastrop, some of whom jumped from the nearby passing trains and hid under the house for shelter. Minnie fed and tried to help them.[46] Pete Griesenbeck died in 1947, and Minnie died in 1956.

Their daughter Ethel Griesenbeck Tarver inherited the home in 1956 and had the stilts removed in the 1970s. Ethel holds the record for the longest service to the state of Texas as a district court reporter—fifty-seven years. Her husband, Hall Tarver, was Bastrop County chief deputy sheriff under Sheriffs Jimmy Nutt and Ira Hoskins and was the first to bring a livestock auction sale to the county.[47] Ethel's only child, Shirley Tarver Edwards, inherited the house from her mother, and she and her husband, Freddie, lived there until they passed away. In 2020 their children—Ethel and Hall's grandchildren, Carol Shull, Rusty Edwards, and Gary Edwards—continue to own the home.

Carol Shull was the keeper of the National Register of Historic Places and managed the National Historic Landmarks program. In 2012 the secretary of the interior recognized Carol's service in the historic preservation programs with the Distinguished Service Award. She retired from the National Park Service in 2015.[48]

The home is listed in the National Register of Historic Places and is a City of Bastrop Historic Landmark.

## Jung-Pearcy House

*909 Pecan Street / 1873*

The red-brick cottage on the corner of Chestnut and Pecan was built in 1873 by Joseph Jung for his bride, Elizabeth "Lizzie" Schwitzer. Joe was born in 1844 and came to America in 1853 from Bohemia, Czech Republic, with his parents, Anton and Anna Jung.[49] In 1857 his twin brothers, Alf (Adolph) and Gus, were born in Bastrop. Anton Jung owned a brickyard outside town and taught his three sons to be brick masons. Several businesses in downtown Bastrop were built by the Jungs.

Joe and Lizzie's house consisted of only two rooms and a hall. The bricks were large and sun-dried, made by Joe's father and his brother Gus. In 1889 a three-room annex was built. Joe's brother Alf did this brick work using smaller, standard-sized, kiln-dried brick. It is interesting to compare the two styles. The kiln-dried bricks are very hard, while the sun-dried bricks can be easily grooved with a fingernail. Other interesting features are the three layers of bricks just below the eaves and the arched, vertical bricks over the windows.[50]

Joe was Bastrop County sheriff from 1869 to 1871 and served as Bastrop County judge from 1874 to 1876. Joe died in 1898; Lizzie, in 1933.

In 1936 Ernest and Ruby Pearcy purchased the house, which remained in their family until 1988. Ernest was first assistant cashier at First National Bank. However, he resigned in 1939 because of his appointment as Bastrop postmaster—serving in that

position from 1939 to 1964.[51] He was also city secretary and was elected to the Bastrop City Council. Ruby Tracy Pearcy was the daughter of a "hell-fire and brimstone" Methodist minister.[52] She was a beloved schoolteacher and the First United Methodist Church's organist for forty years.

Jung-Pearcy House, 909 Pecan Street.

The home is listed in the National Register of Historic Places (listed as the Joe Jung House), is designated a Recorded Texas Historic Landmark (listed as the Jung-Pearcy House), and is included in the Historic American Building Survey (HABS). It is a City of Bastrop Historic Landmark.

## Dyer Moore–O. P. Jones House

*1009 Pecan Street / Circa 1872–1875*

In 1872 Henry and Caroline Koppel bought a vacant lot for $250 and built a one-story cottage that they sold in 1875 to Robert Gill for $1,800. Gill sold the home to Judge Dyer Moore for $2,350 in 1881.[53]

Dyer and Marion Virginia Heise McRae Moore, with their four-month-old daughter, Margaret "Belle," moved to Bastrop in 1872. He served as Bastrop County judge and was elected to that office for six consecutive terms (1876–83). The Bastrop County Courthouse burned on January 1, 1883,[54] and Judge Moore immediately began plans for a new building. Under his leadership, the new courthouse was built within a year, on the same site, and it is still in use today (2019). For many years Dyer was president of the Bastrop School Board of Trustees and the mayor of Bastrop, donating his salary to the public library and the cemetery association.[55]

The 1883 Bastrop County Courthouse. Photo courtesy of the Bastrop County Historical Society.

In 1895 Belle married Oliver Pennington Jones, operator of a Main Street grocery store, Peoples Cash Grocery, and the couple lived in the home with Belle's parents. Marion Moore died in 1910, and Dyer Moore, in 1919. Belle Moore Jones inherited the home. A teacher in the Bastrop schools for forty years, Belle taught first in the Bastrop Academy and later in Bastrop public schools. She was among the teachers who accompanied the student body as they went ice skating on the Colorado River in 1899 when the river froze during a temperature of ten below zero. Belle taught music, including piano and violin lessons, in her home after school. She was a composer and wrote, among others, "Dear Bastrop High," adopted and used for many years as the official school song. She was president of both the Bastrop Harmony Club and the Bastrop Ladies Reading Circle.[56] Bastrop historian Nell Herndon, in an interview in the *Bastrop Advertiser*, said, "Mrs. Oliver P. Jones . . . probably was the one, if we give credit to one, who did the most for the library all of her life. I don't remember anyone who took part in it as much as Mrs. Jones did, but she took part in everything cultural around town."[57]

In 1911 Belle and Oliver Jones added a second and third story to the home. Oliver died in 1922, and Belle continued to live in her childhood home until her death in 1961.

Dyer Moore–O. P. Jones House, 1009 Pecan Street.

O. P. Jones, center, owner of Peoples Cash Grocery, circa 1910. Photo courtesy of the Bastrop County Historical Society.

Their only child, Charles Heise Jones, was born in 1912, and in 1946 he established a corner grocery at 1602 Main, now known as Tracy Chalmers' Drive Inn, still a neighborhood grocery store and a Main Street landmark.[58]

In 1989 a fire raged through the second story and rendered the home uninhabitable. The structure was purchased and rescued from demolition by Dooley Ann and Wilfred Navarro and, after seven months of restoration, was occupied by them in January 1992.[59] They sold to Sammy and Marilyn Callihan in 1997.

Under the ownership of the Callihams the home became important to the young people in the neighborhood. The Callihams joined a national program called the Little Free Library, a free neighborhood book-exchange program designed to increase children's access to books. The Callihams installed a book-sharing box near their front sidewalk. It is filled with children's books and displays the words "Leave or Take."[60]

The home is listed in the National Register of Historic Places (listed as the Oliver P. Jones House and dated 1904).

Neighborhood children are encouraged to "Leave or Take" a book.

## Zeiten-Morris House

*1010 Pecan Street / 1903*

The Zeiten-Morris House was built in 1903, but not at its present location. It was originally built on the northwest corner of the intersection of Chestnut and Pecan Streets and remained there until World War II.[61] In 1903 Leo and Louise Zeiten hired local contractor Joe Pfeiffer to build their eclectically styled Queen Anne home with wide gingerbread porches, two fireplaces, built-in china cabinet, birch wainscoting, three sets of matching pocket doors, golden oak fireplace mantel, and elaborate millwork. Included was a service porch so that ice could be delivered without the deliveryman having to enter the house. Because Zeiten was an amateur photographer, the house included a darkroom.[62] For reasons unknown, the couple sold the home only three years later, in October 1906.

A. T. "Taylor" and Mabel (Mae) Hutchison Morris bought the home for three thousand dollars,[63] and they moved in with their four sons, Edwin, Earl, Jesse, and Charles, and Mabel's mother, Susan Hutchison.[64] Taylor was Precinct 1 county commissioner, constable, deputy sheriff, and a member of the Bastrop Fire Department. He owned a livery, a feed-and-sale stable, and a large blacksmith shop.[65] Earl Morris inherited the house. He and his wife, Hazel Hemphill Morris, moved in January 1, 1929, with their children: Rose Lee, Ann, Charles Bob, Patsy Earl, and Iva Mae.[66]

The Zeiten-Morris House was moved from its original location on Chestnut Street to make way for a new bus station and movie theater for soldiers training at Camp Swift. Courtesy of the Bastrop County Historical Society.

During World War II there were thousands of soldiers in Bastrop because of its proximity to Camp Swift. The decision was made to move the house back to 1010 Pecan Street and sell the vacated lot where a movie theater and bus station were to be built to accommodate the troops. The house was moved with mules and logs about one hundred yards north. Hazel Morris sat on her front porch drinking tea during the ordeal.[67] Within a year of the move Hazel, a modern woman, removed three levels of original gingerbread porch railing and trim to achieve a more "Southern" look.[68]

Subsequent owners include Judge Jack and Ruby Griesenbeck, who purchased the home in 1948; Joe and Iris Shirley and family; Ophelia Roy and Kate Walker; Anton (Tom) and Viola Bartsch; and Gerald and Brenda Wagner. The Wagners turned the home into a children's art museum, Hands around Texas.[69] Shawn and Bill Pletsch

Zeiten-Morris House, 1010 Pecan Street.

Decorative bargeboards.

purchased the house in 1986 and established a bed-and-breakfast, the Pecan Street Inn. Bill is famous for his pecan waffles.

The home is erroneously listed in the National Register of Historic Places as the J. C. Buchanan House. The Buchanan home burned in 1902, and Minnie Buchanan Schaefer died in the fire. The Zeiten-Morris House was rolled backward onto the lot that had been occupied by the Buchanan House. The Zeiten-Morris house is also a City of Bastrop Historic Landmark.

## Jenkins-Moore Home

*1102 Pecan Street / 1921*

This classic Arts and Crafts bungalow was built by Jack and Julia Belle Jenkins in 1921. Its gently pitched broad gable, with rafters and purlins extending beyond the roof-line, covers the large, open L-shaped porch. The floor plan has stayed much the same as when it was originally constructed, with the front door opening into a large living room that spans the front of the house. A central fireplace stands on the opposite wall. The dining room and kitchen are through the door to the left with the bedrooms to the right, all opening into a central hallway.[70]

Jack, who had served as both county and district attorney, died of appendicitis shortly after its construction. In 1925 Belle sold the house to William T. and Julia Placke, who owned a local grocery store. Unfortunately, during the Depression, the Plackes lost their home to the bank.[71] Following the foreclosure, they moved to Austin, where William worked as a grocery store manager. They are buried in Fairview Cemetery in Bastrop.

Robert E. and Bernice Hasler Jenkins purchased the property at the foreclosure sale on the courthouse steps in 1938 from the Home Owners' Loan Corporation. Robert, a World War II veteran, was the Pearl Beer distributor for the Bastrop area for about forty years and also worked with his wife's family's funeral home for about thirty of those years.[72] Bernice taught school from 1930 to 1942, left the profession to help manage the family funeral home during war years when Robert was in the army, and then returned to teaching in 1947. After 1944 the Jenkinses enlarged and enclosed the back porch to add a second bathroom and laundry area. They sold the house in 1966, having owned it for twenty-eight years. Bernice died in 1980; Robert, in 1982.

Ellen Moore, well-known in Bastrop for her popular, weekly gossip column in the *Bastrop Advertiser*, purchased the bungalow in 1974. She married Bob Hoover in 1978, and together they lived in it for nearly forty years. Ellen had attended Wellesley College, worked in the editorial department at *Glamour* magazine, and was well traveled.[73]

Jenkins-Moore Home, 1102 Pecan Street.

In 2015 Sherri Gilmore purchased the home from the Moore estate and began a renovation of its interior, leaving the original longleaf pine floors, ceilings, fireplaces, and footprint in homage to its original design.[74]

## A. A. Erhard House

*1106 Pecan Street / 1850*

There are two homes listed in the National Register in honor of Adolph A. Erhard. This National Register home was purchased by Adolph and Sarah Erhard in 1870, and the family lived here while their house at 1205 Pecan was under construction. After moving into their new home, the Erhards kept this home for rental property. It passed to their son, Chester, and then to Chester's brother, John Erhard.[75]

This small Folk house in the National style has a board-and-batten facade and a central hallway with flanking rooms, each with an outside door. The building's foundation is built with notched and pegged, hand-hewn cedar logs, and the flooring is center-cut, longleaf Bastrop pine. The fireplace is located on an interior wall, one side facing the parlor, the other facing the main bedroom. It was common practice for early carpenters to put a construction date in a hidden location somewhere within the walls of a home, and the date 1850 was discovered behind the fireplace.[76] In the backyard is the original outdoor kitchen, one of the few remaining in Bastrop.[77]

The home is listed in the National Register of Historic Places and is a City of Bastrop Historic Landmark.

A. A. Erhard House, 1106 Pecan Street.

# T. A. Hasler House

*1109 Pecan Street / Circa 1910*

In 1906 the Colorado River flooded, and townspeople lined up on the 1890 bridge to watch the churning water. Sixteen-year-old Mary Hasler and her boyfriend (future husband), Powell Perkins, decided to row across the river. Mary's father, Theodore A. Hasler, who was on the bridge, spotted the couple as they launched their little boat. He began waving his arms, frantically jumping up and down, trying to get their attention. Mary and Powell safely returned to shore. Hasler scrambled down the bank and, to her embarrassment, spanked Mary on the spot.[78] Theodore A. Hasler, born in Switzerland in 1848, arrived in Bastrop penniless in 1861. By 1885 he owned Hasler's Corner, located at the intersection of Main and Chestnut Streets: a saloon, dry goods store, groceries, warehouse, and general store. He became one of Bastrop's leading businessmen.[79]

T. A. was active in civic and charitable causes, serving as county commissioner for Precinct 1 and as treasurer for the Friend in Need Society of Bastrop County. He was elected president of a fifteen-member committee responsible for raising funds and soliciting bids for the construction of the first bridge across the Colorado River at Bastrop in 1890,[80] and he served more than twenty years as vice president of the First National Bank.

He married Marie Hoppe in October 1872 and bought this property in 1880; early photographs show a farmhouse-style home on the property. Here, they raised their sons, Ernest, Walter, Joe, and Bruno, and daughters, Annie and Mary. T. A. Hasler died in 1909, and one year later Marie began renovating and enlarging the home. The leaded-glass windows placed in the two parlors and over the front door were acquired during a trip to Switzerland. Among the upgraded features were flooring, woodwork and wainscoting of longleaf pine, pocket doors, tin ceilings, a built-in china cabinet, and a broad porch wrapping around half the house.[81] Mary Hasler and her husband, Powell Perkins, lived in the home and took care of Marie until her death on December 27, 1926. The couple inherited the home and raised a family of their own: two daughters, Theo Perkins (married to W. B. Townsend) and Dorothy Perkins (married to John Vernon Ash Jr. but divorced in 1972).

Subsequent owners made contributions to the house, including dividing the large upstairs into living spaces and screening part of the porch. Joseph and Ann Emmert owned the home from 1986 to 1992, followed by Mayor Terry and Dr. Patricia Orr,[82] who

owned the home until 2015. The Orrs planted large rose gardens in front of the home. The house was the primary location for the 2011 motion picture *Fireflies in the Garden*, which starred Julia Roberts, Ryan Reynolds, and Willem Dafoe. Glenn and Deborah Johnson purchased the home in 2015.

The home is listed in the National Register of Historic Places and is a City of Bastrop Historic Landmark.

T. A. Hasler House, 1109 Pecan Street.

# McLavy-Cochran-Claiborne Home

*1202 Pecan Street / 1894*

Arthur B. "A. B." and Effie McLavy purchased the eastern one-half block on Pecan Street in 1889.[83] After Effie died in 1892, A. B. married Elnora "Ella" Eckel and built this home on the property in 1894.[84] Ella, A. B., and his children by his first marriage, Raymond and Arthur, lived in the home. A. B. was in the insurance business, and Ella taught fourth grade in Bastrop for approximately thirty years.

Although it was common practice for commercial structures to be made of brick, it was unusual for residences in Bastrop in 1894. Since A. B. was in the insurance business, he was keenly aware of the lowered fire risk of brick structures. Projecting, fish-scale-shingled gables accent the hipped roof structure on all sides. Beneath the front gable sits a large arched window, while the side gables contain very small arched windows centered over a pair of narrow arched windows on the first floor. The front facade features a square columned porch and a simple front door with window lights above.

Ella McLavy, faculty photo, 1925. Courtesy of Wm. Terry Sanders.

A. B. McLavy died in 1928. After Ella died in 1939, the McLavy children sold the home to Samuel and Ethel Hickman Cochran.[85] The Cochrans had three children, two of whom survived to adulthood, Ora Dell and Marion. The Cochrans moved into the McLavy house, divided the remaining property, and built a duplex on the north side for rental income to supplement their grocery store business (Cochran's Grocery) on Main Street.[86] Samuel managed the store, and Ethel was a clerk.[87]

Samuel Cochran died in 1941. Ethel then was a volunteer for the USO, earning a commendation letter from Senator Lyndon Johnson.[88] She was a member of the First Methodist Church choir, where the new minister, Clarence Otto "C. O." Boatman, met and fell in love with her. He was a recent widower with three children of his own.

In 1943 Reverend Boatman left Bastrop for training as an army chaplain near Boston, Massachusetts, and later was stationed at forts and camps near Chicago. Lieutenant Boatman became known as the "Chaplain on Wheels," operating out of a trailer complete with desks, chairs, altar, organ, and pulpit.[89] He traveled with the Third War Bond Show (which included the popular Wayne King Orchestra) throughout the northern United States, returning to Bastrop in December 1944 to marry Ethel before completing his World War II service in France, Belgium, and Germany.

McLavy-Cochran-Claiborne Home, 1202 Pecan Street.

The original red brick before the home was painted, circa 2013. Courtesy of Tommy Claiborne.

After the war C. O. was assigned to the Government Hill Methodist Church in San Antonio, and the couple became traveling evangelists.[90] Ethel sold the house to Jack Dyer Claiborne in 1954.[91]

Jack Dyer Claiborne and Eulalia Kimbrough, both from Alum Creek, married in 1935.[92] Eulalia worked for the *Bastrop Advertiser*, and in 1936 Jack began work at the post office. During World War II he was the superintendent of the Camp Swift Postal Complex. The post office employed sixty-five civilians who worked ten to twelve hours, seven days a week, to keep up with the volume of mail. There were days when they processed up to three boxcars of mail per day. After the war Jack transferred back to the Bastrop Postal System and was a postal clerk another thirty-four years.[93]

Retirement was spent in his garden in the backyard of his Pecan Street home, where he had "some plants 30 years old." There were bromeliads, cannas, geraniums the size of bushes, river ferns, begonias of all shades, gladiolas, and a twenty-five-year-old fig tree.[94] When interviewed by the *Bastrop Advertiser*, he said, "I've always grown plants, but then I like to do most everything. When we bought the house I did the sheetrock, then I did the painting and plumbing and flooring."[95]

The home was sold to Miles Hanson in 2013.[96]

## Adolph A. Erhard House

*1205 Pecan Street / 1870*

In the late 1830s the Erhard family immigrated to Bastrop from Germany. In 1839 both parents died on the same evening, leaving two orphaned children: eight-year-old Adolphus Antonio Erhard and his seventeen-year-old brother, Cayton.

The two boys were taken in by James Nicholson, the owner of a local hotel, where they waited tables, chopped wood, and carried out a variety of chores in exchange for room and board. Young Adolph had quite a personality and was reported to be a favorite of the politicians, lawyers, businessmen, stagecoach drivers, and ministers who were hotel guests. James Nicholson eventually became the young boy's legal guardian.

Adolph married Sarah Beavers in 1853, and together they had four children: Chester, Mary, Susie, and John. Adolph was a blacksmith in partnership with J. R. Nichols to forge barrels for rifles for use by the Confederate Army during the Civil War, but the partnership ended when Adolph left Bastrop to join the Confederate States Army, serving in Captain Morgan's Company, Daniel's Cavalry Regiment.[97] By 1870, at age thirty-nine, he was again a blacksmith in Bastrop and a civic and business leader. He owned large tracts of land outside town, owned a small home in town, and purchased

a six-acre lot where he began construction of this home.[98] He selected this site because it had not flooded when the Colorado River overflowed in 1869.[99]

Adolph A. Erhard House, 1205 Pecan Street.

The architectural style of the Erhard home is Italianate. This lovely style was popular in England in the 1820s; reached America by the 1850s; and, thanks to Adolph and Sarah, arrived in Bastrop in 1870. The two-story home has thirty-seven hundred square feet of living area, including four bedrooms, formal living and dining rooms, a breakfast room, a game room, two staircases, two fireplaces, and three porches. The original Victorian cast-iron trim adorns the front porches and balcony. Glass set in the hand-carved double doors is etched with the Erhard name.[100] When the house was built in 1870, there were only a few two-story homes in Bastrop; most were simple one-story farmhouses, cottages, or upgraded dogtrot cabins. Legend is that this home caused quite a stir when built because it was "too fancy."

The home remained in the family for four generations. It became the property of Mary Erhard Trigg (married to Thomas Jones Trigg), an Erhard daughter, and then it went to Mary's niece, Mary Bell Murchison Brieger (married to Richard Hasler Brieger).[101] After the death of Mary Brieger, her heirs sold the house in 1977 to William C. Barbee, an architecture student at the University of Texas, who rehabilitated the house for his master's degree thesis.[102]

The home is listed in the National Register of Historic Places (listed as the Adolph Erhard House) and is designated a Recorded Texas Historic Landmark (listed as the A. A. Erhard House). It is a City of Bastrop Historic Landmark.

## Cochran-Watson Home

*1206 Pecan Street / Circa 1940*

The Cochran-Watson home was built near the time that World War II–era Camp Swift was under construction north of Bastrop. With the influx of approximately eighteen thousand equipment operators, engineers, laborers, telephone operators, postal workers, typists, highway contractors, and utility workers, rental property was in high demand. This house was built on a large lot purchased in 1939 by Samuel R. and Ethel H. Cochran.[103] The Cochrans divided the oversized property into three separate lots and built this home, originally a duplex, on the northernmost lot for rental income. Each side of the duplex encompassed a small living room, bedroom, bathroom, and kitchen. The hardwood floors were installed before the interior walls were built. Each kitchen opened to the backyard, where there was one single-car garage with an apartment above.

Samuel Cochran was born in 1876; Ethel, in 1895. The marriage was considered a "marriage of convenience" since Ethel was almost twenty years younger than Samuel.[104] In addition to owning their rental property, the couple owned and operated a grocery store on Main Street. Samuel died on May 29, 1941. Ethel remained active in the First Methodist Church and the USO and continued to operate the grocery store and rent out the property.[105] She married a widowed army chaplain, Clarence Otto "C. O." Boatman, in 1944.

When the soldiers started arriving at the camp in 1942, the garage apartment was rented to officers and their families. Among them were Dr. Robert Wells Loveless and his wife, Eloise.[106] Eloise was one of the "original Camp Swift ladies" who established the Ladies Luncheon, which began in 1942 as a way to introduce officers' wives to the women in town.[107] After the war, Robert returned to Eloise and to Bastrop and established a local medical practice under Gordon Bryson, taking over his practice in

Cochran-Watson Home, 1206 Pecan Street.

1947.[108] Eloise was still a member of the monthly Ladies Luncheon when it celebrated its fiftieth anniversary in 1992.[109]

Later owners, Robert C. and Ruth E. Watson, married in September 1941. Robert was employed by the Coca-Cola Bottling Company at 603 Chestnut Street and left his job to join the US Army Air Corps, serving in the Philippines and New Guinea. At war's end Robert and Ruth rented half the duplex, and Robert returned to his job at the Coca-Cola Bottling Company.[110] In 1957 they purchased the duplex from Ethel Cochran Boatman and converted it to a single-family residence.[111]

Robert Watson was among only five or six employees who worked at the Coca-Cola plant,[112] where each Coke was bottled by hand. The process involved filling each eight-ounce glass bottle with a ready-made syrup, adding carbonated water, crimping the cap, and finally placing each bottle into a wooden case. The ready-made syrup was shipped to Bastrop in barrels from other plants in Texas. Employees were not allowed to know the recipe for the syrup. On a very hard day, they could produce five hundred to six hundred cases of Coke, twenty-four bottles to a case. This amount was usually more than enough to keep up with local demand in Bastrop, Elgin, and Smithville.[113] Robert retired after working twenty-eight years for the company. By that time, the company had added a conveyor belt and the number of employees had doubled.

Ruth Watson was an operator for the telephone company at Camp Swift, living with a number of female telephone operators in town while Robert was away. After the war, Ruth worked for the telephone company in Bastrop but was transferred to the Austin Southwestern Bell Telephone offices after the dial phone was adopted.[114] The Watsons had two sons, William (Buster) and Robert (Bobby).

In 1963 the Watsons "modernized" the exterior wood siding on the front, sides, and master bedroom walls of their home with Permastone. Three houses in Bastrop were "modernized" due to the efforts of the 1960s Permastone salesman. In 1964 the construction trades class of Bastrop High School extended the rear roofline and built an enclosed back porch onto the house.

Four generations of Watsons had owned the home when it was sold in 2009 to Sue Ann Fruge. Sue Ann initiated an extensive repair and renovation of the home as well as reconstruction of the badly deteriorated garage and its apartment. Sue Ann's love affair with older homes began early, as she had grown up in an 1897 National Register "Territorial Home" in Wagoner, Oklahoma.

## Fowler-Jenkins House

*1302 Pecan Street / 1906*

Constructed in 1906 at a location four blocks west on Wilson Street, this home was a wedding gift from John Preston Fowler to his son, John Preston Jr., and his wife, Calela (Lela) Brown. Joseph Pfeiffer was the builder and architect. Within a few years of construction, the newlywed Fowlers moved to West Texas and, in 1912, sold their home to Hartford Jenkins. The house was placed on logs and rolled down dirt streets to its present location, pulled by two or three sets of mules. As the logs were rolled forward, the exposed back log would be carried to the front. This exchange was repeated over and over. The progress was but a few feet per hour and took several days.

The house demonstrates Bastrop's version of late Victorian, or turn-of-the-century, architecture, as seen in the small porch, gingerbread trim, and turned porch columns and railings. The facade, including the carpenter's sunrise/sunset above the gable windows, is similar to that of the architect's own home (the Pfeiffer House at 1802 Main Street). Unlike the Pfeiffer House, this house features horizontal gable windows and dentil molding along the cornice. When the house was moved, it consisted of a living room, entry hall, bedroom, parlor, kitchen, and dining room. Hartford and his neigh-

Fowler-Jenkins House, 1302 Pecan Street.

When the Fowler-Jenkins House was moved to its present location on Pecan Street, it was placed on high brick pillars so hunting dogs could live underneath. Photo courtesy of Ann Adams Miller.

bor Senator Paul Page were avid hunters and shared hunting dogs, so Jenkins raised the house on brick pillars so the dogs could live under it.[115] An original cupola tower above the front porch was removed in 1918.[116] Later, a downstairs bedroom and bath were added, and the attic was converted into two upstairs rooms—a bedroom and a gun room, where Jenkins spent hours cleaning and polishing his guns. It is unknown when the house was lowered to its present height.

Hartford Jenkins was the great-grandson of Edward and Sarah Jenkins, who came to Texas as colonists in 1831 and settled an area that became known as Jenkins Prairie. In 1903 he married Beulah Alice Hemphill, a descendant of early settlers in nearby Hemphills Prairie. Hartford was the first county superintendent of schools, county judge, county commissioner, and district clerk. Hartford and Beulah had two children: Robert E. Jr. and Beulah Grace. Beulah Grace recalled that the dormers were added in World War II so that rooms could be rented to contractors and families of soldiers at nearby Camp Swift.[117]

The home was inherited by Robert E. and Bernice Jenkins, who restored it in 1966. In turn, their son, Robert E. Jenkins Jr. (Bobby), and his wife, Stephanie Jackson Jenkins, inherited the home and undertook major renovations in 1994, including adding a new garage and replacing the more than seventy-five-year-old Mansfield slate roof with tin. In 2005 they created a secret room in the attic for their grandchildren, Allie, Taylor, and Jackson. The entrance was behind a picture titled *Lillies of the Valley*. Stephanie recalled, "Many good times were spent by children in this room, especially on Halloween."[118] Bobby practiced law thirty-six years in Bastrop, and Stephanie taught school for many years at St. Andrew's Episcopal School in Austin.

The home is listed in the National Register of Historic Places and is designated a Recorded Texas Historic Landmark (named the Hartford Jenkins House).

## Klockman-Elzner House

*1303 Pecan Street / 1895*

In 1894 Minnie Klockman purchased land for a new home, and by 1895 she and her husband, Henry, had built this typical middle-class family home and added a blacksmith's shop on the south side of their property. Henry died suddenly in 1897, and Minnie, to support her son, Leon, took in boarders. After Leon left home, to keep propriety and reduce town gossip, Minnie's nieces came to live with her.[119]

The house was a one-story frame Folk Victorian. It had a large dogtrot hall, was constructed of local pine with a wood shingle roof, and had five large rooms heated by three coal-burning fireplaces. The original front porch had an ornate, angled entry.

Klockman-Elzner House, 1303 Pecan Street.

Early photograph showing the angled entry onto the front porch. Courtesy of Robbie Sanders.

Minnie married Reinhart (Reinhold) Gemeinert in 1908 and sold her home to Paul Otto Elzner Jr. in 1910. The Elzners lived in the home a number of years; however, after World War I it was most likely rental property. The house caught fire in the spring of 1926 and sustained significant damage. The high school was across the street, and many students helped fight the fire. Robert E. Jenkins Sr. told of jumping out of the first-story window during his English class to race across the street to fight the fire.

Later that same year, 1926, Daniel P. and Leilah Holland purchased the house and undertook its first major remodeling. Will Hoffmann, Duval C. Higgins, and Arthur Hoffmann of Bastrop did the remodeling. Leilah Holland wanted a large front porch with a swing; thus, the entry to the front porch was rebuilt in its current design rather than in its original angled configuration.

Leilah rented bedrooms to support herself during the Depression of the 1930s. From 1942 to 1946 many officers' wives stayed here while their husbands trained at Camp Swift, a military training facility six miles north of Bastrop. During these years, Leilah also rented cots on her side porch for fifty cents a night to GIs on leave. Leilah Holland died in 1959.

In 1960 Clyde and Karen Clardy purchased the house. They added a metal roof and undertook extensive foundation work that saved it from structural deterioration. Clyde had numerous businesses in Bastrop County, including the Bastrop Meat Market on Main Street. Clyde and Karen's regular lunch crowd entered through the back door of the Meat Market, and Clyde served brisket, sausage, ribs, pickles, and onions on a sheet of brown paper. Karen ran the cash register. More than thirty years after the Clardys retired, Bastrop's old-timers still reminisced about Clyde's barbecue at "the ol' meat market."

The home remained the property of the Clardy family for approximately fifteen years until 1976, when it was purchased by Robert Hunt and Betsy Owens Carpenter. The Carpenters upgraded the utilities and made significant additions that included a four-hundred-square-foot room, a side porch, and a nine-hundred-square-foot garage. They designed and created a water garden on the northeast side of the house that features a waterfall and native plants selected to attract birds and butterflies.[120]

The house is listed in the National Register of Historic Places (named the Prince Elzner House) and is recognized by the Texas Historical Commission as the home of "significant persons" (named the Klockman-Elzner Home). It is a City of Bastrop Historic Landmark.

## Thomas Bell Taylor Home

*1305 Pecan Street / 1892, 1902, 1908, 1919*

Thomas Bell Taylor completed medical school at Tulane University and in 1885 began his medical career at the Olive-Sternenberg lumber milling camp in Hardin County, Texas. In 1887 he married Pauline Fulton in Fayette County. In 1892 he opened a medical office and drugstore in Paige, Texas, and "was determined to build a fine house there."[121] He obtained East Texas pine from Hardin County for the construction of his two-story Texas Colonial home. It had front and back galleries and a detached bathhouse with all the amenities for bathing, a luxury for the time in a country house.[122]

In 1902, when he moved his practice to Elgin, he moved his house as well. It was dismantled, shipped by rail, and rebuilt on a lot at 100 North Avenue B in Elgin. This time,

Thomas Bell Taylor Home, 1305 Pecan Street.

Moving Thomas Taylor's home, circa 1908. Courtesy of the Bastrop County Historical Society.

however, it resembled a Texas Victorian house with bays, gables, wraparound porches, and gingerbread trim.[123]

Thomas needed more space for his gardens and orchards, so in 1908 he moved the house across Elgin, intact except for the chimneys, to a larger lot at 1011 North Main Street. It was a huge undertaking. The *Elgin Courier* reported on March 5 that the work had begun, and almost one month later, on April 2, the newspaper reported that the house had moved forward only two blocks with ten more blocks to go. The house was reassembled exactly as it had been.[124]

Thomas moved his practice again in 1919, this time to Bastrop. Once more, he completely dismantled his house and shipped it to 1305 Pecan Street, where the house was rebuilt into a "four-square" structure—two stories with a pitched roof and with the galleries relegated to the back. It was covered with gray stucco. The porch columns and window trim were painted white.[125]

The Taylor children were daughters Mary Beth, Ethel Louise, Eleanor, and Tannie and son, Thomas Bell Jr. Thomas Taylor was secretary of the Bastrop County Medical Society, organized the yearly spring cleanup to remove trash and debris from Bastrop's residential district, was chairman of the City Improvement Committee of the Chamber of Commerce,[126] was the local physician for the MKT Railroad, and served as Bastrop County health officer.[127] He retired in 1943, and the home was sold to Edward "Ed" Duvall and Dinora Young McWilliams Cartwright in the same year.[128] Thomas died in 1950; Pauline, in 1959.

Ed was Bastrop County sheriff from 1932 to 1952. For the first ten years of his tenure, Sheriff and Dinora Cartwright lived on the first floor of the old Bastrop County jail, which was located on the courthouse lawn at the corner of Pine and Water Streets in Bastrop. (The prisoners were housed on the second floor.) Dinora cooked for the prisoners. Their daughter, Ethel, spent her teenage years in the jail building. In later years, Ethel told of being afraid for her father when he left to set up roadblocks for the infamous Bonnie and Clyde.[129]

Suitors had to go to the jail to "call" on Ethel. At age nineteen, in 1940, Ethel married Warren Higgins. The married children from Dinora's first marriage, Bill McWilliams and Elizabeth Lyle, did not live at the jail but had homes of their own.

When Ed and Dinora moved from the old jail into their newly purchased home at 1305 Pecan Street, they immediately took in families who were in need of housing because of the acute shortage created by the influx of contractors and families attached to troops stationed at Camp Swift. One family, Jim Miller and his wife and their daughter, Martha, of Benton Harbor, Michigan, liked Texas and the Cartwrights so much that they returned to Bastrop after the war and spent weekends with them while looking for a home in Austin so that Jim could attend the University of Texas.[130]

After the war, Dinora finally had space to entertain in her home. She often hosted meetings of the Lost Pines Garden Club, the "42" Club, and the Woman's Society of Christian Service of the Methodist Church, where she served coffee from a silver service on her lace- covered dining table with a crystal candelabra. After the death of Ed (1961) and Dinora (1967), their children sold the home to John Corby and Elaine K. Weiss in 1968. The Weiss children are Dale Anthony, Corby Dean, Patricia Ann, Matthew Ernest, and Earle David.

## Jones-Herndon House

*1311 Pecan Street / 1925*

In 1909 Tignal "Tig" and Nell Nash Jones moved into an old home (circa 1860s) located on this site. In 1925 they razed the old home and built a one-story red-brick home with a front double gable and half-hipped roof.[131] Nell Nash Jones was descended from the Nash families who operated the "Nash Ferry," which crossed the Colorado at Utley before the construction of the first Colorado River bridge in Bastrop in 1890. Nell Nash Jones died in 1955. After Tig graduated from Waco Business College, he spent the rest of his life employed by Bastrop County. His first job was county deputy tax assessor, which required him to travel the entire county on horseback. In 1910 he became deputy county clerk and, in 1920, county clerk, an office he held until his death in 1960.[132]

Jones-Herndon House, 1311 Pecan Street.

Original red brick, before restoration in 1973, 1311 Pecan Street. Courtesy of Joe and Nancy Beal.

"Tig" and Nell had a daughter, Mary Nell Jones (born 1909), also called Nell. She attended Bastrop High School, where she graduated in 1926 as both valedictorian and class president. She attended the University of Texas at Austin, where she met her future husband, Grief Perkins Herndon, from Dublin, Texas.[133] Nell and "Perk" were married in 1933 by the Episcopal bishop, the Right Reverend Clinton S. Quinn, and remained married for more than fifty years.

Nell and Perk moved into the old Jones family home in 1973. They remodeled the fifty-year-old house under the supervision of the architectural firm of Marvin Beck and Associates: an extension and bay window were added on the north side, a bedroom was extended on the south, and a substantial addition was made at the rear. A swimming pool, pool house, and workshop were also added. The exterior of the house was painted stonebridge gray because the deteriorating red brick and its mortar could not be matched.[134]

Nell was awarded "Most Worthy Citizen" in Bastrop in 1984. She was a tireless volunteer, a supporter of civic activities, and active in the Historical Society and the library. She was an "avid Longhorn fan. On a winning Saturday, there were orange lights not only on the UT Tower in Austin, but also at 1311 Pecan."[135] Perk died in 1983. Nell died May 21, 2005, seven days short of her ninety-sixth birthday.

In November 2005 Joseph and Nancy Beal bought the home. They converted a screened porch into a family room, added a master suite and exterior office, and converted the existing workshop into a studio for Nancy, who is an artist. She designed nine large, stained-glass windows that were permanently incorporated into the upper walls of the Firewheel Restaurant at the Hyatt Regency Lost Pines Resort and Spa, a destination hotel and conference center west of Bastrop. The theme of the windows is "wildflowers." She also designed several stained-glass windows for Bastrop's Calvary Episcopal Church when it was rebuilt and expanded in 1998.[136]

Joe Beal served seven years (2008–15) on the Bastrop City Council, four years on Bastrop's Planning and Zoning Commission, and two years on the board of the Bastrop Economic Development Corporation. He was a cofounder of Bastrop's Frontier Bank of Texas and general manager of the Lower Colorado River Authority, Austin, for nine years.[137]

The home is a City of Bastrop Historic Landmark.

## Fehr-Haynie-Allbright House

*1404 Pecan Street / 1935*

Thomas Powell "T. P." Haynie Sr. married Tillye Clara Elzner in Bastrop in 1905. Their only child, T. P. Haynie Jr., was born the next year. In 1934, T. P. and Tillye hired the Austin architect Arthur Fehr to design this Tudor cottage to replace their previous home on the property. That same year, Arthur was selected to design the cabins, refectory, and picnic shelter overlooks at Bastrop State Park.[138]

Arthur Fehr (1904–69) was born in Austin. He received his bachelor of science in architecture from the University of Texas at Austin in 1925 and did graduate work at Columbia, the Beaux Arts Institute of Design, and New York University. He worked in New York City before returning to Texas, where he was commissioned to design Bastrop State Park in 1934. After the Bastrop projects, Arthur went on to partner with Charles Granger, and together they designed Concordia Lutheran College, St. Stephen's Episcopal School, and the Terminal Building at Robert Mueller Airport, all in Austin.[139]

Wrought-iron door hinges and cast-iron hasp similar to the hardware seen in structures at Bastrop State Park.

Fehr-Haynie-Allbright House, 1404 Pecan Street.

Built in 1935, the home has a Tudor design that showcases a steep, sloping roof; an arched bedroom doorway; purple heart cedar floors in the living and dining rooms; and a wooden front-entry door with wrought-iron hinges and a cast-iron door knocker similar to the hardware and random-width clapboard siding seen in the park structures.

Tillye served as president of the Ladies Reading Circle from 1915 to 1917. She taught music, played the piano, and sang at weddings. T. P. was a longtime car dealer in Bastrop. By 1933 he had obtained the exclusive Chevrolet dealership. It has been noted that by 1936 T. P. had sold "almost 10,000 cars." He served as mayor from 1929 to 1934.[140] T. P. passed away in September 1941. Tillye sold the house five years later and moved to Austin, where she became a "housemother" for various college fraternities.[141]

Subsequent owners include William Ireland and Jonnie Marguerite Williams Allbright, who added an expansive den, a bathroom, a laundry room, and a large back porch.[142] The cottage remained in the Allbright family for fifty-seven years before it was sold to Daniel G. and Ruby M. Scott in 2003.[143]

Benjamin and Kay Wesson purchased the property in April 2016.[144] Benjamin, now retired, is a US Army veteran who worked as the director of the City of Smithville Electrical Department and of outside operations for the City of Bastrop Electrical Department. Kay, a licensed realtor, served as chair of the Bastrop County Historical Commission for sixteen years. A forty-year member of the Daughters of the American Revolution, she was the organizing registrar for the Lost Pines Chapter of the National Society of the Daughters of the American Revolution (NSDAR) in Smithville, the first chapter in Bastrop County, and in 2016 was the organizing regent for the King's Highway Chapter NSDAR, the first chapter in Bastrop.[145]

The home is designated a City of Bastrop Historic Landmark.

## John and Willie Belle Kennedy House

*1405 Pecan Street / 1922*

The home built by John and Willie Belle Kennedy is described as a Craftsman bungalow, an architectural style popular during the American Craftsman era. Craftsman characteristics are evident in the off-center, wraparound porch; large protecting overhang; and a roof with hipped peaks and prominent corbels.[146] John Kennedy died in 1924, two years after the home was built, and Willie Belle never remarried. She continued to live in the home until she died unexpectedly at age eighty-four in 1975. The home remained unoccupied for fifteen years after her death.

Their son, John Kennedy Jr., eventually sold the home to Catherine and Helen Moran, mother and daughter, in 1996. The next owners were Tom A. and Sarah Scott in 1998, followed by Ann and Larry Brown, who purchased the house in 2004. Each owner made improvements to the home, including upgrading the plumbing and electrical wiring, adding air conditioning, and remodeling the kitchen. In 2005 Larry Brown added a garage and designed a new, one-thousand-square-foot addition that included a master bedroom, master bath, exercise room, and expanded deck.[147]

Ann teamed with her neighbors, Judi Hoover and city council member Joe Beal, to establish a recreational water park for children, which opened in June 2012 in the city's Fisherman's Park. Ann also served on the board of directors of the Lost Pines Art League from 2016 through 2019 and played a significant role in the startup and completion of the Lost Pines Art Center, which opened in December 2016.[148]

The home is a City of Bastrop Historic Landmark.

John and Willie Belle Kennedy House, 1405 Pecan Street.

# P. C. Maynard House

*1408 Pecan Street / 1916*

A young attorney, Powell Maynard, brought his new bride, Clara Lockett Maynard, home to Bastrop in 1913. The couple lived with Mary Young, the recent widow of Mark H. Young, while Clara planned every detail of their future home.[149] Their Texas Prairie-style home was built in 1916 by contractor Joe Pfeiffer for five thousand dollars. The style is a departure from the classical Greek Revival and ornate Victorian styles evident in many of Bastrop's historic homes. Instead, it reflects the influence of the Foursquare/Prairie architectural styles developed around the turn of the century. In this home, the Prairie style is tempered with a classical Greek element known as "entasis," a slight convex curve to the columns supporting the front porch.[150]

Powell and Clara had been in their new home only a few years when, uncomfortable using the new indoor toilet facilities with Clara's friends in the house, Powell had an outdoor privy built in the farthest corner of the backyard.[151] He also loved to get up early, saddle his horse, ride out to the woods and cook breakfast, and watch the sun come up over his pasture and cattle.[152]

Powell was county attorney and mayor of Bastrop, and Clara was active in Bastrop's civic affairs. Family members recount the numerous gatherings of state officials in the house during the administration of Governor Pat Morris Neff in the early 1920s.[153] While on vacation at the 1934 Chicago World's Fair, Powell was fatally injured as he tried to protect Clara from being struck from behind by a streetcar.[154] Clara remained alone in the big house for almost fifty years. As a widow, she was founding president of the Bastrop County Historical Society and taught Sunday school at the Methodist Church for more than twenty-five years. During World War II, she hosted luncheons and teas for officers stationed at Camp Swift, an infantry training camp located six miles north of Bastrop.

Clara was ninety-eight years old when she died in 1982. The home remained vacant until family members sold it in 1992.[155] When the new owners, Bill L. Ennis and Dan Hays-Clark, discovered the little outhouse, it was in its original location, surrounded by tall weeds and brush. They moved it nearer the house and gave it a place of honor next to the barbecue, in memory of Powell Maynard.

The home is listed in the National Register of Historic Places and is a City of Bastrop Historic Landmark.

P. C. Maynard House, 1408 Pecan Street.

Powell Maynard's privy.

## Mary Blanche Duval House

*1502 Pecan Street / 1896*

Mary Blanche Higgins Duval, called Blanche, was the daughter of Republic of Texas pioneer and prominent businessman J. C. Higgins. Her relatives described her as a "real sensible lady." She purchased this home in 1908, one year after the death of her husband of twenty-six years, Brooke Clay Duval. Their twins, Jacob and Mary, died in infancy, and son, Hugh, died in 1936.[156] Blanche married a second time to Robert A. Myers. However, he also predeceased her.

Originally built by J. B. Price in 1896,[157] the home was constructed during the transition period from the ornate Victorian era to the tailored Edwardian era. The original, simple, Victorian detail on the front porch and the minimal use of 105-inch "walk-through" windows are a reflection of the "sensible" architecture and charm that appealed to Blanche Duval when she bought the home. She lived here until her death in 1937.

Her estate included the home, 429 acres of land, and two old mules valued at fifty dollars. This was a considerable estate for a widow in a sensible home.[158] The watering trough for the mules still stands behind the barn on the southwest side of the home, now a koi pond complete with water lilies.

In 1937 "J. V." and Amy Ash purchased the home. Among his many accomplishments, J. V. served a two-year term as a member of the Texas legislature, served more than thirty years on Bastrop's city council and school board, and developed Bastrop's first subdivision, Riverview Heights, commonly referred to as the "New Addition." Amy was one of the original founders of the Bastrop County Historical Society and Museum. J. V. and Amy enlarged the kitchen and added a second bath, bedroom, and breakfast room to the original home.[159] Their daughter, Lucille Ash, a talented artist who studied at the School of the Art Institute of Chicago, taught art to children and adults for twenty-eight years. Classes were taught in the sitting room (now a bedroom), the backyard, or in an original board-and-batten outbuilding, which was converted into her art studio. She lived in the home until 1990.

Subsequent owners include Allen and Marjorie McMurrey, who converted an outside porch into a master bath and a larger master bedroom and added a large game room for Allen's huge collection of animal mounts; Dawn and Christopher Kana, who added a swimming pool; and Mark and Ella Bedford, who purchased the home in

October 2011 after their home burned in the Bastrop County Complex fire. The current owners (2019), Joseph Stanfield and Kitty Barnes, bought the home in 2017.

The home is listed in the National Register of Historic Places (dated 1900) and is a City of Bastrop Historic Landmark.

Mary Blanche Duval House, 1502 Pecan Street.

## E. C. Erhard House

*1507 Pecan Street / 1887*

This home was built in 1887 by E. Chester Erhard for his wife, Mary Trigg Erhard, and their seven-year-old son, Earl C.. The home was originally built with a modest front porch, a front bay window, and ornate metal fretwork. Major exterior changes were made in 1898.[160] In 1889 Chester and several prominent investors, including his two cousins, Albert and Louis Erhard, were among the original shareholders and organizers of the First National Bank. In 1890 Chester and Albert became directors.[161] Chester was appointed the bank's cashier. The Bastrop Advertiser reported, "Cashier Chester Erhard, A. C. Erhard, and T. A. Hasler have private telephones extending from their places of business to their residences, each telephone connecting with the First National Bank." The bank's phone number was 1, and Chester's was 2.

The 1949 premier for the movie *Rio Grande*, starring Evohn Keyes (Evohn Rosanky Moore), was held at Bastrop's Tower Theater. Courtesy of the Bastrop County Historical Society.

Mary died in 1917; Chester, in 1929. Earl was raised in the home, and in 1907 he married Annie Pearl (called Pearl) Windrow.[162] The dramatic wraparound galleries were added to the house in preparation for their wedding.[163] The couple lived in Palestine, Texas, a number of years and, in the fall of 1912, returned to Bastrop to live with Earl's parents. Earl managed Bastrop's Home Hardware Store. In 1921 their only child, Mary Pearl Erhard, was born.[164] Earl became a director of the First National Bank in 1921 and its president in early 1951. He held this position until his death in 1967. Pearl Erhard died in 1963.

In 1938–40 Mary Pearl attended the Mount Vernon Seminary, a finishing school in Washington, D.C. Letters written from Mount Vernon to her parents were found in the attic of the home in 1990 by Jim and Lisa Laughead, who owned the home at the time. Most of the letters discussed boys, clothes, trips to West Point Academy, art symposiums, and her zoology and swimming classes. One letter of particular interest described a luncheon she attended at the Washington Hotel: "There were about 100 people there. The luncheon was given by the 75 Club [wives of members of the 75th Congress] for Mrs. Roosevelt. We sat very close to Eleanor, and she was a lot nicer looking than her pictures. She had on a black suit with red front in it, and a large black straw hat." Mary Pearl signed her letters to her parents with the closing, "Oceans and Oceans of love, Baby."

E. C. Erhard House, 1507 Pecan Street.

At age nineteen, Mary Pearl graduated from the Mount Vernon Seminary and started school at the University of Texas. At a luncheon in Bastrop, she met her future husband, Captain Kenneth R. Duff, who had been assigned to the hospital unit at Camp Swift. They married in December 1942. Mary Pearl and Kenneth returned from their honeymoon to live in the "Honeymoon Hut"—a small building built at the back of the property years earlier (907 Cedar) for the Erhard family cook, Julia Howe.[165] The Honeymoon Hut had been redecorated especially for Mary Pearl and Kenneth.

Within a year, Kenneth was assigned to Fort Sam Houston and from there shipped overseas. He was discharged from the army with the rank of lieutenant colonel. He and Mary Pearl moved to Warm Springs, Georgia; New Orleans; and finally to Houston in 1950, where he was an orthopedic surgeon with his own practice. While living in Houston, Mary Pearl sold her childhood home in Bastrop. Mary Pearl died in 1989; Kenneth, in 2010.[166]

Walter Rosanky bought the home from Mary Pearl in 1970 as a gift for his daughter Evohn Rosanky Moore. Walter, who had a large cattle operation, pampered Evohn throughout her entire life. When she was sixteen, he gave her a Buick Roadster, and one Christmas, among her gifts, was a large Christmas tree with one-hundred-dollar bills tied to every branch.[167]

Evohn replaced a low iron fence surrounding the home with the present (2019) brick and wrought-iron fence and added a swimming pool. She is remembered for her acting role with Hollywood star Sunset Carson in the 1949 movie *Rio Grande*. Her stage name was Evohn Keyes.

The home is listed in the National Register of Historic Places and is a City of Bastrop Historic Landmark.

## Hubbard-Trigg House

*1508 Pecan Street / 1890*

Robert W. Hubbard left his large tract of land in nearby Hills Prairie and built this late Victorian home on Pecan Street in 1890. Robert owned the home with his sister, Cynthia Lawrence. The house was originally L-shaped, consisting of a widow's walk, three fireplaces, two bedrooms, entrance hall, parlor, dining room, pantries, a kitchen, and an L-shaped gallery that extended the length of the house. This gallery later became an interior hall.

Robert Hubbard was a Confederate veteran who was in the last battle of the Civil War, the Battle of Palmetto Hill, May 12 and 13, 1865.[168] This battle was fought near Brownsville, Texas, thirty-four days after General Robert E. Lee surrendered at Appomattox because "Rip" Ford, commander, did not know the war was over. Robert moved to Kyle, Texas, where he opened a mercantile store. He sold the home in 1894 to his daughter, Mary Willis Hubbard, and her husband, Kleber Miller Trigg. The Triggs and their children, Robert Marshall, Kleber Miller Jr., and Annie Mae, left their farm and moved into the home. They enlarged and modernized the house and added two more fireplaces.

The Triggs, believing in a rugged way of life despite their affluence, slept on their screened-in-porch much of the year and drew water from their bricked well. The well later became part of a second porch. Wood was chopped at their farm and brought to town for four of the fireplaces. The living room fireplace burned coal.[169]

Annie Mae Trigg Birmingham (married to Frank Birmingham) inherited the home and, after living twenty years in West Texas, returned to her childhood home in 1961.

Hubbard-Trigg House, 1508 Pecan Street.

She began refurbishing and remodeling by modernizing the kitchen and converting the fireplace to gas. A major endeavor was enclosing the back porch and installing jalousie windows.

The home is listed in the National Register of Historic Places and is designated a Recorded Texas Historical Landmark. It is a City of Bastrop Historic Landmark.

# J. H. Pearcy House

*1602 Pecan Street / 1910*

In 1904 the Onalaska Lumber Company, Onalaska, Arkansas, sent thirty key men to establish a new operation in Texas. James Henry Pearcy was the company bookkeeper and was one of those men who transferred to the new community of Onalaska, Texas.[170] In 1910 James and Elizabeth "Lizzie" Cline Pearcy moved to Bastrop with their three children, Bessie, Ruth, and Ernest, and hired contractor Joe Pfeiffer to build this classic two-story, late Victorian home using plans drawn to replicate a house they had owned in Onalaska, Texas. Though late Victorian, it has dentils along its cornice, a wraparound porch, and Prairie-style elements such as "cottage" windows.

James was bookkeeper for one of the growing and profitable coal mines six miles north of Bastrop. In April 1911 he joined with Marvin Booth to establish Pearcy and Booth, a general merchandise store on Bastrop's busy Main Street. James was bookkeeper for their business.

In 1911 their daughter Bessie married James Clinton "Clint" Orgain, and the newlyweds built a new home next door. However, Clint was in poor health, so the couple sold their home and moved to Marfa, Texas, where Clint became the town's first mayor.

Pearcy and Booth, 1005–1007 Main Street, circa 1912. Courtesy of the Bastrop County Historical Society.

Their daughter, Ruth, married Henry P. Berry and moved to Los Angeles. In 1915, at age seventeen, their son, Ernest, began working as a clerk at the First National Bank. He remained with the bank for twenty-five years. Ernest married Ruby Tracy in 1923, and the couple lived in this home for thirteen years until 1936, when they bought their own home at 909 Pecan. Ernest was later to become Bastrop's postmaster.[171]

J. H. Pearcy House, 1602 Pecan Street.

Lizzie Pearcy died in 1930, and James married Mary "Angie" Starcke in 1933. James died in 1938.

In 1946 J. P. "Pinky" and Ida Maude Sharp purchased the home. They owned a downtown business, Sharp Furniture Company, which supplied furniture and General Electric appliances to most of the homes in the Bastrop area during the mid-twentieth century. The house remained in the Sharp family for forty-five years.[172]

The home is listed in the National Register of Historic Places and is a City of Bastrop Historic Landmark.

# Trigg-Crider House

*1606 Pecan Street / 1913*

Newlyweds James Clinton "Clint" and Bessie Pearcy Orgain built their new home next door to Bessie's parents in 1913. Clint was a young bank teller, and Bessie taught music and expression, which is the teaching of techniques for reading aloud a passage or poem with proper enunciation and emotion. The new house included the modern convenience of indoor plumbing. Bessie's father paid for the septic tank, which was intended to be used by both houses.[173] The carpenter, William Schilling, left his signature, dated 1913, on the chimney bricks inside the house. Located in the kitchen and upstairs bathroom, the chimney vents for the heaters were exposed during restoration done by later owners, Michael and Deborah Jones. The architecture is Eclectic in the Neoclassical style with an asymmetrical, one-story, pedimented portico with double columns.

Clint and Bessie moved to Marfa, Texas, where Clint became Marfa's first mayor. About 1921 the couple moved to El Paso, where Clint served eighteen years as district clerk.[174] They sold their Bastrop house in 1915 to John H. and Helen Scott Mettenheimer. John owned the Powell Oil Mill in Bastrop, a cottonseed oil mill.[175]

In 1917 Robert Marshall and Annie Gamble Higgins Trigg purchased this home from the Mettenheimers, who moved to Dallas. Robert was a stockman and farmer, and the young couple began their married life on his farm outside town. They moved to town when their daughter approached school age. A few years later, Annie's sister, Mary Rebecca Higgins Page, and her husband, Paul Page, built a home next door at 1702 Pecan.

Annie Trigg was an avid gardener, and the 1920 census shows Sid and Harriet Peterson, a gardener and a cook, living in the household. Between 1921 and 1934 a portion of the porch on the south side of the house was enclosed to provide a downstairs bathroom. By 1934 Annie had built a garden shed on the lot.[176]

Annie and Robert's only child, Ann Higgins Trigg, was born in 1911 and graduated from the University of Texas at Austin in 1933. (Family referred to her as Annie Higgins; friends and teachers, as Ann.)[177] Ann met an aspiring young attorney, Bower H. Crider, at UT, whom she later married. He went into practice with Judge Paul Page, his wife's uncle.

Bower served with the Fifth Army in Italy during World War II, earning the Bronze Star in 1945. While he was away, Ann moved in with her parents. During the war the Triggs housed officers stationed at Camp Swift in the servants' house behind the main

Trigg-Crider House, 1606 Pecan Street.

home. Robert Trigg died in 1945, and Bower moved into the house with Ann and her mother when he returned from the war. Bower served as Bastrop city attorney and as county judge (1952–55). Ann taught school in Bastrop and, like her mother, loved to garden.

Annie Trigg died in 1965, and Bower Crider died in 1969. Ann remained in the home until her death in 2001. Michael and Deborah Jones purchased the home in 2003 from the Crider estate. Michael is a filmmaker, and Deborah is a litigation appraiser. Deborah "fell in love" with the yard and restored it to its original design and materials.[178]

The home is a City of Bastrop Historic Landmark.

## Paul D. Page House

*1702 Pecan Street / Circa 1920*

This elegant red-brick Prairie-style house was built by Senator Paul DeWitt Page and his second wife, Mary Higgins Page. The home was built about 1920 while Page was serving as state senator, an office he held continuously from 1914 to 1922. Page was first married to Blanche Garwood, who died in 1911, and during their marriage he served as Bastrop County attorney (1898–1904) and Bastrop County judge (1904–9).

Paul Page is identified with Bastrop's advancement during the first half of the twentieth century. He took a leading role in securing Bastrop State Park and Camp Swift, a World War II infantry training camp located just six miles north of Bastrop. It is now the Camp Mabry National Guard training facility. He was a founder of the Citizens State Bank in 1909 and served as its president until his death at age seventy-six in 1945.[179]

The historic Page House is two stories with low gables, tiled roof, wide overhanging eaves on rafters, and a deep wraparound porch of parquet brick. It has a basement with a single fireplace flue that extends from the basement to the second floor. The flue opens into a fireplace on each floor. Originally, the basement was for storing coal and for housing a coal-burning furnace. Deliveries of coal were dropped down a chute to an interior coal bin. In the winter, Paul hired a man to sleep in the basement and stoke the furnace during the night. Outbuildings included a single-car garage with adjoining maid's quarters.[180]

Paul Page was described as a "feisty little Irishman." He never learned to drive a car—a chauffeur, Isaiah, drove him everywhere.[181] He was fervently patriotic. He was a member of the Bastrop Gun Club and jointly owned several hunting dogs with his neighbor, Hartford Jenkins. Mary Page would not allow the dogs at their home, so they were kept at the Jenkins home at 1302 Pecan.[182] Mary hired cooks and maids to help

Paul D. Page House, 1702 Pecan Street.

run the house. She was fond of entertaining her bridge club and of serving very formal dinners. Tablecloths and napkins were monogrammed, and finger bowls were used, "especially when Bishop Quinn came to town."[183] There was a foot button underneath the dining room table, a bell button in the upstairs hall, and one in the breakfast room to call the maid. A box on the kitchen wall indicated which bell was ringing.[184]

Soon after Mary died in 1970, the house was sold. Subsequent owners include Dr. Bill Jack and Mary Lee Cannon Marshall, who purchased the home in 1970; and Gary and Rae Lynn Morris, who bought the home in 1998. Jay and Maxann Collins purchased the home in 2004. They updated the interior, added an architecturally compatible porch on the building's west side, and enlarged the single-car garage. Jay took charge of the old coal basement. Now, an interior winding staircase leads down to a temperature-controlled wine cellar and tasting room. The "preserved" coal-burning furnace provides nostalgia and ambiance. Under Jay and Maxann's ownership, the home became the setting for many fund-raising events in support of the Lost Pines Arts League and the Lost Pines Art Center.

This home is listed in the National Register of Historic Places and is a City of Bastrop Historic Landmark.

## Long House

*1706 Pecan Street / Circa 1916–1921*

Mellie Duval Higgins, a widow, purchased the vacant lot next to the home of her daughter and son-in-law, Mary Higgins Page and Paul D. Page, in August 1916 for six hundred dollars.[185] Mellie's husband, William T. Higgins Sr., had died only two months earlier. It is unclear when Mellie built her new home. However, it is shown on the 1921 Sanborn Fire Insurance Map.[186] According to a Higgins descendant, William T. Higgins V, the home was built by J. T. Peterson, a carpenter/contractor who emigrated from Sweden and later served as mayor from 1934 to 1940. This Craftsman-style bungalow has a side-gabled roof with decorative braces, an asymmetrical front door with sidelights, cottage windows, and an asymmetrical dormer on the front facade. The bay window on the right side may have been added between 1921 and 1934.[187] Mellie died in 1939, and her children sold the home to Cecil and Ida Lou Long for twenty-five hundred dollars in December of the same year.[188]

Cecil B. Long and Ida Lou Andrews married in Lampasas, Texas, in 1933. Ida Lou had a young daughter, Virginia, from a previous marriage. In 1935 the couple moved to Bastrop, where Cecil had a farm and began raising dairy cattle and other livestock. He managed and later owned the Elkins 5-10-25 Cent Stores in Bastrop, Elgin, and La Grange.[189] Although they bought this home in town in 1939, Cecil continued the dairy and ranching operation at the farm. Cecil and Ida Lou's son, Robert K. "Bob," was born in 1943.

Bob Long later recalled that his father bought the first window air-conditioner in town, a Fedders, from Cecil's brother, C. A. "Dude" Long, who owned the Western Auto Associates Store. As a child, Bob would go into his parents' bedroom and play in the chilled room. Prior to installing the window unit, the entire house was cooled with an attic fan that "would suck the wallpaper off the walls if there weren't enough windows open."[190] Cecil then bought the town's first under-the-dash automobile air-conditioner for their 1955 Chevrolet station wagon. Western Auto sold that, too.[191]

Cecil Long headed up the USO, an entertainment center for servicemen during the years of World War II when Bastrop was swamped with soldiers from Camp Swift.[192] He was elected to the board of directors of the First National Bank of Bastrop in 1946, became chairman of the board in 1967, and became president in 1972. Long was a member of countless civic organizations, serving on the Bastrop City Council and as a member of the Bastrop Fire Department. He was appointed to the Lower Colorado River Authority (LCRA) board of directors in 1961 and was subsequently reappointed

Long House, 1706 Pecan Street.

by four Texas governors. In 1992 an office building in the LCRA's Austin headquarters complex was named in his honor.[193]

After his death in December 1993, Cecil Long was remembered as much for his quiet political acumen, business savvy, and efforts to promote the economic well-being of Bastrop as for his good-natured wit and humanitarian actions.[194] A light was placed in the seldom-noticed windows in the steeple of the historic Bastrop Christian Church as a perpetual memorial to him. The glass windows had never been illuminated; now they shine from dusk to dawn in his honor.[195] Reverend Bob Long delivered the eulogy at his father's funeral.

Ida Lou taught music in the Bastrop School District for forty years. Once segregated with separate schools for African American and Mexican American students, in the early 1930s the district constructed a three-room schoolhouse, at first called the "Mexican School" but later named the Mina Ward School. The school was located on North Main Street, serving about forty students at a time from the first to the seventh

Bastrop Christian Church, built 1895.

Illuminated windows in the steeple of the Bastrop Christian Church in honor of Cecil Long.

grades.[196] Ida Lou taught at the Mina Ward School, where teachers stressed the importance of learning English since many students entered first grade speaking only Spanish. Ida Lou used children's songs to help them learn the new language. She wrote the Mina Ward school song.[197]

The school closed as a result of the historic *Delgado v. Bastrop Independent School District* federal court ruling that required an end to all segregation of Mexican American students in Texas by September 1949. Young Minerva Delgado, for whom the landmark case is named, began her formal education at the Mina Ward School but moved with the other students to the now-integrated Bastrop schools. Ida Lou went on to teach at Emile Elementary School and continued teaching there until her retirement.[198] Ida Lou Long died April 1, 1995.

The home is now (2019) owned by Cecil and Ida Lou's granddaughter, Rebekah Wilson Herrick, who received it from her father, Reverend Robert K. Long, in 1996.[199] The house has been in the Long family for seventy years. In 1991 the home was the site of several scenes in the made-for-television thriller *In Broad Daylight,* starring Brian Dennehy and Cloris Leachman.

The home is a City of Bastrop Historic Landmark.

## Louis Baron House

*1707 Pecan Street / 1872*

Louis and Augusta (sometimes Auguste) Lang Baron are remembered as hardworking and honest with no luxury in their lives.[200] Louis, a furniture maker and carpenter, built this typical four-room dogtrot farmhouse in readiness for their marriage in December 1872. The ceilings are ten feet high; the foundation and roof, cypress; the floors, doors, trim, and framing, longleaf pine.[201] There was a detached kitchen and a barn where he kept his tools. Four children were raised in the home, who, as adults, became educators. A fifth child, Ida Meta, died in 1888 at the age of five, and the Barons bought a site on the highest hill in Fairview Cemetery so they could see her grave from their back door. They were buried beside her—Louis in 1932 and Augusta in 1936.

The home sat on nine acres,[202] where Louis tended his pecan orchard and his many rows of grapes from which he made wine that was kept in a cellar under the house. He kept pigeons in cages under a big elm tree—it is not known if they were for food or sport. Since the area behind the house was swampy and he loved to hunt, many cold mornings he would creep out at dawn to go duck hunting in his backyard.[203]

The Barons had a large vegetable garden and a few cows. Augusta had a horse-drawn grocery wagon and each morning sold vegetables, honey, milk, butter, and cheese throughout the residential areas of town. She would not take her horse onto Main Street because there were too many other horses hitched along the roadway and she was afraid her horse would get nipped or hurt. Instead, she used the neighborhood streets and alleys. She rang a handbell when she stopped at a customer's back door. Since it could be heard from several houses away, it alerted people in advance that Augusta was on her way.[204]

The home was purchased by Beulah Grace Adams in 1948 and by Robert Runkle in 1990. Bill and Pat Crawford purchased the house on October 31, 1992, and each year marked the day of their purchase with very elaborate Halloween decorations.

The home is listed in the National Register of Historic Places (named the August Baron House) and is a City of Bastrop Historic Landmark.

Louis Baron House, 1707 Pecan Street.

Seven-foot-tall Halloween witch. Courtesy of Bill and Pat Crawford.

# Pine Street

## Wallace-Holme House

*907 Pine Street / 1839*

L. B. Harris, a medical doctor, was approximately twenty-six years old when he built this house. When he sold it in 1839, he referred to it as a "new framed house, new and recently built, the dimensions of said house being sixteen feet by twenty."[1] L. B. Harris served as a Bastrop city alderman in 1840, 1843, and 1844.

Later occupants of the house were James P. and Harriet Wallace. Harriet purchased the home in 1848. James Wallace was one of the first Texas Rangers, organized in 1835 to fight Indians guilty of "outrages and depredations."[2] James served the Rangers under Captain Robert Morris Coleman and was injured in a "fierce and heavy fight" with an overwhelming number of Indians at Tehuacana Springs in Limestone County. James lost an eye in the battle and was subsequently referred to as "One-eyed" Wallace.[3] He later served as Bastrop County district clerk from 1847 until his death in 1855. Harriet married A. O. Beck that same year.

Harriet and James Wallace raised two children in the home, Josephine and Phebe (Phoebe) Irene. The sisters married brothers Neil and Robert F. Campbell, respectively. Robert was Bastrop County clerk (1868–74) as well as Bastrop district clerk (1870–74) during the difficult years of Reconstruction following the Civil War. Robert and Phebe moved to El Paso in 1881, where he served as county commissioner, mayor, and postmaster.[4]

James S. and Mollie Holme bought the home in 1920. James Holme was an "Englishman," a brick mason by trade, and supervised the Civilian Conservation Corps' con-

Wallace-Holme House, 907 Pine Street.

struction of the rock entrance to Bastrop State Park in the 1930s.[5] The Holmes and their descendants owned the house until 1985, a tenure of sixty-five years.

Tom and Nancy Scott purchased the home in 1986 and continue to live here today (2019). They built a guest cottage and a gazebo and, using native plants, relandscaped the property. Nancy, recognized for her community service, was awarded the Community Builder Award and the Chamber of Commerce Woman of the Year. Tom was Bastrop mayor from 1998 to 2008 and is a supporter of many service organizations. He joined with Elroy Williams to lead the effort to restore the historic 1914 Kerr Hall. In 2019 Tom was honored at the Bastrop Chamber of Commerce's annual banquet with the its Lifetime Achievement Award.

The home is designated a Recorded Texas Historic Landmark and is a City of Bastrop Historic Landmark.

Harriet Wallace Beck. Harriet lived in the home from 1848 to 1865. After the death of James, she married A. O. Beck. Courtesy of Nancy and Tom Scott.

Sixteen-member Bastrop Lawn Chair Brigade, organized by Nancy Scott, photo circa 1995. Courtesy of Nancy Scott.

## Erna Griesenbeck House

*908 Pine Street* / 1912

The first owners of this home were Erna and Haynie O. Griesenbeck. Erna Walthers was orphaned at the age of thirteen in 1906 and three years later married Haynie Griesenbeck. Haynie was a wholesale grocer who later served as a Bastrop County postmaster (Hills Prairie). On August 23, 1912, the couple contracted with J. L. Wilbarger Lumber Company to build a one-story, "five-room, frame, shingle-roof dwelling house" for twenty-four hundred dollars. The carpenter for the project was John T. Peterson, a Swedish immigrant who later became mayor of Bastrop. John finished construction in six weeks.[6] This late Victorian–style home has a "pinwheel" floor plan, a tall hipped roof, entry sidelights, a front bay window, and Doric columns on a curved ell porch.[7]

Wilma Watson Arbuckle, a young widow, purchased the ten-year-old Griesenbeck house in 1922. A beloved teacher, she taught first grade for fifty-one years, initially in Elgin and from 1923 to 1957 in Bastrop. Although she had no children of her own, she was known by generations of Bastrop families as "Nanny."[8] After Nanny's death in 1965, the house passed to her grandnephew, Charles Rabensburg. He undertook a major renovation in 1982–83 that included the addition of a second story. Dick and Duffy Smith purchased the home in 2005.[9]

The house is listed in the National Register of Historic Places and is a City of Bastrop Historic Landmark.

Erna Griesenbeck House, 908 Pine Street.

## Wertzner Home

*909 Pine Street / 1890*

Built in 1890 by Charles and Mary Wilke Kleinert, the original cottage was approximately 750 square feet and consisted of a foyer entrance flanked by two rooms. This footprint went unchanged through a succession of early owners.[10] In 1898 Otto and Mary Kleinert Griesenbeck purchased the house for $5 and an agreement that Mary Griesenbeck's mother, then a widow, would have six months' board and lodging. In 1904 the Griesenbecks sold the house to J. A. Wilson for $500. In 1908 Wilson sold the house to Hugo and Ida Agnes Wertzner for $850.

This last sale signaled the beginning of a new era for the house, in which it was significantly expanded and served as home to the Wertzner family for seventy-two years. They added several rooms, including a screened porch on the east side of the house. This porch, now glassed in and functioning as a sunroom, was the site of weekend band concerts, musical events that may not have been fully appreciated by the neighbors. According to one account, Ida would play the piano in the room off the foyer and the band would play German "oompah" music on the screened porch, a concert that often "got pretty rowdy."[11]

Ownership of the house passed to their son, Arthur "Dutch" Wertzner, who was three years old when his family moved in; he would continue to call it home until his death in 1980. In the decades in between, Dutch became all but a living legend in the community. He sustained his family's commitment to Calvary Episcopal Church and was credited with almost single-handedly maintaining the church during the Depression and World War II when money, labor, and materials were in short supply.

An electrician at Camp Swift during World War II, he later served as dispatcher for the Bastrop County Sheriff's Office and was a longtime volunteer fireman. For many years, he was a familiar figure at high school football games—a member of the "chain crew," marking downs. In 1964 Dutch sold his house to his friend Ingrid Kouba,[12] who with her husband, Richard, had come to live with him several years earlier. The selling price was one dollar, with the proviso that Dutch be allowed to live there until his death.

At the time of his death at age seventy-five, Dutch was the oldest living member of the Bastrop Volunteer Fire Department. In recognition of that distinction, his body was carried to Fairview Cemetery on the 1929 Seagraves fire engine, which he had driven many times.[13] After his death, the house went through a period as rental prop-

erty and fell into disrepair until it was purchased in 1990 by sisters Lucy Keller and Coco Harrison, who were Houston antique dealers and used the house as a weekend retreat and "project." Owners Rob and June Pace purchased the house in 1998 and picked up where the sisters left off, continuing with renovations, including rewiring and replumbing.[14]

Wertzner Home, 909 Pine Street.

## House at 1002 Pine Street

*1002 Pine Street / Before 1900*

Dr. Henry Burris and Maude Combs owned this home from 1900 to 1911.[15] Whenever he was allowed, Henry would name the babies he had delivered after himself. Also, after delivering a baby, he often bought a tree, planted it in the yard, and gave the tree the same name that had been given to the baby. In 1907 Burris Schaefer was born. As an old man in his eighties, Burris would drive by this home and point out the tree that bore his name.[16] It is not known if Burris knew that he and the tree had been named after the doctor who delivered him.

The home was sold to Paul Dewitt Page in 1911 for fifteen hundred dollars.[17] At that time, Paul was a widower; his wife, Blanche, had died only six months earlier, leaving him with two children, Paul Jr. (age eleven) and Wilmer (age nine). The family moved into this one-story, wood-frame home, which has coupled windows on the projected wing of an ell. Over the coupled windows is a Juliet metal awning.

Paul was founder and president of the 1909 Citizens State Bank of Bastrop and served as county attorney (1898–1904) and county judge (1904–9). In 1914, while living here, he was elected state senator and held that office until 1922.[18] He married Mary Higgins and sold the home in 1918 to W. T. and Julia Placke.[19] They, in turn, sold it in 1925 to Angus Malcom and Mary Belle Alexander Oldfield for twenty-five hundred dollars. Malcom and Belle had three children, Mark Edward, Mary Belle, and Johnelle. Malcom was a building contractor who during World War II worked for Taylor Burns Construction Company at nearby Camp Swift. Belle died in 1948. When Malcom's only son, Mark, married Doris Burns in 1949, Malcom asked the couple to live with him.[20]

Malcom Oldfield died in 1950, and Mark and Doris continued to live in the home. Their children were Deborah, Mary Elizabeth, and Sheila. Mark served in the US Army as a medical corpsman with the 216th General Hospital in Europe. He returned to Bastrop and worked in Austin as a medical technologist until he retired. He was an "avid baseball player, golfer, and domino player." Mark died in 2008.[21]

Doris Oldfield worked for Bastrop County twenty-six years in the tax office and clerk's office and was elected Bastrop County treasurer in 1982, serving four terms. As of 2019 Doris is ninety-three years old, is active in the community, and lives in the home. The home has been in the Oldfield family since 1925, some ninety-four years. The only changes have been the removal and rebuilding of the original kitchen and, unfortunately, the removal of several old trees.[22]

House at 1002 Pine Street.

This house is listed in the National Register of Historic Places as "House at 1002 Pine Street." However, when it was originally listed in 1976, it was named the "Paul Page House" and incorrectly dated as built in 1910. It is a City of Bastrop Historic Landmark.

# Beverly and Lula Kerr House

*1305 Pine Street / 1910*

Beverly and Lula Kerr purchased their lot from Beverly's brother, Robert A. Kerr, on January 11, 1893.[23] Robert Kerr was elected to the Texas House of Representatives in 1881 and served on the Bastrop School Board, during which time he helped establish Emile School, one of the earliest high schools in Texas for African American students.[24] Beverly was a barber, a band teacher at Emile School, and a versatile musician and band leader for Kerr's Orchestra. Lula, also an excellent musician, was the first primary-grade teacher at Emile School when it opened in 1892 and a piano teacher for more than fifty years.[25]

In 1910 Beverly and Lula hired J. L. Wilbarger and Company to build a raised, one-story frame, shingled-roof house, twenty-four by forty-eight feet, and twenty-two feet high. In 1914 they remodeled, "making changes and additions to their one-story dwelling house."[26] This Victorian home has a hipped roof with a side gable, an L-shaped porch, and square columns. The architecture's simple lines are interrupted by wide front steps leading to the home's modest front door with transom. Its raised foundation creates aboveground storage underneath.

The Kerrs saw the need for a social center for the African American community and in 1914 built what was then called Kerr Hall—a two-story, frame structure that became the heart and soul of Bastrop's black community. The building was constructed on the back half of their property and faced Walnut Street. It was a center for social, civic, educational, and musical gatherings. Over the years, many entertainers performed there, including Roosevelt Williams, the "Grey Ghost," a master of the blues piano.[27]

Beverly Wilford Kerr died in August 1941; Lula, in 1944. Lula's sister, Viola B. Shepard, became heir to the home and sold it to Theophilus Clay "T. C." and Olivia Franklin in 1947.[28] T. C. was a longtime educator and local historian. He taught in Bastrop County schools from 1928 to 1930, followed by schools in Elgin, Taylor, and Jefferson, and was principal of Garland High School in DeKalb, Texas. He earned a master's degree from Prairie View A&M College in 1948. He was superintendent of Bastrop County's African American schools for seventeen years, at one time supervising some twenty-two schools. Afterward, he taught education at Huston-Tillotson College in Austin. He wrote two histories of Bastrop's Emile School.[29] The heirs of T. C. and Olivia sold the home in 2001.[30]

The house is listed in the National Register of Historic Places.

Beverly and Lula Kerr House, 1305 Pine Street.

The 1914 Kerr Hall at 1308 Walnut Street, later named the Kerr Community Center.

# Walnut Street

## William Kesselus House

*1002 Walnut Street / Before 1891*

Wilhelm Kessel, a tailor, immigrated to New York City from Prussia and moved "out west" to Bastrop in 1853, changing his name to William Kesselus. The "us" is said to have been for "United States."[1] By 1858 he had his own tailor shop on Main Street in Bastrop. William purchased a lot on Walnut Street from John L. Moncure in 1860.[2] He then served in the Bastrop German Rifle Company and in Company A, 3rd Regiment of the Texas Infantry during the Civil War. After returning to Bastrop, he married Anna Keil in November 1865. They settled into the older portion of this home, where they raised their children: William, Hugo, Helen, Hettie, Adelia, and Erna. (Their son, Rudolph, age twenty-five, died while trying to rescue a cow from the flooding Colorado River, and little Anna, age three, died on the front porch from choking on a piece of corn.)[3]

Around 1891 the house was renovated, and a Victorian facade and rooms facing Walnut Street were added. After the renovation, the house featured a central hallway with the parlor dominantly projecting into the front facade on the right side and the front porch, with its jigsaw-cut brackets and turned balustrade, on the left. Above the parlor was a prominent gable with a decorative truss. The roof was shingled. The Kesselus homestead remained in the family for approximately seventy-seven years until 1937, when it was sold to Bascom and Ima Hodges.[4]

Bascom "Bass" Hodges came to Bastrop from Rockland, Texas, about 1896 when he was six years old. He married Ima Lawson in 1927, and together they operated a dry-cleaning business on Main Street for thirty-four years. Ima made all of the alter-

William Kesselus House, 1002 Walnut Street.

ations. She was at one time the extension service agent, once called the county demonstration agent.[5] Bass and Ima raised three children in the home: Bascom Jr., Lula Jo, and Elma.[6] Bass was eighty-three years old when he died in 1973. He was described as quiet and unpretentious, believing in hard work and fair play; his word was his bond.[7] Ima was eighty years old when she died in 1979. The home remained in the Hodges family for sixty-eight years.

The house is listed in the National Register of Historic Places and is a City of Bastrop Historic Landmark.

## Thomas H. Mays House

*1008 Walnut Street / Circa 1850s*

Located in the front yard of this historic house, the Texas Historical Commission marker reads: "Thomas H. Mays was born in 1802 in Virginia and emigrated to Texas from Tennessee in 1830. In 1834, he became Bastrop's first municipal surveyor and platted the city's new streets. Two years later, he was wounded in the leg at the Battle of San Jacinto while serving in the Texian Army with the 'Mina Volunteers' led by Col. Edward Burleson. Upon his return to Bastrop, he became deputy surveyor for Bastrop County. He also held political office in Bastrop as city alderman (1838) and associate justice (1839). He wed Arie C. Ellis, and the couple reared their children in Bastrop, establishing a large homestead, including this site, in the mid-1800s. Mays died on April 18, 1862, but his burial location is unknown."

The original four-room house, with its two large rooms divided by a foyer that might have been a dogtrot, is now (2019) a seven-room house with one bedroom, sitting room, dining room, kitchen, bath, back entrance or mud room, and living room.

The site is a Recorded Texas Historic Landmark.

Thomas H. Mays House, 1008 Walnut Street.

## Jennie Brooks House

*1009 Walnut Street / Circa 1890*

This vernacular board-and-batten cottage is significant for its association with Jennie Brooks, an early African American settler in Bastrop, who was born into slavery in 1863.[8] Jennie purchased the lot and built her home around 1890. It is one of the oldest houses in Bastrop built by an African American family, and Jennie was one of Bastrop's few African American home owners at that time. A widow, she supported her three children, Lizzie, Lena, and Robert, and her mother, Janie Black, by taking in washing and ironing and by selling jams and jellies made from her backyard orchard.[9] Rather than use a bank, she kept her money in a pouch on her belt around her waist.[10]

With her hard-earned money she purchased a piano and parlor furniture. Her daughters learned to play the piano from Lula Kerr, who lived a few blocks away. Lizzie preferred ragtime music and played every Saturday night for the city dances at Kerr Hall, while Lena was drawn to the classical side and played for programs and the choir at Paul Quinn African Methodist Episcopal Church, when Lula Kerr was unavailable.[11]

The house is listed in the National Register of Historic Places and is a City of Bastrop Historic Landmark.

Paul Quinn African Methodist Episcopal (AME) Church, 1108 Walnut Street.

Jennie Brooks House, 1009 Walnut Street.

# Water Street

## Chalmers Home

*1702 Water Street / 1917*

Calhoun and Susan Holman Chalmers married in 1878; Susan was twenty, and Calhoun was twenty-seven. They had seven children: Mary, Owen, Bessie, Mattie, Maggie, Tom, and Fay. The family moved from McDade to Bastrop in 1905 after Calhoun was elected Bastrop County treasurer.[1] They built their new home in 1917; however, Calhoun died only five years later while still serving as county treasurer.

Susan Chalmers remained in the home, and Fay lived with her for the next thirty years.[2] During World War II, Susan rented part of the downstairs to contractors and support personnel who were working at Camp Swift. From time to time, before and after the war, she took in boarders.[3] Susan died nearing age ninety-six in 1953.

After her mother's death, Fay Chalmers continued to live in the home until 1988, when she moved to a nursing home for health reasons. She died in 1995 and left the home to her nephew, Thomas C. Chalmers. In 1998 he sold it to his cousin, Forrest T. Chalmers, and his wife, Karen Fittz Chalmers,[4] who had three children: Forrest Tracy III, Kallie, and Marlayna.

Forrest and Karen added Prairie School influences to the home, building a deep entry porch along the entire front of the house, an attic dormer, and heavy square columns. The triple window pattern was part of the original construction. Forrest is the great-grandson of the original builders, Calhoun and Susan Chalmers. Five generations of the family have lived in the home.[5]

Chalmers Home, 1702 Water Street.

Forrest Chalmers's 1946 Ford F1 is often parked in front of the home. When the Chalmers family was landscaping, they dug up an old pistol, also dated 1946. Unable to repair it, it now (2019) hangs on the truck's stick shift. Courtesy of Forrest and Karen Chalmers.

# Wilson Street

## Allen-Fowler House

*1404 Wilson Street / 1852*

William J. Hancock, from Aberdeen, Mississippi, was hired to be headmaster of a new school, the Bastrop Academy. In February 1852 he purchased a six-acre lot across the street from the academy and built a two-story home that was a combined family residence and boarding house for out-of-town students attending the school.[1] The house was described as having a two-story front with galleries. There were two large rooms upstairs and two large rooms downstairs separated by a wide hall. The Hancock family occupied the south front room and the first room in the ell.[2]

In 1857 the Bastrop Academy was converted into the Bastrop Military Institute, and William Hancock was replaced by Colonel Robert Thomas Prichard Allen. (He is not to be confused with his son, Major Robert D. Allen, who was commandant of the Military Institute.) Robert T. P. Allen was a graduate of West Point and owned and published the San Francisco *Pacific News* before moving to Bastrop. He was a civil engineer, astronomy professor, and Methodist preacher. "Young men from other States came, and soon more than one-hundred young men were cadets—the finest young men in the country." Although loved and honored by the cadets, Robert was called "Rarin', Tearin', Pitchin' Allen" behind his back.[3]

Robert and Julia Allen bought the Hancock home in 1857 and continued to operate it as a boarding house while living there. Among the important guests in the Allen home was Governor Sam Houston, whose sons were cadets at the Military Institute.[4] When the Civil War broke out in 1861, the cadets of the Military Institute were in demand as drill masters and left the school. Robert left to serve as mustering officer at military

Allen-Fowler House, 1404 Wilson Street.

Bargeboards featuring Texas stars.

camps in Texas and was appointed colonel of the 17th Regiment, Texas Infantry, CSA (Confederate States of America). In 1863 he was given charge of Camp Ford, a prisoner-of-war camp near Tyler.[5]

Located in the front yard of the Allen-Fowler House is a historical marker erected to honor Julia Allen. It describes Julia as "an angel of mercy" to prisoners at Camp Ford. "She nursed the ill, consoled the homesick, cheered the despondent, attended church services with the prisoners; she was so much esteemed and loved that one of the Federals wrote a poem in her honor."[6] At the end of the war, Robert and his son moved to Kentucky and reopened the Kentucky Military Institute.

The home had three different owners before it was sold to attorney John Preston and Maud Maynard Fowler in February 1876. About 1880 the Fowlers added first- and second-story galleries, front and side bay windows, and a side porch on the north. In keeping with the exuberant Victorian style of the time, they added fancy, ornate trim on the exterior. Windows were "framed with paneled pilaster jambs and archtrave [*sic*] with cornices."[7] These architectural features remain today (2019), as do the original five-light transom and sidelights that surround the front doors.

John Preston Fowler was known as "Pet" Fowler. He graduated from the Columbia Law School, Washington, D.C., and established the Bastrop law firm Fowler and Fowler with his attorney sons, Wallace and John Preston Jr. Pet was mayor of Bastrop (1874), was Bastrop County attorney (1873–76 and 1880–81), and was elected Texas state senator (1883–85).[8] Pet and Maud Fowler raised six children in their home. Maud died in 1916; Pet died at age seventy-eight in 1927. The home remained unchanged until 1994, when owners Joe and Nancy Beal added an architecturally compatible master suite to the back wing of the house.

Geoffrey S. Connor, an Austin attorney, purchased the home in 2006. As a historian and former Texas secretary of state, he was particularly drawn to the house for its political, military, and historic background.[9] He retained professional help to remodel the entire interior of the home using 1850s colors and designs and filled the home with books, antiques, art, rugs, and antiquities collected over the decades. Added to these collections are international hunting and fishing trophies and memorabilia and souvenirs of his experiences in law, politics, the military, and academia.[10] He frequently uses the home for political and charitable events.

The house is listed in the National Register of Historic Places and is a designated Recorded Texas Historic Landmark. It is a City of Bastrop Historic Landmark.

## Jones-Powell Home

*1406 Wilson Street / Circa 1850*

William D. C. and Racheal Burleson Jones arrived in Bastrop County in 1848 and settled eight miles south of Bastrop, where they eventually built this small home and engaged in farming. They raised ten children in the house. The home served four generations of the Jones family and became known as the "Stagecoach House" due to its proximity to the Alum Creek Way Station. The old homestead was inherited by the Powell family of Smithville, descendants of W. D. C. Jones.[11]

It began as a simple single-pen cabin of long, straight pine logs with precise dovetailing, cedar-pole rafters, and huge cedar logs for floor joists. The front door was flanked by two windows.[12] The second phase of construction was the addition of a dogtrot and board-and-batten frame structure, the same size as the original. It was constructed of pine with pegged doors of hand-planed longleaf yellow pine. About 1880 phase three gave the structure a Victorian look with the addition of a room with an octagonal bay. A front porch was added with details in keeping with the popular Victorian architecture of that time. In 1984 the old home, long abandoned and threatened with destruction due to the relocation of Highway 71, was sold to Gerald Wagner and moved to its current location.[13]

After a succession of owners and a use as rental property, the home was purchased in 2013 by Karol Rice and Victor Gonzalez, who lost their home in the 2011 Bastrop County Complex fire.

Jones-Powell Home, 1406 Wilson Street.

## Prenzell-Tuck Home

*1503 Wilson Street / 2008, construction incorporating early structures*

This farmhouse-style residence blends old structures and materials with new. It is the work of local reconstruction specialists Tommy and Judi Hoover. "The heart of the house is believed to have once been a medical office at nearby Camp Swift, a US Army infantry training center during World War II and currently a training site for the Texas National Guard."[14] After the war it was moved to Hoffman Road, where it was a residence for many years until the Hoovers moved it to Wilson Street in 2007. A new second floor was created over the Camp Swift building. The original building was so sturdily constructed that it was possible to detach the roof, lift it as a unit by crane, frame in the new second floor, and reposition the original roof atop the new second-floor framing.[15]

The adjoining section, the large master bedroom, dates from before 1880 and was originally a four-room house on Main Street owned by Antone and Terressa Prenzell. The Prenzell house was bought by Richard and Clara Burger in 1890 and was the home for their daughter, Mina, and her husband, Hugo Kesselus. David Gholson purchased the building in the 1970s from William Kesselus for three hundred dollars and moved it to a site on the southwest corner of Spring and Church Streets, where it became Dawn's Early Light bakery. The building passed through a series of owners until purchased by the Hoovers.[16]

The kitchen and dining room are new construction; their ceilings and the kitchen wall are of beadboard from a country store in nearby String Prairie. Reconstruction was completed in 2008. With its blended components the home was purchased from the Hoovers by local attorney Joe Grady Tuck.[17]

Prenzell-Tuck Home, 1503 Wilson Street.

## Crocheron-McDowall House

*1506 Wilson Street / 1857*

Mary Ann and Henry Crocheron's new home was under construction when a hurricane blew into Texas and scattered it over their twelve-acre lot. They gathered up the lumber and began again. By 1857 the home was completed and has since been labeled by the US Department of Interior as one of the finest examples of Texas Greek Revival in the state.

Little is known of Henry Crocheron's early years. Of Dutch descent, he came to America and first settled on Staten Island, New York, and later moved to Montgomery, Alabama, where he opened a mercantile business. In 1837 Crocheron bought twelve slaves and moved to the village of Bastrop in the new Republic of Texas. He later sold the slaves and bought land in various parts of Texas at twenty-five to fifty cents an acre. He went into partnership with L. C. Cunningham and owned several stores, including the Bastrop Steam Mill, Inc., the first industrial enterprise in Bastrop.[18]

Mary Ann Tipple and her widowed English mother and younger sister, Ruth, left London and settled on Staten Island, where Mary Ann supplemented their income with dressmaking. The family set sail in 1839 for Texas to join Ruth's husband, James Nicholson, who had selected the settlement of Bastrop for their new home. After six weeks at sea, they arrived in Galveston and rode horseback to Bastrop. Mary Ann wrote that they were met at the edge of town by some "fine-looking gentlemen on handsome horses." One of the gentlemen was Henry Crocheron, with whom Mary Ann fell in love and married.[19]

Henry owned a cedar brake north of town and a sawmill, so he was able to handpick the logs for their new home. George Orts, the carpenter, made nearly everything of cedar, pine, and walnut. Piers and fireplace foundations were field stone from the property. The six-over-nine window lights, the hand-carved walnut banister, and the window weights (the first in Bastrop) were shipped from New York to Galveston and then by rail and freight wagon to Bastrop. The most unique feature of the two-story house is the novel foyer that runs across the entire front of the house rather than from front to back.

The original structure consisted of the existing two-story building and a one-story ell section at the rear and contained approximately twenty-seven hundred square feet. The original dentil molding surrounds the entire structure. The home is dominated by a two-story central portico supported by four square, one-story wood columns on each floor. The house was for many years the social and intellectual center of Bastrop.[20]

Crocheron-McDowall House, 1506 Wilson Street.

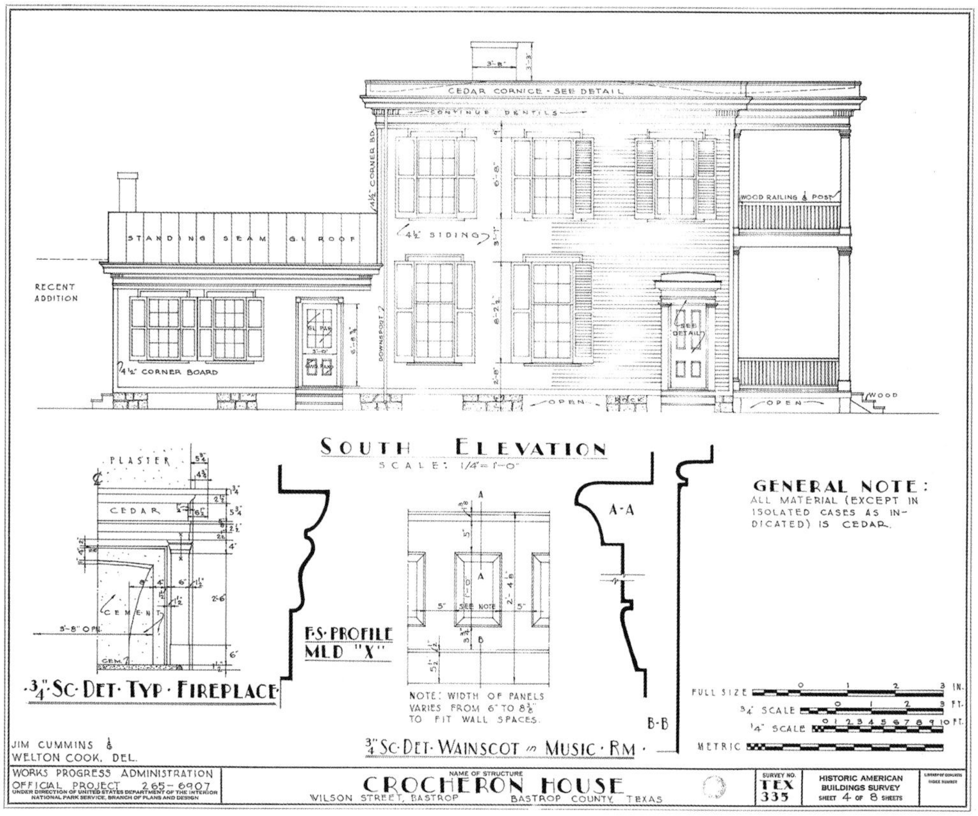


Crocheron House, south elevation, November 1936, Historic American Buildings Survey. Drawing by Jim Cummins and Welton Cook.

Mary Ann and Henry had no children, but after Mary Ann's sister Ruth died, Ruth's three children, Billy, Mary Ann (Mollie), and baby Ruth, moved into the Crocheron home, where they were provided the best of everything. Mollie Nicholson, born in Bastrop in 1843, was pampered by her aunt and uncle. She was sent to the prestigious Bastrop Academy, and for her first piano concert there, Mollie proudly wrote that her aunt put her hair into forty ringlets and that her pantalettes reached down to the top of her shoes. By the time she was sixteen years old, Uncle Henry had bought her three pianos, the last one being the first upright in Bastrop.[21]

In 1861 Mollie's brother, Billy, was among the Bastrop boys who enlisted in the Southern Army. In her memoirs, Molly Nicholson (McDowall) wrote about the night they waited with Billy for the midnight stage to Houston, where he was to join with other volunteers from across the state:

> This is the picture of the last evening. By the East window of the long wide hall my aunt sat in her Boston rocker; uncle, now on the gallery with his pipe, now

Crocheron House, south elevation of hall stairway, September 12, 1936, Historic American Buildings Survey. Arthur W. Stewart, photographer.

> seated inside in his great rocker; we girls, Ruth and myself, trying to be cheerful, but failing utterly; on the lounge, brother William in travel clothes, with his valise, packed to bursting, near the front door; the lamp on the table unsteady, wavering; conversation started, forgotten; aunt's hands busy with some kind of needle work, then lying idly in her lap; and the clock ticking louder and louder as the short hand moved from XI to XII. Impulsively, I picked up the scissors from my aunt's basket and, going to the lounge where my brother lay, clipped off a lock of his hair; quickly he turned, and sadly smiled. Now is heard the stage horn, as the lumbering coach-and-four climbs the bank of the river and enters town. Hearts beat fast; a choking sensation is in the throat; words and kisses of goodbye; the stage coach is at the gate; a last look into eyes, and the soldier brother is gone.[22]

The tradition of clipping a lock of hair from a loved one had two meanings. It could be carried in a trunk or pocket, sometimes tied with a ribbon or framed like a photograph, as a reminder of a loved one. Or, if the person was deceased, the lock of hair would be placed inside a specially designed piece of jewelry called a mourning locket and worn as a necklace. When Billy arrived in Houston, he joined with Terry's Texas Rangers, eleven hundred strong. He was in constant service throughout the four years of the war, received one slight wound, and had three horses killed under him. During the last year of the war he drew a furlough that he gave to a friend, a married man, so his friend might go see his wife and children. Near Rome, Georgia, while the Rangers were covering the retreat of the Southern Army, a shot pierced Billy's left side. He handed his pistols to one of the boys, saying, "I am shot, boys," and rode off into the woods, where he died.[23]

The same year, 1864, while accompanying her uncle on a business trip to Matamoras, Mollie met an Englishman named William McDowall. They were married four years later and eventually settled in London. William died of yellow fever a year after their marriage, and in 1869 Mollie and her three-month-old-daughter returned to Bastrop to live with her uncle.[24] When Henry Crocheron died in 1873, he willed the house to Mollie. She supplemented the family income by teaching music. She was a gifted musician and added much to Bastrop's cultural and social life. Her *Memoirs of Mollie McDowall* was published in 1978 and continues to serve as an excellent resource for local historians. Mollie played the organ for the Methodist and Episcopal churches and taught piano for fifty-six years. She moved to Houston in 1897, where she became the founding president of the Young Women's Christian Association (YWCA), the first in Texas.[25]

The home is listed in the National Register of Historic Places, is designated a Recorded Texas Historic Landmark, and is included in the Historic American Buildings Survey (HABS). The address was originally 1502 Wilson Street; however, the city later changed the address to 1506 Wilson Street.

# Governor Sayers House

*1703 Wilson Street / 1868*

This modest home with its long, inviting, red-brick sidewalk, was built in 1868 by Major Joseph Sayers for his bride-to-be, Ada Walton, who died in 1871. The Greek Revival home is one story, on brick piers, with a pedimented portico supported by four square columns and pilasters.

Joseph Draper Sayers, the son of David and Mary Peete Sayers, was born in 1841 in Grenada, Mississippi, and educated in Bastrop, where he attended the Bastrop Academy, which became the Bastrop Military Institute in 1856.[26] At the time of his graduation in 1860, he was commissioned as a lieutenant by Governor Sam Houston.[27] Although opposed to secession, at the outbreak of the Civil War he joined the Confederate Army. He was severely wounded several times, but he returned to the battlefield each time.[28] He was promoted to the rank of captain for gallantry at the Battle of Val Verde and to major in 1864.

After the war, Joe returned to Bastrop and was elected to the state Senate, where he served from 1873 to 1879 and was chairman of the Democratic State Executive Committee from 1875 to 1878. He then served as lieutenant governor from 1879 to 1881. Elected to the US House of Representatives in 1885, he resigned on January 19, 1899, to become governor of Texas.[29]

If ever Texas was plagued by misfortune, it was during the Sayers administration. The Brazos River overflowed in 1899, flooding its valley from near Waco to the Gulf of Mexico. In 1900 a powerful hurricane made landfall at Galveston and resulted in the deaths of eight thousand citizens and untold loss in property. Then the destructive boll weevil and two years of drought destroyed Texas' main money crop, cotton. Joe personally organized fund drives to raise millions in aid to help his beloved state recover from these disasters. He was referred to in a newspaper article as the "Governor [Who] Never Let the People Down."[30]

In 1879 he married Orline "Lena" Walton (sister of his first wife, Ada). When Joe was elected governor, the couple sold their Bastrop home and moved into the Governor's Mansion in Austin. Lena Sayers was the ultimate hostess and became known as the Dolly Madison of the mansion.[31]

Longtime home owners include Scott and Dessie Millington, who bought the home in 1937 and immediately began restoration. The home became rental property for a few years after Dessie and Scott moved to Angleton, where he was county agricultural agent. After retirement, they returned to Bastrop. Scott died in 1972, and Dessie remained in the home until 1994, when she sold it to Linda and Michael Moorcock.

Governor Sayers House, 1703 Wilson Street. Courtesy of the Bastrop County Historical Society.

Governor Joseph D. Sayers House, March 13, 1934, Historic American Buildings Survey. L. C. Page Jr., photographer.

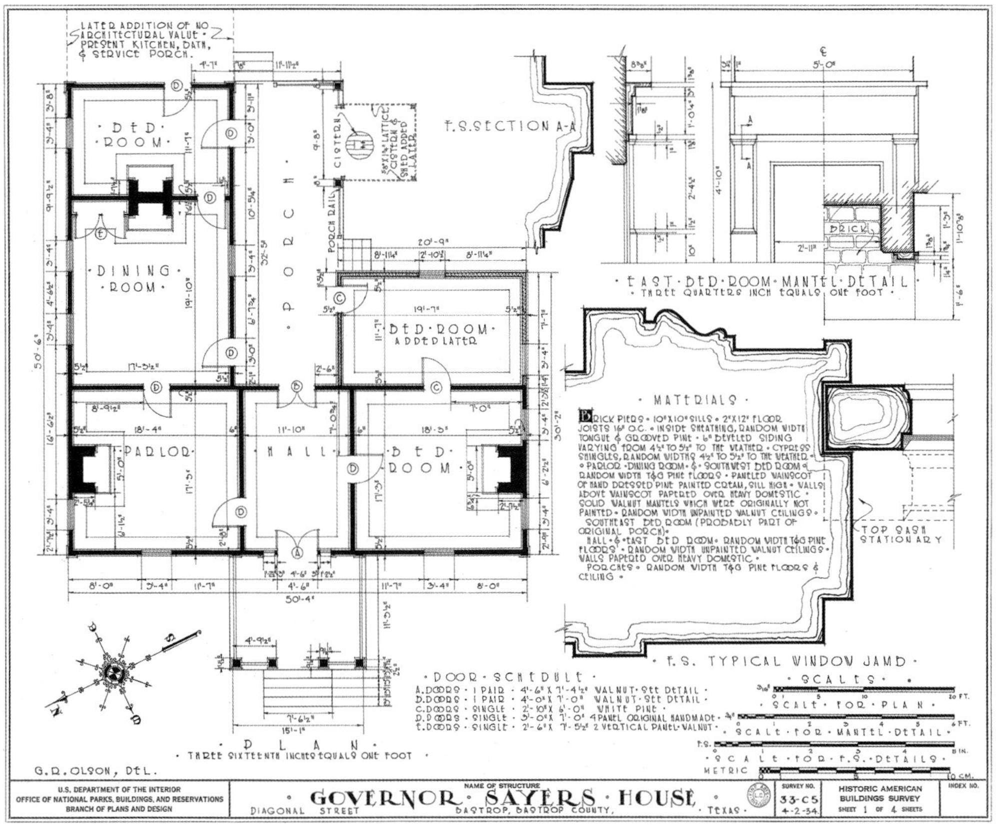


Historic American Buildings Survey, April 2, 1934. Drawing by G. D. Olson.

Michael and Linda moved to Bastrop from London in 1994. Michael is a writer, journalist, editor, and musician. Author of more than one hundred books, he was named by the *London Times* as among the fifty best writers since 1945. He has won and been shortlisted for many literary prizes. He has received several Lifetime Achievement awards in France, England, and the United States and has also been inducted into the Science Fiction Hall of Fame. Michael's notable creations include the characters Corum, Hawkmoon, Jerry Cornelius, and, most famous of all, the tragic albino prince, Elric of Melniboné. He performed onstage in Austin in 2019 at the North American Space Odyssey and recently put out a new album, *Live at the Terminal Cafe*, from Cleopatra Records.[32]

The building is listed in the National Register of Historic Places, is designated a Recorded Texas Historic Landmark, and is included in the Historic American Buildings Survey (HABS).

# Notes

## *State Highway 304*

1. John Holmes Jenkins III, ed., *Recollections of Early Texas: Memoirs of John Holland Jenkins* (Austin: University of Texas Press, 1977), p. 17.

2. "Henry Arthur McArdle," Wikipedia, accessed May 28, 2019, https://en.m.wikipedia.org/wiki/Henry_Arthur_McArdle.

3. "Eva Hill LeSueur," notes and written articles located in the personal files of Libby Sartain. Sartain credits descriptions of the early home to her great-grandfather, Reverend Benjamin O. Hill, and to Eva Hill LaSueur, who provided her memoirs and wrote extensively for the *Bastrop Advertiser* about the house and family. Eva was the poet laureate of the Daughters of the Confederacy and published a book of poems, *Leaves of Ancient Oaks*.

4. "Eva Hill LeSueur."

5. Historic American Buildings Survey, HABS, was a program established in 1933 by the National Park Service for the purpose of documenting a representative sampling of America's architectural heritage. Records consist of measured drawings, archival photographs, and written reports.

6. Elizabeth "Libby" Sartain, interview by Robbie Sanders, May 15, 2019, notes in the personal files of Robbie Sanders.

7. Elizabeth "Libby" Sartain, interview.

8. Webster Gregg, *From a Prince to a Slave* (Lake Mary, FL: Creation House, 2009).

9. Bastrop County Deed Records (BCDR), Vol. K, p. 509, June 15, 1857.

10. Bastrop County Probate Records (BCPR), Vol. G, p. 6, December 5, 1866.

11. Eugene Young, "My Grandfather—My Father's Father," September 30, 1981, Minifred Trigg personal files and Trigg file, Bastrop County Historical Society (BCHS) Museum Archives.

12. Bastrop County Marriage Records, Vol. A, p. 452.

13. Eugene Young, "My Father," September 30, 1981, Minifred Trigg personal files and Trigg file, BCHS Museum Archives.

14. Eugene Young, "My Grandmother (My Father's Mother)," September 30, 1981, Minifred Trigg personal files and Trigg file, BCHS Museum Archives.

15. Bastrop County Probate Minutes (BCPM), Vol. M, pp. 286, 287, October 24, 1910 (last will and testament).

16. Young, "My Father."

17. BCDR, Vol. 150, pp. 535–37, October 29, 1959 (176 acres).

18. BCDR, Vol. 151, p. 294, February 4, 1960 (176 acres). Nine acres were lost to the Highway Department for right-of-way for Highway 304.

19. Minifred Trigg, interview by Robbie Sanders, June and July 2019, notes in the personal files of Robbie Sanders.

20. "Train Crash Takes Life," *Bastrop Advertiser*, August 20, 1990, pp. 1, 2.

21. Minifred Trigg, interview.

22. Reid Sharp and Cindy Sharp, *Aldridge-Fitzwilliam-Sharp, "Wexford" 1852—1872—1990, Bastrop, Texas: One Hundred Forty-Three Years of Texas History at Wexford*, revised 2016, booklet in Hwy 304 file, Aldridge-Fitzwilliam House, BCHS Museum Archives.

23. Sharp and Sharp, "Aldridge-Fitzwilliam-Sharp."

24. Sharp and Sharp, "Aldridge-Fitzwilliam-Sharp."

25. Sharp and Sharp, "Aldridge-Fitzwilliam-Sharp."

26. BCDR, Vol. 580, p. 770, August 24, 1990.

27. Reid Sharp, interview by Robbie Sanders, June 5, 2019, notes in the personal files of Robbie Sanders.

28. Steve Cocheo, ed., "Bringing Santa to Bastrop," *ABA Banking Journal* (December 2010): 56.

## Cedar Street

1. BCDR, Vol. K, p. 465, September 9, 1850; and Vol. N, p. 227, October 24, 1866.

2. Augustus Koch, *Bird's Eye View of Bastrop—Bastrop County, Texas, 1887*, BCHS Museum Archives.

3. BCDR, Vol. 54, p. 679, December 4, 1906.

4. "Mrs. W. F. Tribble Is Buried Here Saturday," *Bastrop Advertiser*, February 9, 1961, p. 1.

5. "Bastrop Is Growing," *Bastrop Advertiser*, July 28, 1911, p. 2.

6. Judy Edwards, telephone interview by Robbie Sanders, June 6, 2009, Church Point, Louisiana. Edwards is the niece of Ferrell and Susie Smith.

7. Tracy Chalmers and Mary Jean Chalmers, interviews by Sandra Chipley, 1993 and 2010, notes in the personal files of Sandra Chipley.

8. BCDR, Vol. L, p. 173, December 18, 1858. The deed describes the location of a nearby property that was sold by Samuel and Gabriel Friedberger to Alexander Dobe. Moore's residence is used as a reference point in that deed.

9. Anonymous, "Moore, Littleton Wilde (1835–1911)," *Handbook of Texas Online*, published by the Texas State Historical Association, accessed June 13, 2019, http://www.tshaonline.org/handbook/online/articles/fmo33.

10. Ethel Mary Franklin Smith, ed., *Memoirs of Mollie McDowall* (Austin: National Society of the Colonial Dames of America in the State of Texas, 1978), p. 26.

11. Anonymous, "Moore, Littleton Wilde."

12. BCDR, Vol. N, pp. 286, 287, January 10, 1867.

13. "Mrs. Sarah J. Orgain," *Interstate Index: A Journal of Progress* 2, no. 5 (1920): 11.

14. Bill Moore, *Bastrop County 1691–1900*, rev. ed. (Wichita Falls, TX: Nortex Press, 1977), p. 133.

15. "Sarah Jane Orgain," 602 Cedar Street file, BCHS Museum Archives.

16. "Former Bastropian Writes of Fascinating Early Days in Old Town," in *In the Shadow of the Lost Pines: A History of Bastrop County and Its People*, comp. and pub. R. E. Standifer, Amy S. Standifer, and R. E. Standifer Jr., publishers of the *Bastrop Advertiser* (Bastrop: 1955), p. 6. The booklet is a collection of articles and stories related to Bastrop County history.

17. US Census, 1930.

18. Sandra Chipley and Robbie Sanders, "Honeymoon Hut," 2013 Holiday Homes Tour, 907 Cedar Street file, BCHS Museum Archives.

19. Mary Jane Davis, interview by Robbie Sanders, October 15, 1993, notes in the personal files of Robbie Sanders. Mary Jane Davis was one of the local residents involved in the preparations.

20. Janean Whitten, interview by Robbie Sanders, February 6, 2019, notes in the personal files of Robbie Sanders.

## Chestnut Street

1. Augustus Koch, *Bird's Eye View of Bastrop—Bastrop County, Texas, 1887*, BCHS Museum Archives. The drawing shows a vacant lot where the Dawson House now stands.

2. "City of Bastrop 1892–1908, Block 27 East of East Main," in *Assessor's Abstract of City Lots, Bastrop County*, p. 78. The assessment for 1892 shows that two homes were on the land owned by Bastian. The *Assessor's Abstract* is owned by Robbie Sanders, a gift from Clyde Reynolds.

3. Mary Jane Davis, interview by Robbie Sanders, January 22, 1993, notes in the personal files of Robbie Sanders.

4. Marilee Spooner Smith, letter to Robbie Sanders, January 1993, personal files of Robbie Sanders.

5. Smith, letter to Robbie Sanders.

6. Smith, letter to Robbie Sanders.

7. US Census, 1870.

8. US Census, 1880.

9. The lumberyard was located on the northwest corner of the intersection of Spring and Water Streets.

10. BCDR, Vol. 10, p. 575, June 21, 1887.

11. US Census, 1900. Griesenbeck's occupation is district clerk.

12. US Census, 1910; and BCPM, Vol. U, pp. 100–103.

13. Jacqueline Hastay, interview by Robbie Sanders, May 4, 2019. Emilie married W. A. Hasler, Bruno married Alma Murchison, Haynie married Erna Walthers, and Rufus Jr. married Agnes Koenig.

14. Jacqueline Hastay, interview.

15. William "Terry" Sanders, interview by Robbie Sanders, June 4, 2019, notes in the personal files of Robbie Sanders.

16. Charles "Chuck" Bunte, interview by William "Terry" Sanders, June 26, 2019. Chuck is the son of Granville Bunte.

17. Laurie Schneider, interview by Robbie Sanders, May 4, 2019, notes in the personal files of Robbie Sanders.

18. Nancy Klauber, "Victorian Simplicity in Haralson Home, *Smithville Times*, September 18, 1974.

19. Mrs. Fred Haynie, "The Haralson House," application for Texas Historical Building Medallion (#6948), Texas State Historical Survey Committee, Austin, November 13, 1962.

20. Haynie, "The Haralson House."

21. Marguerite Sanderson, interviews by Robbie Sanders, 1993 and 2009, notes in the personal files of Robbie Sanders.

22. Mary Jane Davis, "The George W. Davis House," National Register of Historic Places, Inventory-Nomination Form, December 18, 1976, BCHS Museum Archives.

23. Mary Jane Davis, interview.

24. Mary Jane Davis, interview.

25. "Miss Mary Jane Davis Wins Chronicle Prize," *Bastrop Advertiser*, April 9, 1931, p. 1, https://texashistory.unt.edu/ark:/67531/metapth206735/m1/1/?q=Davis.

26. Betty Gurwitz, interview by Robbie Sanders, September 1, 2019, notes in the personal files of Robbie Sanders. Betty was a student living in the Scottish Rite dorm on the UT campus when Davis was a counselor there.

27. Mary Jane Davis, interview.

28. Willie Delarosa, interview by Robbie Sanders, August 31, 2019, notes in the personal files of Robbie Sanders.

29. Sandra Chipley and Robbie Sanders, "The George W. Davis House," 2014 Holiday Homes Tour, 1010 Chestnut Street file, BCHS Museum Archives.

## Church Street

1. BCDR, Vol. I, pp. 75, 278, March 15, 1851.

2. Kenneth Kesselus, *Bastrop County: 1846–1865* (Austin: Jenkins Publishing, 1987), p. 191.

3. American Society of Arms Collectors, "N. B. Tanner & Company," BCHS Museum Archives. James R. Nichols was in partnership with Adolph A. Erhard in the blacksmithing business. After Adolph volunteered to serve in the Confederate Army, James wrote the Texas Military Board that he needed Adolph to detach from the army and rejoin their blacksmithing partnership in Bastrop to forge barrels for Tanner's rifles. There is no evidence that the request was granted.

4. *Bastrop Advertiser*, December 20, 1902, p. 2, 1207 Church Street file, BCHS Museum Archives.

5. Neil Gurwitz, interview by Robbie Sanders, March, 2019, notes in the personal files of Robbie Sanders.

6. BCPR, Vol. 28, pp. 770–75, September 6, 1975.

7. Reid Sharp, "Claude 'Red' Sharp," a press release of the obituary for his father, Claude Harris Sharp, July 24, 2011, Reid Sharp personal files, Bastrop.

8. Sharp, "Claude 'Red' Sharp."

9. Reid Sharp, untitled press release of the obituary for his mother, Effie Davis Sharp, April 28, 2010, Reid Sharp personal files, Bastrop.

10. "Bastrop Is Growing," *Bastrop Advertiser*, July 28, 1911, p. 2. The article states that the "palatial residence of Dr. H. B. Combs, south of Methodist church, is in course of erection and will be completed within thirty days."

11. "The Dr. H. B. and Maude Combs House," 1208 Church Street file, BCHS Museum Archives.

12. Dick Smith, "The H. B. Combs House, 1208 Church Street," press release to the *Bastrop Advertiser*, 1208 Church Street file, BCHS Museum Archives.

13. "Burned to Death," *Bastrop Advertiser*, May 13, 1905, p. 3.

14. Nancy Juarez Gutierrez Bulak, "Macario Juarez (Mike), April 10, 1893," BCHS Museum Archives.

15. Laurie Liriano, interview by Robbie Sanders, September 5, 2019, notes in the personal files of Robbie Sanders; and BCDR, Vol. 2185, p. 76, October 26, 2012.

16. Anonymous, "Risher and Hall Stage Lines," *Handbook of Texas Online*, published by the Texas State Historical Association, accessed September 2, 2019, https://www.tshaonline.org/handbook/entries/risher-and-hall-stage-lines.

17. BCDR, Vol. P, pp. 203, 204, February 19, 1870.

18. Joseph Draper Sayers, future governor of Texas, and his brother, William Branch Sayers, were the sons of David and Mary Peete Sayers. The brothers were adults living elsewhere when their father purchased this home.

19. DeLea Sayers, interview by Robbie Sanders, August 2018, notes in the personal files of Robbie Sanders.

20. Catine E. Perkins, letter to Mrs. Keefe, July 4, 1964, 1307 Church Street file, BCHS Museum Archives. The letter appears to be a follow-up to the application to the Texas Historical Commission for a historic marker for the home.

21. "Some Rooster," *Bastrop Advertiser*, April 14, 1921, p. 2.

22. Eliza Perkins, email to Robbie Sanders, May 29, 2019, BCHS Museum Archives.

23. Eliza Perkins, letter to Robbie Sanders.

24. Eliza Perkins, letter to Robbie Sanders.

25. Eliza Perkins, letter to Robbie Sanders.

26. Eliza Perkins, letter to Robbie Sanders.

27. Alfred E. Menn, "Oldest Texas Drug Store in Bastrop," undated newspaper clipping, in Cayton Erhard Collection, Dolph Briscoe Center for American History, University of Texas at Austin. Alfred Menn interviewed Cora Erhard, who stated that her mother built their home in 1889.

28. Fairview Cemetery, Section Fb, Row 17, Bastrop.

29. Marilyn Whites, "The Harriet Erhard House," 1999 Holiday Homes Tour, 1401 Church Street file, BCHS Museum Archives.

30. Sandra Chipley, "Narrative to the Application for a Recorded Texas Historic Landmark Marker," 2010, 1402 Church Street file, BCHS Museum Archives.

31. Chipley, "Narrative."

32. "City Council Proceedings," *Bastrop Advertiser*, August 12, 1905, p. 5, https://texashistory.unt.edu/ark:/67531/metapth205916/m1/6/?q=council.

33. BCDR, Vol. 97, p. 283, August 1, 1936.

34. Eliza Lee Beyer, "Coal & Lignite Mining in Bastrop County," Coal Mines file, BCHS Museum Archives.

35. Mary Ann McDowall, "A Little Journey through Memory's Halls," 1931, pp. 46, 47, Mary Ann McDowall file, BCHS Museum Archives.

36. McDowall, "A Little Journey," p. 84.

37. US Census, 1860. Sallie Bell was fourteen years old in the 1860 census and listed with her mother, father, and brothers. She married John Howard Allen, the son of Julia and Colonel R. T. P. Allen, in Bastrop on October 26, 1865. Sallie and John Howard Allen moved to Paducah, Kentucky, and then to Orlando, Florida, where she died in 1888 at age thirty-seven. John was the second mayor of Orlando.

38. Henry Newton Bell III, notes and corrections regarding the history of the Allen-Bell House, August 24, 2019, personal files of Robbie Sanders.

39. Henry Newton Bell III, interview by Robbie Sanders, August 27, 2019, notes in the personal files of Robbie Sanders.

40. "From McDade: Fatal Shooting Affray," *Galveston Daily News*, January 24, 1874, https://texashistory.unt.edu/ark:/67531/metapth461565/m1/1/zoom/?q=McDade&resolution=3&lat=6288.589931071322&lon=3447.1011979374784; "McDade, Where Santa Scheduled a Visit, but the Devil Came Instead," 2008, "Items of Interest in McDade, 1874," p. 165, McDade Historical Society.

41. "Bell Family History," n.d., Bell Family files, BCHS Museum Archives.

42. M. S. Staples, "Elegant Landmark Houses Three Bell Generations," *Bastrop Advertiser and County News*, February 26, 1981.

43. Henry Newton Bell III, interview.

44. Henry Newton Bell III, interview.

45. "Bell Family History," p. 1.

46. US Census, 1900.

47. Henry Newton Bell III, notes and corrections.

48. Henry Newton Bell III, notes and corrections.

49. Henry Newton Bell III, notes and corrections.

50. "Green's Great Granddaughter Tells Family's Coming to Bastrop," *Bastrop Advertiser*, August 2, 1956, Pioneer Homecoming ed., p. 21.

51. "Green's Great Granddaughter," p. 44.

52. Kenneth Kesselus, *The First National Bank: A Century of Progress and Service in the Bastrop Community*, August 13, 1989, pp. 21, 27, BCHS Museum Archives. This booklet was written for the centennial celebration of the First National Bank of Bastrop.

53. Mary Jane Davis, interview by Robbie Sanders, February 12, 1994, notes in the personal files of Robbie Sanders.

54. Shudde Bess Bryson Fath, "Griesenbeck-Bryson House," BCHS Museum Archives. Shudde wrote that Joe Pfeiffer had built or designed the Rufus Green House. He evidently added the second story.

55. Kesselus, *First National Bank*.

56. BCDR, Vol. H, p. 387, July 2, 1852; and Augustus Koch, *Bird's Eye View of Bastrop—Bastrop County, Texas, 1887*, BCHS Museum Archives.

57. Bill Moore, *Bastrop County 1691–1900*, rev. ed. (Wichita Falls, TX: Nortex Press, 1977), p. 131.

58. BCDR, Vol. 41, pp. 169–70, June 8, 1906. Dora Perkins Partain sold the home to Lucy V. Luckett in June 1906 for one thousand dollars. Lucy owned the home for four months and sold it to J. M. Holt for eleven hundred dollars in October 1906.

59. "Sale of Sales," advertisement, *Bastrop Advertiser*, December 13, 1902, p. 1, https://texashistory.unt.edu/ark:/67531/metapth205621/m1/1/?q=Meyers.

60. "Turner Family of English Origin: Comes to Bastrop County in 1894," *Bastrop Advertiser*, August 2, 1956, Homecoming ed., p. 5, https://texashistory.unt.edu/ark:/67531/metapth237594/m1/5/zoom/?q=Turner&resolution=4&lat=3836&lon=2628.5.

61. Mary Jane Davis, interview by Robbie Sanders, January 1993, notes in the personal files of Robbie Sanders; "Purely Personal," *Bastrop Advertiser*, December 22, 1906, p. 3, https://texashistory.unt.edu/ark:/67531/metapth205678/m1/3/zoom/?q=Holt&resolution=4&lat=5063&lon=2800.5.

62. BCDR, Vol. 88, pp. 59–60, April 19, 1930.

63. BCDR, Vol. 97, p. 261, August 10, 1936.

64. Mrs. Benj. D. Orgain, *From Dawn to Eventide* (New York: Eaton and Gettinger, 1918), p. 38, BCHS Museum Archives/Library.

65. Orgain, *From Dawn to Eventide*, p. 51.

66. Cynthia S. Lalla, "The B. D. Orgain House," application for Official Texas Historical Marker (history no. 6161), November 17, 1980, Texas Historical Commission, Austin.

67. Kesselus, *First National Bank*, p. 8.

68. Sue Ransome Denman, "The Bastrop Cemetery," November 1957, BCHS Museum Archives. This is a paper prepared for the November 1957 program of the BCHS.

69. "Fairview Cemetery, Bastrop, Texas" (narrative history), March 2003, Historic Texas Cemetery Designation, Texas Historical Commission.

70. "Bastrop Mourns the Passing of Beloved Pioneer," *Bastrop Advertiser*, July 9, 1931, p. 1.

## Elm Street

1. Flo Barker and Bobby Felts Terrell, "The Margaret Chambers Home," application for Texas Historical Building Medallion

(history no. 6006), August 10, 1962, Texas State Historical Survey Committee, Austin.

2. Mary Ann Nicholson McDowall, "A Little Journey through Memory's Halls," 1927, pp. 57–58, Mary Ann McDowall file, BCHS Museum Archives.

3. J. W. Wilbarger, *Indian Depredations in Texas* (Austin: Steck, 1935), pp. 7–14.

4. "Another Landmark Gone," *Bastrop Advertiser*, January 16, 1897, p. 3.

5. "The Margaret Chambers House," handwritten letter presumed to be written by Rubelle Norment McMillan, 502 Elm Street file, BCHS Museum Archives.

6. Barker and Terrell, "The Margaret Chambers Home."

7. BCDR, Vol. I, p. 768, January 1857.

8. Wilbarger, *Indian Depredations in Texas*, pp. 614–16.

9. Sandra Chipley, "The Chambers House," 2019 Holiday Homes Tour, 502 Elm Street file, BCHS Museum Archives.

## Farm Street

1. US Census, 1900. Dick Burger stated that he immigrated in 1850.

2. Kenneth Kesselus, interview by Robbie Sanders, July 13, 2019, notes in the personal files of Robbie Sanders.

3. Judith K. Hoover, "The Richard Burger House, Bastrop," application for Official Texas Historical Marker (history no. 5645), March 8, 1979, Texas Historical Commission, Austin.

4. Kenneth Kesselus, interview.

5. Hoover, "The Richard Burger House."

6. Kenneth, interview.

7. Hoover, "The Richard Burger House."

8. Hoover, "The Richard Burger House."

9. BCDR, Vol. 1897, p. 463, February 26, 2009.

10. BCPM, Vol. J, pp. 25–28, July 26, 1909.

11. Sanborn Fire Insurance Map, Bastrop, January 1912, sheet 3, Perry-Castañeda Library Map Collection, University of Texas Library System.

12. Judy McLeod Bland, interview by Sandra Chipley, September 8, 2018, notes in the personal files of Sandra Chipley.

13. Stephanie Jenkins, interview by Robbie Sanders, July 14, 2019, notes in the personal files of Robbie Sanders.

14. Judy McLeod Bland, interview.

15. Judy McLeod Bland, interview.

16. BCDR, Vol. 166, pp. 579–81, September 25, 1964.

17. BCDR, Instrument #2016010035, August 1, 2016.

18. Bastrop County Tax Rolls, 1895 (Grimes owned either one horse or a mule); and US Census, 1900 (which shows his age).

19. BCDR, Vol. 56, p. 211, June 30, 1914.

20. T. C. Franklin, "Two Black Doctors Who Practiced in Bastrop," n.d., 1201 Farm Street file, BCHS Museum Archives.

21. Franklin, "Two Black Doctors."

22. BCPM, Vol. E, p. 376, December 30, 1865; and US Census, 1910, in which Gloeckner stated he immigrated to the United States in 1859.

23. BCDR, Vol. 22, p. 564, February 5, 1895.

24. "City of Bastrop 1892–1908, Farm Lot 36, East of Main," *Assessor's Abstract of City Lots, Bastrop County*, personal property of Robbie Sanders.

25. BCPM, Vol. L, p. 380, October 22, 1917.

26. BCDR, Vol. 153, p. 325, December 20, 1960.

27. BCDR, Vol. 566, p. 505, March 23, 1990.

28. BCDR, Vol. 49, pp. 218–19, June 3, 1911; and Vol. 64, pp. 441–44, November 7, 1913.

29. "Native Citizen Passes Away," *Bastrop Advertiser*, September 4, 1947, p. 1, https://texashistory.unt.edu/ark:/67531/metapth237130/m1/1/?q=Native.

30. Melinda Larson, "Application for Historic Landmark Certificate of Appropriateness, City of Bastrop," Planning and Development Department, March 10, 2017.

## Hill Street

1. John Holmes Jenkins III, ed., *Recollections of Early Texas: The Memoirs of John Holland Jenkins* (Austin: University of Texas Press, 1977), pp. 41–44.

2. Kenneth L. Untiedt, *Legends & Life: Folklore from the Lone Star State, in Stories and Song* (Denton: University of North Texas Press, 2017), pp. 55–62. Mariann Fisk Laughlin, a descendant of Greenlief Fisk, contributed a chapter titled "Did David Crockett Really Stop in Bastrop? Some Facts and Folklore," pp. 55–64.

3. "Davy Crockett Jailed Here on Way to Alamo," *Bastrop Advertiser*, March 19, 1964, p. 4, https://texashistory.unt.edu/ark:/67531/metapth237992/m1/4/?q=Crockett.

4. Enous J. Reed, untitled narrative, application for Texas Historical Building Medallion, February 28, 1964, Texas State Historical Survey Committee, Austin; and "Medallion and Plate for Historic Mina Pioneer House Presented," *Bastrop Advertiser*, November 5, 1964, p. 4, https://texashistory.unt.edu/ark:/67531/metapth238025/hits/?q=Medallion.

5. Cynthia Pence, "Docent Information for the T. C. Osborn House—1002 Hill Street, 2006," 1102 Hill Street file, BCHS Museum Archives.

6. Pence, "Docent Information."

7. Pence, "Docent Information."

8. Admission ticket, 2006 Holiday Homes Tour, BCHS Museum Archives.

9. Admission ticket.

10. Amy S. Standifer, "Green's Great Granddaughter Tells Family's Coming to Bastrop," *Bastrop Advertiser*, August 2, 1956, Pioneer Homecoming ed., p. 21.

11. Sandra Chipley and Robbie Sanders, "The Reynolds House," 2015 Holiday Homes Tour, 1108 Hill Street file, BCHS Museum Archives.

12. Chipley and Sanders, "The Reynolds House."

13. Chipley and Sanders, "The Reynolds House."

14. "A. Griesenbeck, Prominent Bastrop Citizen Died Last Saturday," *Bastrop Advertiser*, February 4, 1926, p. 1, https://texashistory.unt.edu/ark:/67531/metapth206473/m1/1/?q=griesenbeck.

15. "Bastrop Loses One of Oldest Citizens," *Bastrop Advertiser*, November 16, 1950, p. 1, https://texashistory.unt.edu/ark:/67531/metapth237297/?q=Bastrop%20Advertiser%20november%201950.

16. "A. Griesenbeck."

17. Shudde Bryson Fath, "The Bryson House," n.d., BCHS Museum Archives; and "Bastrop Is Growing," *Bastrop Advertiser*, July 28, 1911, p. 2. The article states that the new home of Alf Griesenbeck was completed within the past year.

18. "Former Bastropian Writes of Fascinating Early Days in Old Town," in *In the Shadow of the Lost Pines: A History of Bastrop County and Its People*, comp. and pub. R. E. Standifer, Amy S. Standifer, and R. E. Standifer Jr., publishers of the *Bastrop Advertiser* (Bastrop: 1955), p. 6. The booklet is a collection of articles and stories related to Bastrop County history.

19. Anonymous, "Bryson, James Gordon (1884–1968)," *Handbook of Texas Online*, published by the Texas State Historical Association, accessed June 8, 2019, http://www.tshaonline.org/handbook/online/articles/fbrax.

20. Anonymous "Bryson, James Gordon."

21. Fath, "The Bryson House."

22. BCDR, Vol. 47, p. 318, August 3, 1910.

23. BCPR, Vol. K, pp. 577–80, August Term, 1892. C. B. Maynard died in 1889, but his property was not divided by the courts until 1892.

24. US Census, 1910.

25. US Census, 1920.

26. BCDR, Vol. 48, p. 310, January 10, 1911; and Vol. 48, pp. 455–56, January 27, 1911.

27. BCDR, Vol. 53, pp. 526–27, July 1, 1913.

28. Mary Clements McMurrey, interview by Robbie Sanders, May 7, 2019, notes in the personal files of Robbie Sanders.

29. BCDR, Vol. 104, pp. 264–65, October 5, 1940.

30. Mary Clements McMurrey, interview.

31. Ernest G. Simmons, "Murder of Lucy Rivers Maynard Caused Bastrop to Lose Innocence," in *Memories of Bastrop 1930–1950*, vol. 1, August 1998. Simmons wrote articles about local history in the *Bastrop Advertiser*. Bound copies of his newspaper clippings are in two volumes, BCHS Museum Archives.

32. "County Judge Resigns to Enter Service," *Bastrop Advertiser*, January 14, 1943, p. 1, https://texashistory.unt.edu/ark:/67531/metapth236889/m1/1/?q=resigns.

33. Mary Clements McMurrey, interview.

34. BCDR, Vol. 165, p. 657, July 14, 1964.

35. *Antigonon leptopus*, known as love vine or coral vine but locally called Queen Anne's lace.

36. BCDR, Instrument #201703421, March 13, 2017.

37. BCDR, Vol. 10, pp. 406–8, March 3, 1887.

38. US Census, 1900, Bastrop County.

39. BCDR, Vol. 37, pp. 251–52, February 11, 1902.

40. Thomas Flournoy "Tommy" Claiborne, interview by Robbie Sanders, April 9, 2019, notes in the personal files of Robbie Sanders.

41. "The Claiborne House," n.d., 1402 Hill Street file, BCHS Museum Archives.

42. "C. A. Long Dies," *Bastrop Advertiser*, December 14, 1978, p. 1, https://texashistory.unt.edu/ark:/67531/metapth335033/m1/1/?q=Long.

43. Susan Long, interview by Robbie Sanders, May 29, 2019, notes in the personal files of Robbie Sanders.

44. The property was sold to Jewell Hodges in 1986 for forty-eight hundred dollars; BCDR, Vol. 424, p. 372, June 20, 1986.

45. Cyndi Wright, "Life Spent Breaking Barriers," *Bastrop Advertiser*, February 12, 2009, pp. 1, 5A.

46. Wright, "Life Spent Breaking Barriers."

47. Wright, "Life Spent Breaking Barriers."

48. Debbie Moore, "Bastrop Loses Diminutive Giant," *Austin American-Statesman*, March 14, 2013.

49. Andy Sevilla, "Bastrop County Turns Out to Celebrate Life, Legacy of Jewell Hodges," *Austin American-Statesman*, August 2, 2017, updated September 22, 2018, https://www.statesman.com/news/20170802/ bastrop-county-turns-out-to-celebrate-life-legacy-of-jewell-hodges.

## Jefferson Street

1. Kenneth Kesselus, "Hoppe House," ed. Jodie Slatterfield, application for Official Texas Historical Marker (history no. 06790), November 5, 1990, Texas Historical Commission, Austin.

2. BCDR, Vol. 81, p. 529, May 1, 1926.

3. H. A. Schaefer, [article concerning Maynards], *Bastrop Advertiser*, April 26, 1928, https://texashistory.unt.edu/ark:/67531/metapth206586/m1/7/zoom/?q=Maynard&resolution=4&lat=6300.280386656685&lon=2761.8128047094056.

4. Davis McAuley, "Ed Maynard Dies at 89," *Bastrop Advertiser*, January 3, 1980, p. 1.

5. McAuley, "Ed Maynard Dies at 89."

6. BCPR, Vol. 45, pp. 845–55, October 19, 1982.

7. Clara Maynard, interview by Robbie Sanders, August 2, 2019, notes in the personal files of Robbie Sanders.

## Main Street

1. Mrs. W. E. Maynard, "Bastrop County Museum," application for Official Texas Historical Marker (history no.1458), August 27, 1952, Texas State Historical Survey Committee, Austin.

2. Maynard, "Bastrop County Museum."

3. Dick Smith, "The Richard Starcke House, 703 Main Street," handout for the Bastrop County Historical Society 2008 Holiday Homes Tour, 703 Main Street file, BCHS Museum and Archives.

4. "R & G Starcke, Dealers in Hardware, Stoves, and Cutlery," *Bastrop Advertiser*, March 7, 1891, p. 2, https://texashistory.unt.edu/ark:/67531/metapth205059/m1/2/?q=Stoves.

5. Vina Eskew, interview by Robbie Sanders, July 15, 2008, notes in the personal files of Robbie Sanders.

6. Connie Zinn Olson, interview by Robbie Sanders, July 16, 2008, notes in the personal files of Robbie Sanders.

7. Richard Hawkins, "Historical Narrative—Elzner Home," application for Official Texas Historical Marker (history no. 4485), April 1976, Texas Historical Commission, Austin.

8. Hawkins, "Historical Narrative."

9. "Old Elzner Home," July 22, 1975, 802 Main Street file, BCHS Museum Archives.

10. Sidney Lee Brannon Sr., "A Brief Narrative," unpublished autobiography, 1964, BCHS Museum Archives.

11. Jack Brannon, grandson of Sidney L. Brannon, interview by Robbie Sanders, 2006, notes in the personal files of Robbie Sanders.

12. "Brannon Services Held Here Sept. 22," *Bastrop Advertiser and County News*, September 30, 1971, p. 1.

13. Brannon, "A Brief Narrative."

14. The July 2, 1890, issue of the *Bastrop Advertiser* has the first advertisement for "John W. White Contractor, etc., Plans, Specifications and Estimates made on Application." John White had a separate notice in the same issue in which he advertised to hire "two or three first class carpenters. Permanent employment and first class wages." As of February 4, 1894, he no longer advertised in the *Bastrop Advertiser*, suggesting his business had closed.

15. Frank O. Huffman, "2010 Bastrop County Historical Society Home Tour: A Resource for Docents, White-Turner House at 1307 Main Street, Bastrop, TX," December 2010, BCHS Museum Archives.

16. Huffman, "2010 Bastrop County Historical Society Home Tour."

17. "Wedding Bells," *Bastrop Advertiser*, November 22, 1902, p. 3.

18. Trudy K. Barden, "The White-Turner-Barden House," application for Official Texas Historical Marker (history no. 7198), February 10, 1983, Texas Historical Commission, Austin.

19. "Turner Family," *Bastrop Advertiser* August 2, 1955, Homecoming ed.

20. Karen R. Thompson and Richard L. Scroggins, eds., "Bastrop County Death Records," April 2000, BCHS Museum Archives.

21. Barden, "The White-Turner-Barden House."

22. Dick Smith, "The Amthor Home," 2005 Holiday Homes Tour, 1308 Main Street file, BCHS Museum Archives.

23. Brian A. Ross, "The U.S. Marines of the Legation Guard, Managua, Nicaragua, 1912–1925: A Case Study in Leadership, Professionalism, and Cultural Awareness" (master's thesis, Marquette University, December 2006), pp. 20–22.

24. "Marines' Sentences Cut," *New York Times*, July 7, 1922, p. 19.

25. Smith, "The Amthor Home."

26. Michael Beeman, interview and home tour given to Robbie Sanders, June 2004, notes in the personal files of Robbie Sanders.

27. Sharon Duggan, interview by Robbie Sanders, April 28, 2019, notes in the personal files or Robbie Sanders.

28. BCDR, Vol. H, p. 4, April 17, 1851.

29. Kenneth Kesselus, *Bastrop County 1846–1865* (Austin: Jenkins Publishing, 1987), pp. 60–62; and "Editorial Correspondence," *Weekly Journal* (Galveston), July 16, 1852.

30. [Buildings listed as owned by T. M. House among those burned in fire of 1862, under "List of Sufferers"], *Tri-Weekly Telegraph* (Houston), July 7, 1862, vol. 48, p. 72; and Eric C. Caren, *Texas Extra: A Newspaper History of the Lone Star State 1836–1936* (Edison, NJ: Castle Books, 1999).

31. BCDR, Vol. X, p. 246, October 23, 1865.

32. Ford Dixon, "Notes and Documents: Cayton Erhard's Reminiscences of the Texas Santa Fe Expedition, 1841," *Southwestern Historical Quarterly* 66 (July 1962–April 1963): 425–57.

This is a series of articles written from 1882 to 1884 by Cayton Erhard for the *San Marcos Free Press* and reprinted in the *Southwestern Historical Quarterly*.

33. Ford Dixon, "Erhard, Cayton (1822–1844)," *Handbook of Texas Online*, published by the Texas State Historical Association, accessed June 15, 2021, https://tshaonline.org//handbook/online/articles/fer09.

34. Dixon, "Erhard, Cayton."

35. Cayton Erhard, "Last Wishes," Cayton Erhard Scrapbook, Dolph Briscoe Center for American History, University of Texas at Austin.

36. Alfred E. Menn, "Oldest Texas Drug Store in Bastrop," undated newspaper clipping, Cayton Erhard Scrapbook, Dolph Briscoe Center for American History, University of Texas at Austin. Alfred Menn interviewed Cora Erhard, who stated that her mother built their home on Church Street in 1889.

37. Ray Arbuckle, interview by Robbie Sanders, September 1993, notes in the personal files of Robbie Sanders. Ray, grandson of Florence Erhard, provided many photographs of the home at 1402 Main.

38. BCDR, Vol. 67, pp. 128–29, April 26, 1919 ($1,625).

39. Mary Jane Davis, eighty-four years old, interview by Robbie Sanders, August 16, 1993, notes in the personal files of Robbie Sanders. In the 1920s Mary Jane was one of Ivor Young's piano students.

40. Joseph K. Young Jr., interview by Robbie Sanders, August 17, 1993, notes in the personal files of Robbie Sanders. Joe Young, the son of Ivor and Joe Young Sr., lived at 1402 Main until he was sixteen years old.

41. Joseph K. Young Jr., interview.

42. BCDR, Vol. 146, p. 180, October 23, 1957.

43. Scarlett Clardy Lunsford, interview by Robbie Sanders, August 1993, notes in the personal files of Robbie Sanders.

44. BCDR, Vol. 664, p. 182, April 20, 1993.

45. BCDR, Vol. M, p. 441, January 1, 1861 ($1,800).

46. BCDR, Vol. H, p. 254, October 19, 1866 ($2,500).

47. US Census, 1860, 1870.

48. "Mrs. Norvell Honored," *San Antonio Light*, February 19, 1950.

49. Mary Jane Davis, interview.

50. BCDR, Vol. D, p. 246, September 24, 1976.

51. Ivor Young submitted an incorrect construction date for the Wilbarger House when applying for a Texas Historic Landmark designation. The construction and occupancy dates were corrected by later owners, Tom and Lyn Phillips (history no. 08BP04), October 8, 2008.

52. "Bastrop County Complex Fire," Wikipedia, edited June 4, 2019, https://en.wikipedia.org/wiki/Bastrop_County_Complex_Fire.

53. J. W. Wilbarger, "Josiah Wilbarger," in *Indian Depredations in Texas* (Austin: Steck, 1935), pp. 7–14. J. W. was Josiah's brother.

54. BCDR, Vol. 47, pp. 353–54, August 24, 1910; and "Bastrop Is Growing," *Bastrop Advertiser*, July 28, 1911, p. 2. The article states that the new home of C. L. Moncure on "North Main street was completed within the past year."

55. "C. L. Moncure House," n.d., BCHS Museum Archives.

56. Barry W. Moncure, interview by Robbie Sanders, July 15, 2019, notes in the personal files of Robbie Sanders.

57. "Julia Moncure Dies at 88," *Bastrop Advertiser*, July 17, 1980, p. 16.

58. Houston City Directory, 1932 US City Directories, 1822–1995, https://www.ancestry.com/imageviewer/collections/2469/images/4980925?usePUB=true&_phsrc=uSi2558&_phstart=successSource&usePUBJs=true&pId=400424768; Port Arthur City Directory, 1938 US City Directories, 1822–1995, https://www.ancestry.com/imageviewer/collections/2469/images/4852405?usePUB=true&usePUBJs=true&pId=386922649; Port Arthur City Directory, 1938 US City Directories, 1822–1995, https://www.ancestry.com/discoveryui-content/view/385713450:2469; US Census, 1930, https://www.ancestry.com/imageviewer/collections/6224/images/4547974_00738?usePUB=true&usePUBJs=true&pId=63387021; and US Census, 1940, https://www.ancestry.com/imageviewer/collections/2442/images/m-t0627-04078- 00600?usePUB=true&usePUBJs=true&pId=155197474.

59. Grace Moncure Kunkel, "Leah Moncure, P. E. No. 2250," March 16, 1977, p. 1, personal files of Lisa Lacey Willits, Bastrop (copy at Texas Department of Transportation Archives, Austin).

60. "Women in Engineering: Past, Present and Future," *TN Magazine*, Texas Department of Transportation, May–June 2016, p. 14.

61. "Dies in Austin Hospital Monday," *Bastrop Advertiser*, January 20, 1972, p. 1.

62. Barry W. Moncure, interview.

63. Kenneth Kesselus, *The Citizens State Bank 1909–1984: Seventy-Five Years of Service in Bastrop*, n.d., pp. 3 11.

64. BCDR, Vol. 52, p. 386, June 8, 1911.

65. Kesselus, *Citizens State Bank 1909–1984*.

66. News clipping concerning the hotel under ownership of the Crysup family, provided by Mary Elizabeth Pierce, great-granddaughter of James Travis Crysup, *Austin American-Statesman*, June 7, 1983, p. 5, 1607 Main Street file, BCHS Museum Archives.

67. BCDR, Vol. 289, p. 100, July 15, 1980.

68. Joseph Emmert, interview by Robbie Sanders, July 3, 2019, notes in the personal files of Robbie Sanders.

69. Elbert S. Orgain House, National Register of Historic

Places, Inventory-Nomination Form, December 20, 1976, BCHS Museum Archives.

70. Mary Jane Davis, interview by Robbie Sanders, 1994, notes in the personal files of Robbie Sanders.

71. "Funeral Services Held Saturday for Elbert S. Orgain," *Bastrop Advertiser*, May 18, 1944, p. 1.

72. BCPM, Vol. Y, p. 182, August 7, 1944.

73. Roy Johnson, age ninety-two, interview by Robbie Sanders, January 17, 2019; and Scarlett Clardy, interview by Robbie Sanders, July 25, 1993, notes for both interviews in the personal files of Robbie Sanders.

74. Roy Johnson, interview. Johnson noted that some of the colorful bottles were liquor bottles, which raised a few eyebrows of passersby.

75. Anonymous, "Batts, Robert Lynn (1864–1935)," *Handbook of Texas Online*, published by the Texas State Historical Association, accessed January 21, 2019, http://www.tshaonline.org/handbook/online/articles/fbaal.

76. John Holmes Jenkins III, ed., *Recollections of Early Texas: The Memoirs of John Holland Jenkins* (Austin: University of Texas Press, 1997), pp. 20–21.

77. John H. Jenkins, "The Old Jenkins Home (as Told by John H. Jenkins, III)," application for Texas Historical Building Medallion, March 31, 1964, Texas Historical Survey Committee, Austin.

78. Jenkins, *Recollections*, p. 261.

79. Jenkins, *Recollections*, p. 35.

80. Jenkins, *Recollections*, pp. 232–33.

81. Jenkins, "The Old Jenkins Home."

82. BCDR, Vol. L, p. 213, February 18, 1859.

83. "History of the Waugh Home, Bastrop Historical and Architectural Multiple Restoration Nomination #47," 1801 Main Street file, BCHS Museum Archives.

84. Sandra Chipley, "Narrative to the Application for a Recorded Texas Historic Landmark," H. P. Luckett House, BCHS Museum Archives. Bob and Winnie's son, Alex Waugh, owned the Luckett House.

85. Chipley, "Narrative."

86. "Services Held for Mrs. Waugh," *Bastrop Advertiser*, March 2, 1972, p. 1.

87. Bobbie Felts Terrell, "History of the Pfeiffer Home in Bastrop Texas," application for Official Texas Historical Marker (history no. 5102), June 27, 1977, Texas Historical Commission, Austin.

88. Terrell, "History of the Pfeiffer Home."

89. "Pfeiffer House," n.d., 1802 Main Street file, BCHS Museum Archives.

90. BCDR, Vol. 276, p. 663, June 22, 1979.

91. Kathryn Lang, interview by Robbie Sanders, May 1 and May 24, 2019, notes in the personal files of Robbie Sanders. Kathryn is the Whites' daughter.

### Pecan Street

1. Letter from Gus Jung to Ernest F. Pearcy, April 27, 1936, BCHS Museum Archives.

2. BCDR, Vol. 111, p. 110, April 5, 1943.

3. BCDR, Vol. 1965, p. 80, January 4, 2010.

4. "The Willie Schaefer House," 2005 Holiday Homes Tour, 608 Pecan Street file, BCHS Museum Archives; and Judith Hoover, interview by Robbie Sanders, August 1, 2019, notes in the personal files of Robbie Sanders. Judith Hoover, owner of the home in the 1980s, interviewed Gilbert Schaeffer, son of Willie F. Schaeffer and "Miss Willie" Schaeffer.

5. "The Willie Schaefer House."

6. "The Willie Schaefer House."

7. Sally Keinarth, email to Robbie Sanders, February 19, 2019, BCHS Museum Archives.

8. Sally Keinarth, email.

9. Sharah Johnson, email to Robbie Sanders, February 14 and 15, 2019, BCHS Museum Archives.

10. Mika Spears, "A Look at the Final Three Stops on the Holiday Homes Tour," *Bastrop Advertiser*, December 6, 2007, p. 13A.

11. Sandra Chipley, "The Petty-Prokop Home, 701 Pecan Street," unpublished research paper, personal files of Sandra Chipley.

12. Spears, "A Look."

13. "The Prokop House," n.d., 608 Pecan Street file, BCHS Museum Archives.

14. Spears, "A Look."

15. "The Prokop House."

16. BCDR, Instrument #201609950, July 28, 2016.

17. Amy S. Standifer, "Services Held for Mrs. Gill," *Bastrop Advertiser*, December 5, 1940, p. 1.

18. BCDR, Vol. O, pp. 542–43, May 15, 1869.

19. Mary Jane Davis, interview by Robbie Sanders, January 22, 1993, notes in the personal files of Robbie Sanders. Mary Jane is the granddaughter of Robert and Mary Jane Gill.

20. "Bastrop Woman Who Stitched for Texas Heroes Reminisces," *Bastrop Advertiser*, September 1932.

21. Standifer, "Services Held for Mrs. Gill."

22. Standifer, "Services Held for Mrs. Gill."

23. "Tobe Cook Hangs," *Bastrop Advertiser*, June 11, 1892, p. 3.

24. Oliver Wesley Sumerlin, "History of Bastrop, Texas (1851–1935)" (master's thesis, University of Texas, 1963). Sumerlin references "Aleck Brown Hangs," an article in the *Bastrop Advertiser*, July 29, 1893, p. 3.

25. Mary Jane Davis, interview.

26. Standifer, "Services Held for Mrs. Gill."

27. BCDR, Vol. 47, pp. 77–78, April 29, 1910.

28. BCDR, Vol. 69, pp. 277–78, March 10, 1920.

29. Mary Jane Davis, interview.

30. Charles E. Rabensburg, interview by Robbie Sanders, July 19, 2019, notes in the personal files of Robbie Sanders. Ed Rabensburg sold his business to Adren "Red" Long (Long's IGA) and the building to Charles DeWitt and LaVerne Alexander (Alexander's Feed and Seed).

31. Charles E. Rabensburg, interview.

32. BCDR, Vol. 314, p. 666, November 1, 1983.

33. "Robert Lane Jenkins Rogers 'Miss Bob,'" n.d., BCHS Museum Archives.

34. "Death Claims Former Mayor," *Bastrop Advertiser*, June 4, 1970, p. 1.

35. Thomas Flournoy Claiborne, interview by Robbie Sanders, June 5, 2019, notes in the personal files of Robbie Sanders.

36. "Longtime Resident Dies," *Bastrop Advertiser*, July 10, 1947, p. 1; and "Last Rites Held for Mrs. Pete Griesenbeck," *Bastrop Advertiser*, December 13, 1956, p. 1. The 1947 obituary for Pete Griesenbeck gives his birth and marriage dates, which, when calculated, show he was twenty-one years old. The 1956 obituary for Minnie Griesenbeck states she was nineteen years old when she married.

37. Judge Jack A. Griesenbeck, interview by Robbie Sanders, January 21,1993, notes in the personal files of Robbie Sanders; and "Colorado River Freezes Over in 1899," in *In the Shadow of the Lost Pines: A History of Bastrop County and Its People*, comp. and pub. R. E. Standifer, Amy S. Standifer, and R. E. Standifer Jr., publishers of the *Bastrop Advertiser* (Bastrop: 1955), p. 44.

38. BCDR, Vol. 34, pp. 476–77, June 8, 1901.

39. Shirley Tarver Edwards, interview by Robbie Sanders, January 18, 1993, notes in the personal files of Robbie Sanders.

40. US Census, 1900. Sarah Lockett and her mother, Mary Thedin, were living with Pete and Minnie Griesenbeck. Sarah and Mary were both widows.

41. Obituary for Sarah Lockett, *Bastrop Advertiser*, vol. 52, no. 7, April 30, 1904, p. 7, https://texashistory.unt.edu/ark:/67531/metapth205854/m1/7/?q=fancy.

42. Kenneth Kesselus, comp., *The Citizens State Bank of Bastrop: 1909–1984 Diamond Jubilee*, 1984, p. 6. The anniversary booklet states, "In June of 1910, the Bank purchased from J. L. Wilbarger 'the house and lot, known as the Lockett Restaurant Building for $1,000.'"

43. BCDR, Vol. 46, pp. 597–98, March 16, 1911; and Vol. 50, pp. 490–91, January 17, 1912. These deeds record the rental of the building to E. J. Rabensburg. They state the building is "immediately between the building of Citizens State Bank of Bastrop, on the north, and the building known as the Perkins Market Building on the south." The address today is 926 Main Street.

44. Judge Jack A. Griesenbeck and Mary Jane Davis, interviews by Robbie Sanders, January 11, 1993, notes in the personal files of Robbie Sanders.

45. Judge Jack A. Griesenbeck and Mary Jane Davis, interviews.

46. Judge Jack A. Griesenbeck and Mary Jane Davis, interviews.

47. Rusty Edwards, interview by Robbie Sanders, March 29, 2020, notes in the personal files of Robbie Sanders.

48. "Carol D. Shull," Coalition to Protect America's National Parks, accessed March 30, 2019, https://protectnps.org/centennial-biographies-2/carol-d-shull/.

49. Letter from Gus Jung to Ernest F. Pearcy.

50. "Jung-Pearcy House," application for Texas Historical Building Medallion, September 1, 1962, Texas State Historical Survey Committee, Austin, 909 Pecan Street file, BCHS Museum Archives.

51. Kenneth Kesselus, *The First National Bank: A Century of Progress and Service in the Bastrop Community*, August 13, 1989, p. 24.

52. Allen Pape, *150 Years of Methodism in Bastrop* (Bastrop: Bastrop Stationers, 1985), pp. 39–40.

53. BCDR, Vol. B, p. 397, June 5, 1838; Vol. V, p. 44, December 23, 1875; and Vol. 2, p. 136, September 8, 1881. The large increase in value of the property between the purchases by Henry and Caroline Koppel and Robert Gill shows that the Koppels built the home.

54. "Bastrop, Court-House Burned," *Galveston Weekly News*, January 4, 1883.

55. Amy Standifer, "Tribute Paid to Mrs. O. P. Jones' Father," *Bastrop Advertiser*, April 14, 1955, p. 6, reprint of an article written by Emma Holmes Jenkins.

56. "Many Grieve at Death of Beloved Teacher-Friend," *Bastrop Advertiser*, August 3, 1961, p. 8.

57. "Library's Evolution Traced by Nell Herndon," *Bastrop Advertiser*, June 30, 1988, p. 13.

58. BCDR, Vol. 119, p. 50, May 9, 1946; and Vol. 122, pp. 282–84, September 17, 1947. Heise and Lolita Jones bought the property from J. M. and Martha Mecey for six hundred dollars in May 1946. They sold it to R. W. and Evohn Rosanky Young for sixty-five hundred dollars in September 1947.

59. Dooley Ann Navarro, "The O. P. Jones House," 1009 Pecan Street file, BCHS Museum Archives.

60. Little Free Library, accessed August 24, 2019, https://littlefreelibrary.org/.

61. "Homes," *Bastrop Advertiser*, December 6, 2007, pp. 11A, 13A.

62. Shawn Pletsch, "Zeiten-Morris-Pletsch House," September 2007 (written for the 2007 Holiday Homes Tour), BCHS Museum Archives.

63. BCDR, Vol. 41, p. 377, October 26, 1906; and "Purely Personal," *Bastrop Advertiser*, December 22, 1906, p. 3.

64. US Census, 1910.

65. Margaret Griffin, "A. T. Morris," RootsWeb, accessed September 10, 2019, http:www.rootsweb.ancestry.com/~txmdhms/people_a_t_morris.htm.

66. US Census, 1930, 1940.

67. Shawn Pletsch, interview by Robbie Sanders, June 2019, notes in the personal files of Robbie Sanders.

68. Shawn Pletsch, interview.

69. Shawn Pletsch, interview.

70. Sandra Chipley, admission ticket, "The Jenkins- Moore Home," 2016 Holiday Homes Tour, BCHS Museum Archives.

71. BCDR, Vol. 80, p. 391, January 4, 1926; and Vol. 99, p. 380, January 4, 1938.

72. "Jenkins Sr. Dies in Austin at 70," *Bastrop Advertiser*, May 27, 1982, p. 1.

73. Cyndi Wright, "Beloved Staffer Passes Away," *Bastrop Advertiser*, March 26, 2014, pp. 1, A7.

74. Sherri Gilmore, interview by Sandra Chipley, August 2, 2016, notes in the personal files of Sandra Chipley.

75. Sandra Chipley, Janean Whitten, and Bryan Whitten, "The A. A. Erhard House," 2018 Holiday Homes Tour, 1106 Pecan Street file, BCHS Museum Archives.

76. Myrtle Long, interview by Robbie Sanders, 1994, notes in the personal files of Robbie Sanders.

77. Chipley, Whitten, and Whitten, "The A. A. Erhard House."

78. Mary Jane Davis, interview by Robbie Sanders, October 14, 1993, notes in the personal files of Robbie Sanders.

79. Robbie Sanders and Patricia Orr, "Building Block #4, Lot #1, East of Main—Hasler's Corner," July 2008, BCHS Museum Archives.

80. "Bastrop Bridge Completed in 1890 Enterprise," in *In the Shadow of the Lost Pines: A History of Bastrop County and Its People*, comp. and pub. R. E. Standifer, Amy S. Standifer, and R. E. Standifer Jr., publishers of the *Bastrop Advertiser* (Bastrop, 1955), p. 30.

81. Sandra Chipley, "The T. A. Hasler House," 2014 Holiday Homes Tour, BCHS Museum Archives.

82. BCDR, Vol. 644, p. 838, September 29, 1992.

83. BCDR, Vol. 34, p. 229, July 8, 1889; and Vol. 29, p. 353, July 18, 1889.

84. "City of Bastrop 1892–1908, Farm Lot 1 East of Main," in *Assessor's Abstract of City Lots, Bastrop County*, p. 248, personal property of Robbie Sanders. The taxes for A. B. McLavy jumped from $700 in 1893 to $1,950 in 1894, indicating a home was built on the property in 1894.

85. BCDR, Vol. 102, p. 599, December 21, 1939.

86. David Boatman, email interviews by Sandra Chipley, August 14–28, 2011, notes in the personal files of Sandra Chipley.

87. US Census, 1940.

88. Sue Ann Fruge and Sandra Chipley, "The Cochran/Watson Home," September 11, 2011, personal files of Sandra Chipley.

89. "Chaplain on Wheels," *The Rotarian*, October 1943, p. 50.

90. David Boatman, email interviews.

91. BCDR, Vol. 139, p. 55, April 8, 1954.

92. "Jack Dyer Claiborne, Sr.," *Bastrop Advertiser*, July 7, 2005, news clipping in Claiborne file, BCHS Museum Archives.

93. "Jack Dyer Claiborne, Sr."

94. Ellen Moore, "Garden Tradition Runs Strong," *Bastrop Advertiser*, June 20, 1992, pp. 1–2.

95. Moore, "Garden Tradition Runs Strong."

96. BCDR, Vol. 2279, p. 518, November 15, 2013.

97. American Society of Arms Collectors, "N. B. Tanner & Company," BCHS Museum Archives.

98. BCDR, Vol. P, pp. 10–11, September 15, 1859.

99. Bobbie F. Terrell, "A. A. Erhard Home," 1205 Pecan Street file, BCHS Museum Archives.

100. Terrell, "A. A. Erhard Home."

101. Mary Bell Murchison Brieger was the daughter of Susie Erhard Bell and Durant Hatch Bell. Mary Bell's first husband was Walter Hamilton Murchison (died August 28, 1932). Her second husband was Richard H. Brieger.

102. Terrell, "A. A. Erhard Home."

103. BCDR, Vol. 102, p. 599, December 26, 1939. The Cochrans purchased the property from A. B. McLavy and moved into the McLavy home, dividing the remainder of the property, where they built a rent house.

104. David Boatman, interviews.

105. David Boatman, interviews.

106. Thomas Flournoy Claiborne, interview.

107. Janice Butler, "After 50 Years Luncheon Still Going," *Bastrop Advertiser*, May 14, 1992, pp. 1–2.

108. Ellen Moore, "Shudde Bess Bryson Recalls Memories of Her Mother," *Bastrop Advertiser*, March 24, 1994, p. 7.

109. Butler, "After 50 Years."

110. Buster Watson, interview by Sandra Chipley and Sue Ann Fruge, August 2011, notes in the personal files of Sandra Chipley.

111. BCDR, Vol. 145, p. 328, May 22, 1957.

112. Ernest Goertz, interview by Robbie Sanders, September 2008, notes in the personal files of Robbie Sanders. Goertz was an employee of Bastrop's Coca-Cola plant.

113. Ernest Goertz, interview.

114. Buster Watson, interview.

115. Mary Jane Davis, interview.

116. Mrs. A. F. Adams, "Fowler-Jenkins," application for Official Texas Historical Marker (no. 3374), May 24, 1971, Texas Historical Foundation, Austin.

117. Stephanie J. Jenkins, "The Hartford Jenkins Home—Updated," 2018, 1302 Pecan Street file, BCHS Museum Archives.

118. Stephanie J. Jenkins, interview by Robbie Sanders, April 12, 2019, notes in the personal files of Robbie Sanders.

119. Robert H. Carpenter, "Klockman-Elzner House," application for Official Texas Historical Marker (history no. 5352), July 1, 1978, Texas Historical Commission, Austin.

120. Carpenter, "Klockman-Elzner House."

121. Kitty Kent, "Mobile Home," *Bastrop Advertiser*, October 10, 1998.

122. Kent, "Mobile Home."

123. Kent, "Mobile Home."

124. Kent, "Mobile Home."

125. Kent, "Mobile Home."

126. "Clean-Up Week under the Leadership of Dr. T. B. Taylor," *Bastrop Advertiser*, March 31, 1921, p. 3.

127. Josephine Metcalf Smith, "Thos. Bell Taylor, 1862–1950: The House He Built," 2002, 1305 Pecan Street file, BCHS Museum Archives.

128. BCDR, Vol. 111, p. 315, June 16, 1943.

129. Robert Warren Higgins Jr., interview by Robbie Sanders, March 30, 2019, notes in the personal files of Robbie Sanders.

130. "Local News," *Bastrop Advertiser*, January 31, 1952.

131. "The G. P. Herndon, Jr. Home," n.d., BCHS Museum Archives.

132. "Jones-Herndon House," n.d., 1311 Pecan Street file, BCHS Museum Archives; and "Salmagundi, by the Editor," *Bastrop Advertiser*, February 4, 1960, p. 1.

133. "Mary Nell Jones Herndon," *Austin American-Statesman*, May 24, 2005, p. 16.

134. "The G. P. Herndon, Jr. Home."

135. "Mary Nell Jones Herndon."

136. Nancy Beal, interview by Robbie Sanders, April 4, 2019, notes in the personal files of Robbie Sanders.

137. Joseph Beal, interview by Robbie Sanders, April 4, 2019, notes in the personal files of Robbie Sanders.

138. Arthur Fehr, "Papers and Drawings: Drawings 1931–1941," Austin History Center, accessed July 20, 2019, https://legacy.lib.utexas.edu/taro/aushc/00353/ahc-00353.html.

139. Arthur Fehr, "Papers and Drawings: Biographical Note," Austin History Center, accessed July 20, 2019, https://legacy.lib.utexas.edu/taro/aushc/00353/ahc-00353.html.

140. Ernest Simmons, "The 1936 Bastrop Advertiser Historical Edition," *Bastrop Advertiser*, April 18, 2002.

141. "All U.S., City Directories, 1822–1995 Results for Tillye Haynie," Ancestry.Com, accessed July 2, 2021, https://www.ancestry.com/search/collections/usdirectories/?name=tillye_haynie&event=1952_austin- travis-texas-usa_78510&gender=f&residence=_austin-travis-texas-usa_78510: Austin, Texas, City Directory, 1947, https://www.ancestry.com/discoveryui-content/view/383168296:2469?tid=&pid=&queryId=5d10d75716eb01bef498bb4fcc534faf&_phsrc=uSi2583&_phstart=successSource; 1952, https://www.ancestry.com/imageviewer/collections/2469/images/4804407?usePUB=true&_phsrc=uSi2580&_phstart=successSource&usePUBJs=true&pId=382374423; 1953, https://www.ancestry.com/imageviewer/collections/2469/images/4953670?usePUB=true&_phsrc=uSi2582&_phstart=successSource&usePUBJs=true&pId=397058127; and 1957, https://www.ancestry.com/imageviewer/collections/2469/images/4963691?usePUB=true&_phsrc=uSi2581&_phstart=successSource&usePUBJs=true&pId=398278804).

142. BCDR, Vol. 118, pp. 469–71, April 12, 1946.

143. BCDR, Vol. 1287, p. 663, March 11, 2003.

144. BCDR, Instrument #201604601, April 15, 2016.

145. Kay Wesson, email interview by Sandra Chipley, July 19, 2019, notes in the personal files of Sandra Chipley.

146. Ann Brown, "John & Willie Belle Kennedy House History," n.d., 1405 Pecan Street file, BCHS Museum Archives.

147. Brown, "John & Willie Belle Kennedy House History."

148. Ann Brown, interview by Robbie Sanders, April 2, 2019, notes in the personal files of Robbie Sanders.

149. Robbie Sanders, "The P. C. Maynard House," 2001 Holiday Homes Tour, 1408 Pecan Street file, BCHS Museum Archives.

150. Sanders, "The P. C. Maynard House."

151. Dan Hays-Clark and Bill Ennis, interview by Robbie Sanders, July 31, 2019, notes in the personal files of Robbie Sanders. Dan and Bill garnered much of the home's history from William E. Maynard III, nephew of Powell Maynard.

152. "Powell C. Maynard Home—Built 1916," 1408 Pecan Street file, BCHS Museum Archives.

153. Dan Hays-Clark and Bill Ennis, interview.

154. Sanders, "The P. C. Maynard House."

155. BCDR, Vol. 634 p. 24, May 28, 1992.

156. Robbie Sanders, "Mary 'Blanche' Duval Home," 2003 Holiday Homes Tour, 1502 Pecan Street file, BCHS Museum Archives.

157. BCDR, Vol. 24, pp. 340, 341, 342, February 26, 1896.

158. BCPM, Vol. V, p. 217, May 10, 1937.

159. Sanders, "Mary 'Blanche' Duval Home."

160. Brad Duff, "The Erhards of Bastrop," Brad Duff Collection, BCHS Museum Archives.

161. Kesselus, *The First National Bank: A Century of Progress*, p. 3.

162. Annie Pearl Windrow's mother died when Annie Pearl was eleven years old, and Annie Pearl moved to Bastrop when she was a teenager to live with her aunt and uncle, W. A. and Sallie McCord.

163. Shawn Pletsch, interview.

164. Fairview Cemetery records indicate that three children were previously born to Earl and Pearl. Each child lived only one day.

165. US Census, 1930. Julia Howe, cook, is listed in the household of Earl Erhard.

166. "Obituary, Dr. Kenneth Robert Duff," *Houston Chronicle*, February 3, 2010, https://www.legacy.com/us/obituaries/houstonchronicle/name/kenneth-duff-obituary?pid=139305951.

167. Ben Simmons, interview by Robbie Sanders, December 1989, notes in the personal files of Robbie Sanders. Ben was approximately seventy-five years old at the time of the interview. He had attended the Christmas party in the Rosanky home where Evohn's Christmas tree was the focal point. It was the first time he had ever see a one-hundred-dollar bill.

168. Annie Mae Trigg Birmingham, interview notes titled "Hubbard-Trigg-Birmingham House," n.d., 1508 Pecan Street file, BCHS Museum Archives.

169. "House Undergoes Extensive Refurbishing," *Smithville Times*, October 9, 1974.

170. "Onalaska, Arkansas," Ouachita County Historical Society, accessed June 15, 2021, http://www.ouachitacountyhistoricalsociety.org/Onalaska.pdf.

171. Kenneth Kesselus, *The First National Bank* (Bastrop: Bastrop Stationers, 1989), p. 24.

172. Sandra Chipley, "The J. H. Pearcy House," 2015 Holiday Homes Tour, 1602 Pecan Street file, BCHS Museum Archives.

173. BCDR, Vol. 54, pp. 209–10, October 1, 1913; and BCDR, Vol. 60, pp. 437–38, December 23, 1915.

174. "Service Set for Clint Orgain," *El Paso Herald-Post*, June 10, 1957, pp. 1, 4.

175. "Bought the J. C. Orgain House," *Bastrop Advertiser*, November 19, 1915, p. 6.

176. Sanborn Insurance Maps, Bastrop, Texas, 1921, sheet 5, and 1935, sheet 5, Perry-Castañeda Library Map Collection, University of Texas Library System.

177. Minifred Trigg, interview by Robbie Sanders, June 2, 2019, notes in the personal files of Robbie Sanders.

178. Deborah Jones, interview by Sandra Chipley, September 14, 2013, notes in the personal files of Sandra Chipley.

179. C. W. Webb, "Senator Paul D. Page," BCHS Museum Archives.

180. Blanche Page Wilson, "Dear Mrs. Morris," letter dated March 11, 1999, BCHS Museum Archives.

181. Blanche Page Wilson, "Dearest Becky and Jimmy," letter dated July 18, 1990, BCHS Museum Archives.

182. Mary Jane Davis, interview.

183. Wilson, "Dearest Becky and Jimmy."

184. Wilson, "Dear Mrs. Morris."

185. BCDR, Vol. 61, pp. 61–62, August 16, 1916.

186. Sanborn Fire Insurance Map, Bastrop, Bastrop County, 1921, sheet 5, Perry-Castañeda Library Map Collection, University of Texas Library System.

187. Sanborn Fire Insurance Map, Bastrop, Bastrop County, 1934, sheet 5, Perry-Castañeda Library Map Collection, University of Texas Library System.

188. BCDR, Vol. 102, pp. 596–98, December 13,1939.

189. "Bastrop Mourns Death of Cecil Long," *Bastrop Advertiser*, December 23, 1993, p. 1, Long file, BCHS Museum Archives.

190. Reverend Robert K. Long, interview by Robbie Sanders, July 29, 2019, notes in the personal files of Robbie Sanders.

191. Reverend Robert K. Long, interview.

192. "Bastrop Mourns Death of Cecil Long."

193. "Cecil B. Long," *Austin American-Statesman*, December 22, 1993.

194. "Bastrop Mourns Death of Cecil Long."

195. "Lighted Tower to Honor Long," *Bastrop Advertiser*, December 25, 1993, p. 1, BCHS Museum Archives.

196. Mary Huber, "5 Things You Should Know about Historic Mina Ward School," *Bastrop Advertiser*, September 21, 2017, p. A1, Bastrop County Schools Mexican/Hispanic file, BCHS Museum Archives.

197. Reverend Robert K. Long, interview.

198. Reverend Robert K. Long, interview.

199. BCDR, Vol. 786, p. 855, February 26, 1996.

200. "Louis and Augusta Baron House—Information Gathered from Various Family Members," 1707 Pecan Street file, BCHS Museum Archives.

201. Robbie Sanders, "The Baron House," 2004 Holiday Homes Tour, 1707 Pecan Street file, BCHS Museum Archives.

202. BCDR, Vol. R, pp. 372–73, October 14, 1872 (three acres); and Vol. U, pp. 535–37, December 15, 1874 (six acres).

203. Clyde Reynolds, interview by Robbie Sanders, February 9, 1993, notes in the personal files of Robbie Sanders. Reynolds remembered that when he was a boy, he would sneak into Louis Baron's garden to steal watermelons.

204. Clyde Reynolds, interview.

## Pine Street

1. BCDR, Vol. C, pp. 240–41, September 8, 1839.

2. Tom Scott, "The House at 907 Pine Street—Bastrop, Texas," application form for State Marker Program (history no. 06690), August 1990, Texas Historical Commission, Austin,.

3. Scott, "The House at 907 Pine Street."

4. "Col. Campbell Dies," *El Paso Morning Times*, May 25, 1905, p. 5.

5. Scott, "The House at 907 Pine Street."

6. Sandra Chipley and Dick Smith, "Erna Griesenbeck House" (historical home research paper), 2010, 908 Pine Street file, BCHS Museum Archives.

7. "Erna Griesenbeck House," Inventory-Nomination Form, National Register of Historic Places, recorded December 21, 1976, https://atlas.thc.state.tx.us/NR/pdfs/78003338/78003338.pdf.

8. Chipley and Smith, "Erna Griesenbeck House."

9. Chipley and Smith, "Erna Griesenbeck House."

10. Dick Smith, "The Wertzner Home," 2001 Holiday Homes Tour, 909 Pine Street file, BCHS Museum Archives.

11. Smith, "The Wertzner Home."

12. BCDR, Vol. 163, p. 502, January 4, 1964.

13. "Fire Truck Takes Dutch Home," *Bastrop Advertiser*, April, 10, 1980.

14. "Wertzner Home," 909 Pine Street file, BCHS Museum Archives.

15. BCDR, Vol. 33, pp. 129, 130, November 23, 1900. On November 23, 1900, Henry and Maude Combs purchased the home for one thousand dollars from Mary Russmann. The US Census, taken five months earlier in June, shows that the Combses were renting a house in the same block occupied by this house. It is probable that the house rented by and purchased by the Combses at 1002 Pine is the same.

16. Doris Oldfield, interview by Robbie Sanders, April 27, 2019, notes in the personal files of Robbie Sanders.

17. BCDR, Vol. 50, p. 488, September 30, 1911.

18. *W. St. John Garwood, "Page, Paul Dewitt (1868–1945)," Handbook of Texas Online*, published by the Texas State Historical Association, accessed April 27, 2019, http://www.tshaonline.org/handbook/online/articles/fpa08.

19. BCDR, Vol. 65, pp. 100–101, August 29, 1918.

20. Doris Oldfield, interview.

21. Cyndi Wright, "Mark Edward Oldfield: April 24, 1922–Nov. 17, 2008," *Bastrop Advertiser*, November 22, 2008, p. 14.

22. Doris Oldfield, interview.

23. C. B. Maynard, "Dear Franklin," letter dated February 4, 1947, BCHS Museum Archives. This letter to T. C. Franklin lists all legal transactions regarding ownership of the Kerr home from 1835 to 1947.

24. Tom Scott and Dock Jackson, "The Kerr Community Center & Park," City of Bastrop: Bastrop's 175th Birthday and Juneteenth Celebration, June 2007, pp. 18–19, BCHS Museum Archives.

25. Scott and Jackson, "The Kerr Community Center & Park."

26. Maynard, "Dear Franklin."

27. Scott and Jackson, "The Kerr Community Center & Park."

28. BCDR, Vol. 121, p. 32, February 1, 1947.

29. "Bastrop Civic Leader, Educator Franklin Dies," *Bastrop Advertiser*, July 15, 1999.

30. BCDR, Vol. 1162, p. 896, September 14, 2001.

## Walnut Street

1. Kenneth Kesselus, email correspondence to Sandra Chipley, August–September, 2015, personal files of Sandra Chipley.

2. BCDR, Vol. L, p. 462, February 25, 1860.

3. Kenneth Kesselus, interview by Robbie Sanders, July 3, 2019, notes in the personal files of Robbie Sanders.

4. BCDR, Vol. 99, p. 23, July 27, 1937.

5. Margaret Pfeiffer, "Ima Hodges Remembered," *Bastrop Advertiser*, December 6, 1979, p. 11.

6. "B. C. Hodges Passes Away on Oct. 2," *Bastrop Advertiser*, October 11, 1973, p. 1.

7. "B. C. Hodges Passes Away."

8. US Census, 1900.

9. Terry Hagerty, "Freed Slave's Home under Renovation," *Bastrop Advertiser*, February or March 2007.

10. T. C. Franklin, personal recollections regarding Jennie Brooks, n.d., 1009 Walnut Street file, BCHS Museum Archives.

11. Franklin, personal recollections.

## Water Street

1. "Bastrop's Oldest Citizen Passes Away Friday," *Bastrop Advertiser*, April 23, 1953, p. 1.

2. "The Chalmers House," 2003 Holiday Homes Tour, BCHS Museum Archives.

3. "The Chalmers House."

4. BCDR, Vol. 897, p. 878, March 12, 1998.

5. Forrest T. Chalmers, interview by Robbie Sanders, July 15, 2019, notes in the personal files of Robbie Sanders.

## Wilson Street

1. BCDR, Vol. K, p. 551, February 1852.

2. Mary Nicholson McDowall, "A Little Journey through Memory's Halls," 1931, p. 36, Mary Ann McDowall file, BCHS Museum Archives.

3. McDowall, "A Little Journey," pp. 46, 51.

4. McDowall, "A Little Journey," pp. 64–65.

5. Thomas W. Cutrer, "Allen, Robert Thomas Pritchard (1813–1888)," *Handbook of Texas Online*, published by the Texas State Historical Association, accessed March 19, 2019, http:www.tshaonline.org/handbook/online/articles/fal58.

6. "Julia Dickinson Allen," Open Plaques, accessed June 15, 2021, http:/openplaques.org/plaques/27106.

7. Bobbie Terrell, "Fowler-Malone House," 1404 Wilson Street file, BCHS Museum Archives.

8. "Pioneer Citizen Called by Death," *Bastrop Advertiser*, December 22, 1927, p. 2, https://texashistory.unt.edu/ark:/67531/metapth206568/m1/2/?q=Fowler.

9. Geoffrey S. Connor, email interview by Robbie Sanders, August 27, 2019, notes in the personal files of Robbie Sanders.

10. Geoffrey S. Connor, interview.

11. Bobbie Felts Terrell, "The Jones-Powell House," 2002 Holiday Homes Tour, 1406 Wilson Street file, BCHS Museum Archives.

12. Terrell, "The Jones-Powell House,"

13. Terrell, "The Jones-Powell House."

14. Dick Smith, "The Prenzell-Tuck Home, 1503 Wilson Street," handout written for the 2009 Holiday Homes Tour, BCHS Museum Archives.

15. Smith, "The Prenzell-Tuck Home."

16. Smith, "The Prenzell-Tuck Home."

17. Robbie Sanders, "Prenzell-Tuck Home," 2009 Holiday Homes Tour, 1503 Wilson Street file, BCHS Museum Archives.

18. "Crocheron-McDowall House," Wikipedia, last edited October 5, 2020, http://en.wikipedia.org/wiki/Crocheron-McDowall_House.

19. McDowall, "A Little Journey," p. 7.

20. "Crocheron Plantation, Guided Tour Information—Crocheron House," pp. 1, 2, 1506 Wilson Street file, BCHS Museum Archives.

21. McDowall, "A Little Journey," pp. 40, 41.

22. McDowall, "A Little Journey," pp. 67, 68.

23. McDowall, "A Little Journey," pp. 69–71.

24. McDowall, "A Little Journey," pp. 91–115.

25. Ethel Mary Franklin Smith, ed., *Memoirs of Mollie McDowall (Mary Ann Nicholson): 1843–1934* (Austin: National Society of the Colonial Dames of America in the State of Texas, 1978), p. 89.

26. Anonymous, "Sayers, Joseph Draper (1841–1929)," *Handbook of Texas Online*, published by the Texas State Historical Association, accessed May 10, 2019, http://www.tshaonline.org/handbook/online/articles/fsa41.

27. Bill Moore, *Bastrop County 1691–1900*, rev. ed. (Wichita Falls, TX: Nortex Press, 1977), p. 220.

28. "Joseph D. Sayers," Wikipedia, accessed May 10, 2019, https://en.wikipedia.org/w/index.php?title=Joseph_D._Sayers&oldid=892541828.

29. "Joseph D. Sayers."

30. Siri Lundstedt, "Sayers: As Governor He Never Let the People Down," *Hancock Special* (Austin), May 26, 1974, BCHS Museum Archives.

31. Mary D. Farrell and Elizabeth Silverthorne, *The First Ladies of Texas: The First One Hundred Years, 1836–1936* (Temple, TX: Stillhouse Hollow Publishers, 1976).

32. "Michael Moorcock," Wikipedia, accessed May 10, 2019, https://en.wikipedia.org/w/index.php?title=Michael_Moorcock&oldid=893511652.

# Index